FROM THE

"Holly McClure has become an important resource for millions of American parents who hope to take more constructive control of the media messages their children receive."

—MICHAEL MEDVED, Nationally Syndicated Talk Show Host

"Today's media influences our children and teens—and consequently our collective cultural worldview—in pervasive, persuasive, and powerful ways. Our emerging generation of kids is more media-saturated than any previous generation. Holly McClure will challenge you—as she has me—to know the media so that you'll know what to celebrate, what to lament, and how to respond."

—WALT MUELLER, President, Center for Parent/Youth Understanding
and Author of *Understanding Today's Youth Culture*

"In Death by Entertainment, *Holly McClure combines her historical knowledge of Hollywood with an abundance of analytical data that in the end leaves no doubt as to the tremendous impact that popular culture has on our society—especially on children and teenagers."*

—MARK HONIG, Executive Director, Parents Television Council

"The advertising industry is willing to spend millions of dollars on a thirty second TV commercial because they know how much a mere thirty seconds can affect behavior. Yet we allow our children to watch hundreds of hours of television and movies with little concern for its damaging effects. Holly McClure understands the media's impact on the family as well as anyone in America. This is the book that will change the way you think about today's media, and if you have children, it may be the most important book you'll read this year."

—PHIL COOKE, Television Director

*"*Death by Entertainment *is a book past due, to challenge and encourage parents, kids, and grandparents to media awareness and action. In society today, no family is immune to the influence of media on our lives, but we can be smart about what we watch and what influence we allow it to have on our children. Holly provides practical advise for the family that you just can't miss. So if you care about your family, read the book!"*

—RICK BEE, PH.D., Director of Alumni University
Development Services, Biola University

"Holly McClure has penetrated the veneer of Hollywood and exposed the danger for all who care about the preservation of the established family model. Death by Entertainment *is an act of courage and generosity."*

—JAMES L. HIRSEN, Law Professor,
Talk Show Host and Columnist.

HOLLY McCLURE is a movie critic whose weekly Southern California newspaper column is syndicated across the country in over 360 newspapers. She hosts a radio talk show in San Diego called "Holly McClure Live" as well as a weekend entertainment show called "Holly on Hollywood."

Known as a strong advocate for family values, Holly is a regular guest on *Politically Incorrect* and *The New Movie Show* on FoxFX and has appeared on *CNN & Co.*, *The Charles Grodin Show*, *The Montel Williams Show*, *Equal Time*, and *Real Time*.

Holly is a member of the Broadcast Film Critics Association, serves on the Biola University Film Task force, and is on the Dove Foundation board. She has guest lectured at USC and has been a spokesperson for the Phonics Game and World Vision. A dynamic speaker on family, social, political, and entertainment issues, Holly lends her enthusiasm and sense of humor to messages that encourage both male and female audiences. Her family friendly reviews can be found at www.hollymcclure.com.

She and her three children make their home in Southern California.

Exposing Hollywood's
Seductive Power
Over You and Your Family

DEATH BY

entertainment

HOLLY
McCLURE

LION'S
HEAD
PUBLISHING

TO MY SWEET NATHAN.
Thanks for your endless support,
nightly hugs, daily kisses, and "I love you's,"
for standing by me through the hard times,
loving me no matter what,
reminding me to have fun,
and having the courage to say no.
You truly are my gift from God.

ACKNOWLEDGMENTS

I began the decade of the '90s with a divorce after fourteen years of marriage, in a new city with no friends, no job, and three small children who desperately needed a stay-at-home mom. My education about real life and my journey through careers as a family film critic, local television movie critic, radio talk show host for several Southern California radio stations, and being a regular guest on television shows such as *Politically Incorrect* ended that decade with incredible family support, wonderful friends, and many fellow professionals who helped me along the way. My observations and experiences are what gave me the motivation to write this book, but without loved ones and friends to support me it wouldn't have happened.

I cannot express my huge debt of gratitude to the best friend and best publisher any writer could ever dream of working with—John Peterson and Cliff Ford, respectively. Thanks for sticking by me and making the book possible when it seemed impossible. To Lance Wubbels and Terry McDowell, incredible literary developers who took me from kindergarten through college with this experience while my mistakes nearly drove them insane. Thanks to Lions Head Publishing for all their hard work and for making me look good.

To my family who has encouraged me through every step of my life, long before this book began. To my parents, Mary and Jerry, who have covered me with daily prayer, endless phone calls, and have proven you never stop being a parent—I love you both so much. To my wonderful sisters, who are my constant source of prayer support, emotional strength, and best friends. Amy, you are my touchstone and the best mom I know—I can't imagine a week without your wisdom! Dena, you are my spiritual warrior, standing in the gap and always taking my side—that means a lot to me. Kelly, baby sister, your godly gifts are beautiful to behold—I treasure your prayers, mighty woman of God.

To my dearest friends, Stephanie Pearce and Robin Schrecengost. Stephanie, we have shared laughter, tears, divorce, and life together—

thanks for always being there. Robin, you are my oldest friend—you know me well and still can love me.

There are many others who have encouraged or motivated me along the way. The gang at KPRZ and Mark Larson, Monica Murray, Gloria "Super Glo" Deloney, Terry Frost—thanks for the grace, for covering for me and letting me play "best-of"s to get this book done! My *O.C. Register* editor, Vance Durgin, and OCN producer and supporter, Jeff Rowe—thanks guys! The gang at *Politically Incorrect* who have always treated me like family—Carole, Marilyn, Joy, and even you Bill. Crosswalk.com, Dick Rolfe, Pat and Caryl and Jeremiah Films. My cousin Deborah Johnson, who took a long walk with me years ago and encouraged me to write this book. Dr. Neil Clark Warren—sage and friend whose challenge is to find me the love of my life. Pastor Phil and Jeannie Munsey, who have seen me through it all. Pastors Steve, Dave, Doug and others at The Life Church who have prayed for, counseled, and been spiritual fathers to my children and to me. Most of all I thank Jesus and God the Father for the exciting journey I've had in this life. I am in awe of your protection, blessings, grace, mercy, faithfulness, friendship, being my husband when I needed one, a loving father to my children, and most of all for your constant love. Selah! Jeremiah 29:11-14.

CONTENTS

OUR GREATEST BATTLEFIELD IN THIS NEW MILLENNIUM WILL BE FOR THE MINDS AND HEARTS OF OUR CHILDREN. As parents or concerned family members and friends, we need to fight to protect those minds and hearts and, ultimately, teach them how to fight for themselves. I consider it a battlefield because as a talk show host, film critic, and mother of three, I've witnessed firsthand the headline news that proves an unhealthy entertainment lifestyle can influence people to make life-or-death choices. My passion, purpose, and desire is to help you make your entertainment choices wisely. It's time for you to equip yourself and your children with sound, practical advice from Holly on Hollywood.

Culture war? I think it's more like a "Cultural Holocaust." And the victims are our children.

—Phil Cooke, television director

PARENT TO PARENT

had just finished my Friday night radio show when Nathan, my fourteen-year-old, called to check in. He was at our local movie theater with five of his friends, and the plan had been to see a PG-13 movie. He informed me that his friends wanted to "switch" movies and see either *Freddy Got Fingered* or *Joe Dirt* (neither being a good choice).

I didn't answer for a few seconds because I knew Nathan was standing right next to the buddies he'd been waiting to "hang" with all week. I had a feeling this last-minute switch wasn't his idea because he already knew what my answer would be. Nathan was definitely in one of those tough spots teenagers get into with their peers. And I knew that Nate making that phone call and being truthful wasn't going to win him a popularity contest with his peers.

So there I was . . . a family film critic, an author of a book about empowering your kids in this specific type of situation, but most importantly Nate's mom. I was in a no-win situation with my moral conscience on one side and the thought of being the "mean mom" versus the "popular mom" on the other. Every parent has been there.

I suspected that the boys had already made up their minds to see *Freddy*, and I asked Nathan if that was the case. He paused and said, "Yeah, they're all going to go see *Freddy*." I reassuringly reminded him that there was no way I could give him permission to see that horrendous movie, but he already knew that. Which is why I got the call in the first place. I was Nathan's backup plan for getting him out of a peer-pressured situation. When I asked how the boys planned on buying tickets for this R-rated movie, he told me they were going to "sneak in." I told him I was on my way and to meet me out front.

We went for a hamburger and talked about the situation. I told him how proud I was that he took a stand in front of his friends and chose to call and tell me the truth. He told me one of his friends asked, "Why did you tell your mom the truth? You should have just lied about the movie." Nate replied, "Because I don't lie to my mom. If I got caught, it would ruin my relationship with her *and* my privileges, and it's not worth it. Besides, I don't really want to see that movie."

I had tears in my eyes, a lump in my throat, and I have never been more proud of my son's integrity, values, and character than at that moment. Nathan had proven to me that my message about raising kids to be media savvy and empowering kids with the ability, discernment, and wisdom to say no to peers in tough situations could succeed.

Parents, that is one of the messages I want to get across to you in this book. It's time to not only raise your kids to be aware of just how much the entertainment world influences their lives but empower them with the ability to take a stand in their "peer-pressured world" and make wise choices about their lives. In today's seductive entertainment culture, it's more important than ever to educate yourselves and your children and teenagers about how these influences can and will shape and affect their lives.

I truly believe that many parents don't realize how much America's entertainment- and media-focused culture influences their families, especially morally, ethically, and spiritually. The fundamentals of the world's value system are spoon-fed to kids daily through the movies or television shows they watch, the music they listen to, the magazines they read, the Internet they spend time on, the video games they play, and the friends they associate with. It's time to educate and empower your kids to be aware of all of these.

As a child and teenager, I logged far too many television hours with my four sisters while my mom and dad worked long hours to provide a living for our family. However, things were different in those days—not only was television a tamer beast, but our society was a different gatekeeper! Our culture and media venues as a whole found common ground when it came to cherishing and protecting our children and families. Sadly, those days of valuing and protecting not only our children and families but also the very sanctity of life itself are being redefined by our media-minded society.

The last thirty years have witnessed drastic changes, shocking "firsts," incredible achievements, triumphs, tribulations, and success in the film and television industry. We have eagerly rewarded that industry with our praises, faithful adoration, hard-earned dollars, and perhaps unwittingly sacrificed our children in the process.

Being a movie critic, radio talk show host, and parent of three teenagers has laid the foundation for my suggestions in this book. I know what years of absorbing numerous entertainment choices can do to adults as well as children, and I've seen firsthand how it directly influences our lives. My intent is to give you more than just a glimpse into what's affecting our society and changing our world. I hope to provide you with insight and helpful tools to prepare your children for the world's bombardment.

Your eyes will be opened to the mentality Hollywood has toward you and your children and the pervasive influence the mass media has on our lives. My purpose is not to solely demonize or bash Hollywood. Too many people want to blame the entertainment industry or media for all of our social and cultural ills, and that's irresponsible. There are countless movies, television shows, songs, radio programs, and technological advancements that have brought valuable contributions to our society and impacted our lives in positive ways.

But there is a dark side to the entertainment and media industry, a seductive power that entices all of us. Whether it's material, sexual, emotional, physical, mental, spiritual, or subliminal, you need to be aware just how easy it is to get complacent and drawn into that seductive mind-set, lifestyle, and "entertain-me" world!

My sincere hope is that in unveiling the destructive influences that many entertainment choices bring to our lives, it will educate, influence, and positively change the way you and your family choose to live.

In researching this exhaustive subject of the entertainment and media world, I realized it would take volumes to address every venue thoroughly. I had to narrow my focus to a few specific areas that I felt were the most important issues facing parents today. I am not a sociologist or an expert in the psychoanalysis of how Hollywood is influencing our culture. You will not find complicated graphs or sophisticated theories. I simply bring the professional knowledge and information I have attained through my years of experience as a movie critic, giving you practical ways to teach your children to become "media savvy."

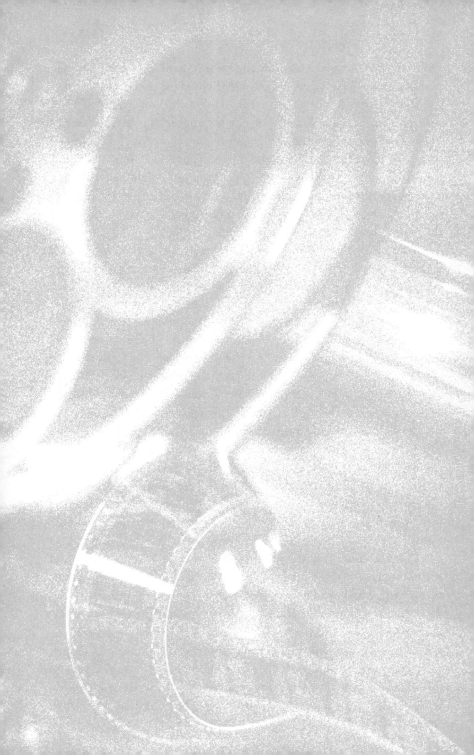

Brothers, what we do in life echoes in eternity.

—Maximus in *Gladiator*

WHO'S WHO?

Franklin D. Roosevelt said, "To some generations much is given, of others much is expected. This generation has a rendezvous with destiny." While we may be fascinated with this idea of the destiny of generations, sociologists are more fascinated with how fast and how quickly our culture is changing and what that means in today's world. Television spin rooms, radio talk shows, advertising agencies, consulting companies, Internet marketing lines, and movie companies are all labeling, quoting, stereotyping, and cataloging the likes, dislikes, behaviors, desires, and ultimately the moods of each demographic group, in hopes that each generation can be marketed to. After all, for the entertainment industry, it's all about money.

We love to put labels on generations. Terms such as senior citizen, mid-life, 40-, 30-, and 20-somethings, teenagers, and children used to describe and categorize our culture. But those terms are quickly becoming passé. According to academics Neil Howe and William Strauss in their book *Millennials Rising: The Next Great Generation,* we currently have five living generations: the GI (1901–1924), Silent (1925–42), Baby Boomers (1943–1962), Xers (1963–1981), and Millennials (1982–present). Demographers seem to differ over the cut-off dates by a year or two, but the term *millennials* actually covers two groups: Gen-Y (1979–1995 by one account), or *echo boomers,* and Gen-I (those born after 1995 and dubbed so because they're growing up with the Internet). Basically, it's the nineteen-and-under crowd that fall in this category.

Why does it seem to matter to the popular culture what groups people fit into according to age? It's because in today's entertainment-saturated society, *age does matter.* Every ad agency, restaurant, Internet site, movie studio, television network, radio station, retail store, and magazine cares, because who you are will determine their success. The exact category that you fit into determines their future and is the capital they're banking on.

Here's how these groups are shaping and changing not only our economy but our culture as well.

THE MILLENNIALS: I & Y

Gen-I is the Internet generation just under Y. These are kids born since 1995 who are learning how to use a mouse and are very familiar with teletubbies. Many can sing you the lyrics to "Oops! . . . I Did It Again" and are extremely savvy about brand names. They live a life of luxury compared to former generations and are considered a lucrative target for most advertisers. The record, movie, and television industries, toy manufacturers, computer games, fast-food chains, clothing companies, and crafty marketers and advertisers are all pursuing this demographic group because of the powerful influence these kids will have on the next trends. Gen-I kids may barely know what's going on, but what they do know is that it's *all* about them.

Gen-Y kids and teens are the second baby boomer kids born from 1982 to present. The nineteen-and-under crowd numbers almost 79 million strong and spent $27.9 billion of their own money, surpassing the 78 million baby boomers and 40 million Gen-X parents. Even more impressive, these techno-wizard, multitasking, media savvy kids got their moms and dads to spend $248.7 billion of their own money just on them in 2000. With a network of Web sites created to cater to their generation's wants and needs (www.snowball.com), this demographic segment of teens has it all.[1]

The good news is that Generation Y, the millennials, is a healthy group poised to become the next great generation, one that will provide a more positive, group-oriented, can-do ethos. The millennials get along well with their boomer and Xer parents and are savvy about their bright future. Not only are their numbers significant for an impressive impact on our future, but their outlook on life is different from their Gen-X and boomer parents. We are also seeing a direct reversal of their behavior from the boomer youth behavior.

As a nation, we've devoted more concern, attention, focus, and money on this generation than any other. Today's teenagers are the wealthiest generation and live in the most prosperous times in our country's history. Over the next decade, their pop music will become more melodic and singable, sitcoms more melodramatic and wholesome, and there will be a new emphasis on manners, modesty, and old-fashioned gender courtesies, with an emphasis on marriage and family. Knowledge is power with this generation.

Neil Howe and William Strauss have this to say about these kids: "Over the next decade, the Millennial Generation will entirely recast the image of youth from downbeat and alienated to upbeat and engaged— with potentially seismic consequences for America. They will rebel against the culture by cleaning it up, rebel against political cynicism by touting trust, rebel against individualism by stressing teamwork, rebel against adult pessimism by being upbeat, and rebel against social injustice by actually going out and getting a few things done."[2]

GEN-X

Gen-Xers can best be described as those who live to work, not work to live. Yes, they like to have fun, are tech savvy, can be demanding, and absolutely want all the amenities life has to offer. They are the latchkey kids whom boomers went to therapy over and upon whom divorce took its greatest toll. Their numbers are small (40 million) due to the availability of abortion and boomer women waiting longer to have children. Their pessimism is a natural reflex, and their individualism and entrepreneurial abilities have prompted businesses to cater to their every whim. Commercials skew to their language and sense of humor. Hotels offer them amenities such as cordless phones, printers, faxes, WebTV, and CD players because they realize this generation is used to all those luxuries. Restaurants and hotel dining facilities are going for a more relaxed feel to accommodate them. Even fitness centers are keen on wooing their hearts for membership. Nightclubs that offer tattooing, herbal teas, and alternative music are in. These are the kids who swore they would never get married so they would never get divorced. They are deathly afraid of making the same mistake their parents made, so even though they work to live, they cherish their children and are desperately trying to reverse the divorce-casualty syndrome. Clearly, since the business world seems to be what Gen-Xers follow after, it's only appropriate that they go in style.

BABY BOOMERS

Modern Maturity, the largest circulation magazine in the world, announced a new magazine aimed at the 50-somethings. Apparently the maturing boomers are having a hard time coming to terms with their age after surviving divorce, aging parents, empty nests, bumpy rides on the stock market, life-threatening illnesses, numerous job changes, and major physical rehaul. Bottom line: boomers don't want to grow older.

Baby boomers are the first generation in American history whose average age will be in the '80s. In fact, the Census Bureau estimates a booming number of boomer octogenarians is approaching. By 2025 there will be 15 million Americans 80 or older and 31 million in 2050. There are 78 million baby boomers that make up almost 40% of U.S. adults today.

Youthfulness is highly valued by boomers these days. Part nature, part neurosis, today's boomers want to remain active, youthful, and hopeful into old age. Antiaging products, nutraceuticals, genetic research, herbs, acupuncture, antistress therapies, alternative medicines, bifocal contacts, hidden hearing aides, cosmetic surgery, and cosmeceuticals will all play a part in how this generation ages gracefully. For a generation who rebelled against authority, these changes are evolutionary, not revolutionary.

Older age for boomers won't be the same as it was for their grandparents. With a better chance at a healthier lifestyle and living longer, boomers' options seem to be booming. After all, the teens of today are still listening to the Beatles, Dylan, Beach Boys, Stones, Simon, Jackson, Clapton, and Aerosmith. Boomers still rule!

OCTEGENARIANS

Will you still need me?
Will you still feed me?
When I'm 64?"

When boomers were young and crooning that Beatles' tune, 64 seemed old because society deemed it retirement age and, psychologically, people thought and acted old. Well, we've come a long way baby, and things have changed! Today, one third of Americans in their 70s consider themselves "middle-aged," as did 22% of those 80 and older.

Nearly half of the 65- to 69-year-olds consider themselves middle-aged and look forward to being a functioning citizen in the 80-plus world. The National Institute on Aging reports that there are 9 million Americans 80 or older. Healthcare for these octogenarians is increasing their life expectancy, and elective surgery is improving their quality of life. There's no better example of how active, healthy, and thriving the 80-plus crowd is going to be in the next quarter of a century than the poster girl for octogenarians, the Queen Mother of England. She lived through the entire twentieth century, reaching a majestic 100 years old as she entered the millennium, and is a royal example that it can be done in a productive way.

It seems an understatement to say that life has drastically changed for octogenarians who lived before WWII. We're talking about a generation who lived in America before there were TVs, electric toothbrushes, radar, or air conditioners. Luxuries such as frozen foods, contact lenses, ballpoint pens, dishwashers, pantyhose, clothes dryers, credit cards, tape decks, electric typewriters, artificial anything, and much, much more were only dreamed of. We're talking before man walked on the moon and gas was 11 cents a gallon. Can you imagine how much more our culture and country will change in the next century? What changes, inventions, and improved lifestyles will the octogenarians reflect on in the year 2025? Only time will tell.

MOVIES HAVE BECOME THE PULPITS TO OUR SOCIETY, teaching their own brand of morality, ideals, religion, and popular opinion. Television is the nanny to our children, the educator to our teens, and a scapegoat for most adults. Music is the Pied Piper of seduction that our children are willingly following, and MTV is the land of no return. The Internet is an information gateway bringing the entire world into the intimacy of homes, streaming megadoses of fantasy and reality into minds, hearts, and souls.

Our Addiction to Entertainment

few years ago I stepped into the restroom in the "Cowboys" restaurant at Universal Studios in California. The walls above the toilets and over the sinks were inlaid with mini-televisions. I recall thinking . . . *only in California!* Did I really need to be entertained while using the restroom or washing my hands? My curiosity got the best of me, so I asked the manager why they had spent so much money on the elaborately equipped bathrooms. His response was as simple as this: "So no customer will miss any part of the entertainment." That pretty much sums up our American culture today. None of us want to miss being entertained!

Do we really need the entertainment luxuries our commercial society inundates us with? Do we really need all the products that pander to our every whim? Could we get by without the Palm Pilots, computers, and fax machines we can hold in our hands. Or ninety-nine television channels with big screens? Or movie theaters with eighteen screens and stadium seating? Or the luxury cars with sticker prices of $300,000 and up? The list goes on and on!

America has entered this new millennium a much different country than our founding fathers ever dreamed it would be. With six billion people on this planet and 282 million living in the United States, the principles, spirit, and standards this country was founded on are quickly and sadly vanishing, being redefined in this unprecedented period of historic change. The Judeo-Christian fundamental values that twelve generations of Americans fought so hard to preserve have been inundated with a popular entertainment culture that has forever changed our families, social life, businesses, and even our religious activities. Our lifestyles have been so saturated with this mind-set that it has become a form of religion in and of itself, a religion that worships the gods of mass media.

At the brink of this exciting new millennium, incredible changes through computer technology, scientific advances, medical break-throughs, and entertainment choices are reshaping our lifestyles. Never before have so many entertainment alternatives been available—movies, television, DVDs, CDs, electronic games, the Internet, not to mention the music and talk radio industry. But how will all of these enter-tainment choices affect our future generations? How has our society already been bombarded with choices that have taken an obvious toll on adults as well as our children?

For the past twelve years that I have reviewed movies, I've seen firsthand the staggering influence that Hollywood has upon our day-to-day lives. I've watched trends come and go in the film industry as well as on television. What used to be an occasional lifestyle choice for a Friday night date, a family outing, or a night spent relaxing on the couch has become a daily way of life in our American culture. Providing escapism and fantasy has become an incredibly lucrative twenty-four-hour-a-day business, and entertainment is the commodity.

IN CASE YOU DOUBT

As a family film critic, I'm well aware of how much our kids love to be entertained and how much Hollywood has an influence on our society, our culture, our religion, our values—especially our children and teens. America's "melting pot" of cultures now simply emulates and epitomizes the entertainment we devour. And we—parents, teens, and children—are addicted to it.

Is *addicted* too strong a word? Take a look at how teenagers spend their free time. By the time your teenager finishes high school, he or she will have watched 23,000 hours of television! Compare that to the 11,000 hours spent in the classroom.[1] More time is spent with the tel-evision than is spent with teachers, friends, or family. Add to that total the hours spent listening to music. How many hours would you say your child or teen listens to music as soon as they get in the car or their room? One, two, three hours a day? From the time a teenager has gone from grades seven to twelve, they will have listened to a whopping 10,500 hours of music![2]

The fact is, what once was a pleasurable novelty for baby boomers has become their children's daily obsession. They *need* to be, *want* to be, and *have* to be entertained! Teenagers love movies so much that 92%[3] of them will choose going to a movie over any other activity, whether it's sports, going to the beach, or spending time with friends. While the average moviegoing adult sees only eight movies a year, the average teenager will see fifty, and the vast majority of those films will be R-rated.[4]

If movies were teenagers' main source of entertainment, that would be one thing, but movies have also become their main source of education. For the teenagers of the twenty-first century, movies are where they learn about life and from which they derive their trends in clothing, their taste for music, the latest hip language, and, of course, their understanding about sex. All entertainment is educational; it's just a question of what subject it's teaching. Movies, television, music, electronic games, the Internet, not to mention MTV or the talk radio industry, are all in tremendous competition with one another. All of these entertainment mediums are vying for our money and diverting our focus from life and consuming our minds. And sadly much of what our youths are consuming, much of what comes into their minds and stays there, is twisted, distorted, and deviant to the core. If the domination of our entertainment culture remains unchecked, the end results can only be blamed on ourselves.

WHAT DO I MEAN BY DEATH BY ENTERTAINMENT?

When I refer to *entertainment,* there are several definitions that are helpful: entertaining or being entertained, amusement, pleasure, something that entertains; especially, a show or performance, music, dramatic performance, oratory, or interesting, diverting, amusing thing that holds interest or attention.[5] And when I refer to the *mass media,* the word *mass* includes the world of movies, television, radio, newspapers, music, and magazines. But entertainment also includes other forms such as MTV, CD-ROMs, the Internet, electronic games, and all instruments of popular communication.

You can see why I refer to the mass media as the "life source" for our popular culture. The *Concise Columbia Encyclopedia* states: "The mass media often function as the locus of social control and the source of popular culture. They help create historical events, teach values, and by virtue of the huge commercial enterprises they represent, affect the viability of free societies."[6] Notice the words: "social control," "source of popular culture," "create events," "teach values."

The many powerful influences behind the mass media subtly permeate and tap into our lives by creating and maintaining a daily drug-of-choice through different forms of entertainment. As a nation, the more we lose our moral compass and objectivity and buy into that shallow, self-serving decadence, the more we will see that behavior reflected in our homes (rebellious kids, husbands hooked on Internet pornography, wives addicted to fantasy soap operas) and our society (teen school shootings, perverse crimes, sexual abuse, etc.).

Why and how does entertainment wield so much power over our everyday lives? Because we as a culture *love* to be entertained. In fact, we love it so much we *worship* the formats that entertainment comes in (movies, TV, MTV, music, sports, etc.). Entertainment delivers pleasure, and we are a nation addicted to pleasure. The level of illusion, deception, fantasy, or perversion that pleasurable entertainment brings you or your family is what ultimately can and will be destructive to you and your family. It's the level and amount to which you allow an entertainment mind-set to control or run your life. Remember, whatever you idolize, love, or worship becomes your god.

So what do I mean when I use the phrase *"death by entertainment"*? I believe that by *constantly* pursuing, consuming, stimulating, and surrounding yourself with an entertainment/fantasy lifestyle, you ultimately wear down your ability to discern what's right or wrong for you as an individual and a family and slowly adopt a new value system of discernment. As you grow callused and even desensitized to things that are harmful or destructive, your moral conscience becomes seared. Once you let your guard down, the death of what you and your household once stood for will slowly become evident. Your values, ethics, standards, and beliefs that are an integral part of who you are will give way to a pleasure-seeking, "entertain me" addictive mentality that I believe has become a sort of religion in this country. All that you held dear or sacred can be slowly corrupted if you're not careful.

Don't let your family get swept into this "entertain me" religion. Choose to be a discerning and responsible media consumer. Train your children in the way they should go so that they too can learn to make wise media choices. And hopefully, by preparing your kids for what they will be bombarded with, teaching them how to handle those choices, empowering them to say no to peers and, more importantly, to themselves, you will spare you and your family a *death by entertainment*.

OUR ENTERTAINMENT MIND-SET

Almost every aspect of our society and daily lives has been inundated with an entertainment mind-set. It used to be said that art imitates life, but these days it's obvious just how much our lives are imitating the art we daily consume through all of these mediums! Many Americans plan their daily routine based on how stimulating, exciting, or fun it will be. Whether it's work, play, exercise, a hobby, school, dining out, or even going to church, we subliminally evaluate time spent on the experience as good or bad, based on how entertaining it could and should be. In fact, unless even the simplest, most mundane of tasks or activities has an entertaining lure to it, most people will replace the activity with something else.

In 2000 director Robert Zemeckis made an interesting movie with Tom Hanks called *Cast Away*, in which the main character is stranded on a desert island for four years. It is fascinating that for about an hour the audience doesn't hear much music or conversation from Hanks. Instead, we watch him adapt to his surroundings and struggle to survive. There is almost no stimuli, noise, or anything from the outside world—just Tom and the island. As I watched the movie, I wondered whether a teenager could go through a situation like that today and survive? Could they do without the constant stimuli and entertainment they've grown accustomed to? Would they make it with just their mind for company?

We now know how easily an entertainment mind-set can permeate and influence our social culture and, most importantly, our family.

But just what effect does this mind-set have on our society today? There are those who blame the entertainment industry for the increase in violence, sex, stress, and depression among our teenagers. Parents are especially concerned about their younger children and how they are being influenced by this media onslaught.

THE MEDIA'S INFLUENCE

Movies, television, music, the news media, advertising, the Internet, and electronic games are all designed to convey information in one way or another. While we are usually aware of the content of the material that is being presented to us, we may not be conscious of the inherent subtleties. For it is from these all-encompassing entertainment mediums that we make our decisions about life, form our opinions, and gather insight into why we think and do the things we do. We learn about love, family, friendships, business, cultural trends, art, fashion, family, diversity, religions, music, and all other aspects of life because the communication is that pervasive.

When we examine closely the entertainment influences in our society, we discover three levels of media influence and communication. The first is *explicit communication*. At this level we observe the surface content of the communication in the various forms of news media and entertainment media—the real world with actual people and actual events. The second level is *technological communication*, which is subtler, and not the real world. The technological media has put together what in essence is a counterfeit world, and viewers see the world through the window they present, which looks like reality but is not. The third level is the *subliminal communication*, which is the most subtle of all. Advertisers, in particular, use it to communicate powerfully, not necessarily by what is said, but more through what is presupposed by the image they present.

While it is obvious that the mass media has not only influenced our entertainment-minded society, it also appears to define it. We know that with the control of the media comes a control of our culture. Many Americans evaluate their quality of life on the basis of the material levels of pleasure and ease in which they live their daily lives. Attaining those levels of pleasure to create those materialistic lifestyles is achieved through many avenues and drastically differs among all of us.

Our society has become a mass melting pot of cultures, religions, and ideals that are powerfully shaped, propelled, and influenced by what we are conditioned with through movies, television, advertising, and the media. America has long been known as "the land of the free," and now it's known for being "the capital for entertainment." The source of this self-indulgent entertainment mind-set comes from a powerful influence with a destructive moral code that has slowly become the Bible for our culture.

Our pleasure-seeking, "entertain me" culture has catapulted into the twenty-first century hooked on the latest conveniences to get us through the day. Cell phones are the modern convenience du jour, with almost as many teenagers carrying them as adults. Electronic gadgets feed us stock reports and e-mail messages, and almost anything else that you want can be obtained from the palm of your hand. The average household television has cable or satellite with ninety-nine channels streaming in twenty-four hours a day with the latest movies, sound bites, sports, gossip, celebrity quotes, inside information, and anything else *Entertainment Tonight, Extra, Showbiz, E-online,* and others can sell. America is the largest exporter of "direct culture" (movies, books, TV, music, newspapers, and magazines) in the history of the world, and our culture is rapidly becoming a global culture, shaping, changing (and being shaped and changed) by the rest of the world.

It's clear that today's technology is transforming tomorrow's possibilities. The lifestyles of average baby boomers and Gen-Xers in America are steadily improving due to drastic technological advancements that will affect every aspect of our lives. We live in an era that caters to personal lifestyles and has achieved a phenomenal quality of life both in and out of the home. And even the American corporate structure is changing with an information age of technology that has redefined the business world along with its leaders and the economy.

HOW HAS THE MEDIA CHANGED AMERICA?

The transition from an industrial to a technological age was revolutionary for our country. In its infancy, the media influence (what was allowed into the home) on a family was still under the control of the parents. With the birth of the media generation, we've leapt into an era with limitless information that has infiltrated and influenced every aspect of our daily lives. Many parents can no longer keep their kids protected from the outside world. Even if a parent can regulate and manage the flow of media content coming into their homes, what about when they walk out the door? What about when their kids go to spend the night at a friend's home, or your teenager goes out with friends to a movie? If they have not been taught to protect themselves from the world's influence by becoming "media savvy," they are easy targets.

Many authorities agree that easier access to violent and sexually explicit material has and is changing the moral landscape of our nation. In the last twenty-five years, the bombardment of entertainment products that have been introduced and marketed to baby boomers and Gen-Xers and Gen-Yers has probably been the single most significant factor in making parenting more difficult. A recent survey showed 44% of adults believe movies and TV are directly responsible for the social, moral, and cultural problems in America.[7] But it's not just movies and television that are to blame for creating this climate. Music, MTV, magazines, books, video games, advertising, and the Internet are all driving forces of a pleasure-seeking society that indulges in self-gratification and satisfaction on many levels.

After years of denying the power of the mass media, more and more people are becoming aware of, and opposed to, the ungodly influence Hollywood has on our society. A *USA Today/CNN/Gallup* poll found:

+ 96% are very concerned about sex on TV.
+ 97% are concerned about vulgar language.
+ 97% are concerned about violence.
+ 68% believe that reducing the amount of sex and violence in movies, music, and on TV would significantly improve the moral climate of the U.S.
+ 65% felt the entertainment industry is seriously out of touch with the values of the American people.
+ 63% felt government should become involved in restricting sex and violence presented by the industry.[8]

Now the industry has grown from a few major studios and television networks to a worldwide multibillion-dollar global business. Gone are the days of a few key studios holding all the power. Now there are countless independent companies contributing worldwide to an industry that's constantly changing, and not for the better.

Movies have become the pulpits to our society, teaching their own brand of morality, ideals, religion, and popular opinion. Television is the nanny to our children, the educator to our teens, and a scapegoat for most adults. Music is the Pied Piper of seduction that our children are willingly following, and MTV is the land of no return. The Internet is an information gateway bringing the entire world into the intimacy of homes, streaming megadoses of fantasy and reality into minds, hearts, and souls.

Celebrities have become as important as politicians, and politicians have become the celebrities. Sports figures, earning the highest-paid salaries in history, along with celebrities are the "heroes" of our children today. Sex and violence are killing the innocence that our children once enjoyed. In today's culture, sex and violence are the staple diet of Gen-Y kids, who are redefining both with their own terms. Our English language has been manipulated, crucified, demeaned, and brought to a new level of translation where even a president gets away with asking what "is" is. Literacy is at an all-time low because kids and teens are choosing entertainment choices over learning.

Even within the traditional family, divorce has ripped the moral and spiritual fiber that once held families together and sustained heritage and values. Parents have abandoned children for careers, forcing their kids to raise themselves at home. America now holds the distinction of having the highest divorce rate with the most children affected by it in the industrial world. Families have also been redefined, reconfigured, and trivialized to the point that anyone, male or female, who clings to someone else for more than a week can call themselves "family." Parental criteria have been redefined with women seeking to have (and raise) children without fathers. Children are growing up too fast, and many parents feel out-of-control.

How has the media and entertainment industry achieved such a hold on our society? By monopolizing our time, money, affections, and, ultimately, our lifestyles. We work hard to make money to buy things from people we don't know . . . with money we don't have . . . for things we don't even need! In other words, we are working longer hours and putting in more time to maintain this lifestyle that's become our source of pleasure. But even more seriously, America's moral fabric, values, ethics, standards, and spiritual truths have undergone a dumbing down with a brainwashing philosophy that accommodates what's culturally popular and politically correct. The presence of the entertainment and media has changed what was once a traditional social structure of family, church, school, and entertainment. Now the entertainment industry has become a teacher in and of itself, not only filling a leisure need but an educational one as well.

WHAT HAPPENED TO RESPONSIBLE PARENTING?

Fame and fortune have always been an American dream, but these days it seems to be an obsession. The quest for instant wealth and attaining fame for the way you do it has become a mantra for the Gen-X and Gen-Y set. Lifestyles are hectic, making *stress* the most widely used term in the '90s to describe our lives. No one has the luxury of time anymore, and a world of constant input, stimulation, and activity has nearly extinguished the peaceful, slower-paced, quiet, bygone America.

Some point a finger at the entertainment industry, blaming it for a plethora of cultural problems, and it certainly plays a significant role. But what about parents? Clearly, a good portion of the responsibility falls upon them.

I've lost track of how many times I go to see an R-rated movie and seated close by is a mother or father (or both) with a child under twelve. When I watched *The Legend of Sleepy Hollow,* I heard a child whimpering and asking to leave. I looked over and watched both parents hush her and say, "Just put your head in my arm and don't look." If you've seen this movie directed by Tim Burton, you'll recall heads rolling, bodies sliced and diced, and depictions of witchcraft too intense for some adults to sit through. But as so many parents do, rather than get a baby-sitter, this couple chose to expose their five-year-old daughter to violence and horror that experts have proven stays in the memory.

The *New York Times* recently reported that children as young as ten are frequenting R-rated films on a regular basis accompanied by a parent, despite the fact that these films routinely include scenes of extreme violence, sexuality, nudity, and profanity.[9] In later chapters

I will speak more to parents on this, but I definitely believe many parents have abdicated their parental roles and responsibilities, both in parenting and disciplining. For the past two decades our country has seen disrespect, violence, loose morality, and horrendous behavior on the rise in young people, and parents must shoulder their part of the burden of responsibility.

OUR ADDICTION TO RICH AND HAPPY?

When I was younger I used to enjoy watching the television show *Lifestyles of the Rich and Famous*. Robin Leach would search out the most exquisite homes, vacation spots, and getaways anywhere in the world. I used to love to watch that show and dream about living in one of those homes or taking a vacation to one of those exotic places. That show made me want to be rich. But more importantly, it convinced me that if I was rich, I would be happy.

I believe that very mentality ("I have to be rich to be happy!") permeates our culture today. As the wealth of our nation increases with one out of five families earning $100,000 a year,[10] so does our appetite for luxury, convenience, excess, pleasure, and the creature comforts of life. We are spending more time pampering and entertaining ourselves, and less time worshiping (daily time has declined 22%)[11] or visiting friends and relatives (down 21%).[12] Many people don't even realize they've bought into the "entertain me" lifestyle, but bought into it they have!

The price of entertainment from cable television to concerts to sporting events, even meals at restaurants, has risen more rapidly than consumer prices over the last few years, and the reason is simple: Americans want to be entertained!

Today's families have an array of entertainment choices not even thought of a few decades ago, and parents are flocking to spend their time and money on those choices with their kids. Aside from movies and cable TV, there are new options such as Internet access, video games, PC games, and pay-per-view that all carry a price tag. In the year 2000 we spent $7.7 billion on movie tickets, which is 2.9% more than what we spent in 1999. The cost of going to the movies has likewise increased 6.3% for an average price of $5.39, the second biggest jump since 1991. In the next few years, projections for global ticket sales are at $21.4 billion and could be more if ticket prices continue to rise.[13]

Theme parks, cruise ships, resorts, and amusement parks have all enjoyed a booming economy, attracting families that can afford the high costs and wealthy clientele looking for their next adventure. Americans are even turning to space for their ultimate fantasy trip. Hilton Hotels are looking at the feasibility of opening a hotel in space or on the moon, which could cost around ten billion dollars. How much would guests pay for this luxurious elite trip? About $20,000 a couple for a week in space.

New Year's Eve 2000 was billed as one of the biggest profit-grossing nights of live entertainment, the most expensive evening of the twentieth century. Celebrities asked astronomical fees to perform in hotels and restaurants, gouging customers who were willing to pay premium prices of as much as $1,000 a ticket just to be memorably entertained. Ironically, people overspent because there was an inkling of false security that the world would be coming to an end, or financial institutions would collapse and not be able to handle the fallout. The expected chaos and upheaval created a false comfort in the fact that everyone could live it up because no one knew what tomorrow would bring. For many it brought more than a hangover—debt and high interest rates on maxed-out charge cards.

So what is the trick to get the public to pay this outrageous amount of money just to be entertained? Advertisers and clever marketers pander to our insatiable appetites for pleasure and fun. But even deeper than that, they tap into a part in all of us that believes we "need" or have to "have" that experience. The entertainment industry creates an elitist mentality, an urgency, if you will, such as a must-see movie, must-see TV, must-see space, must-see Web sites, rides, music, cruises, automobiles, etc.

And who is being affected by all of this passive entertainment? We all are.

I HAVE BEEN AMAZED AT THE LEVEL OF GENUINE, SINCERE, FRIGHTENING HATRED AND HOSTILITY toward religious believers of every stripe that you get from secular extremists right now. It's very scary to me. I think it's the only kind of bigotry that's considered politically correct and acceptable, and you see it in a lot of regards—just utter contempt, hatred, tremendous fear, a total lack of understanding. Part of what is necessary in a pluralistic democracy is that we all respect one another and try to get along together, but that is not the attitude you get from Hollywood. It seems that every time they portray someone in today's world as a religious believer that person is viewed as some kind of a crook, a deviant, a weirdo, an ugly person, or something's wrong with him or her. It's poisonous.

—MICHAEL MEDVED, Nationally Syndicated Talk Show Host[1]

The Hidden Agenda

THE GOLDEN AGE OF HOLLYWOOD

n the spring of 1896, Edison's latest invention, the vitascope, introduced movies that were shown as a novelty in vaudeville houses. They quickly became popular with the working class but were shown mostly on Kinetoscopes in arcades, which became known for their risqué films. As more and better films were made, the popularity of going to the movies spread to the middle class, and vaudeville houses began to combine movies with live acts. Soon the popularity of the movies and the affordability of just showing a film instead of hiring performers paved the way for full-length films and movie theaters. By the 1920s the motion-picture industry had revolutionized the world of entertainment, and movies replaced vaudeville and legitimate theater as a preferred art form with the public. Although the movie was at first thought to be a vulgar medium, eventually it took on a life of its own when various producers stepped in and made quality films.

Theaters began to spread across the United States, and eventually Hollywood became a powerful social institution that communicated its own brand of ideas and values. Even in the early years, the content of movies influenced teenagers and young people in their dating and sexual behaviors, attitudes about racial and ethnic stereotypes, and their disillusionment with their own lives. Love, sex, and crime were the main themes for most of the films produced in the 1920s, which seemed to reflect what was taking place in the Hollywood community. Tabloid headlines announced Mary Pickford divorcing her husband to marry Douglas Fairbanks, scandals about suicide, murder, sex, lavish and extravagant lifestyles, big salaries, and promiscuous actors and actresses. In the era of prohibition, Hollywood was considered an immoral portal of influence, and crusaders rallied against their liberal ideology and declared Hollywood "out of touch" with the realities of American life. Any of that sound familiar?

Attempts to supervise or censor these films by police and censorship boards were handled at local levels but soon proved futile and frustrating. Religious and cultural leaders realized that the movie industry would play a significant role in shaping our national culture, so the question was how to turn this powerful entertainment medium into a tool that could spread moral values that would better society and not destroy it.

With the combined influence of religious, educational, and social groups and the growing threat of social and federal censorship, the movie industry formed the Motion Picture Producers and Distributors Association (MPPDA) under the direction of William Hayes, a lawyer and member of President Harding's cabinet. Unfortunately, the MPPDA had the effect of lulling moral Americans into complacency by making them think something was being done to clean up Hollywood, when in fact very little was.

When sound was introduced to movies in 1927, it further transformed the industry and made going to the movies one of the most popular pastimes. My father told me stories of his mother and father taking him to the movie theater to see silent movies at cheap prices. He remembered that even when they had talking pictures, people still watched silent ones because of the affordability of taking the whole family. By the end of the 1920s, as unusual as it may seem, on the average, every man, woman, and child in America went to the movies about once a week.

ITS EARLY IMPACT

In the 1930s there was so much speculation about the impact of movies on young people that a series of research studies were undertaken.

The studies found film to be a powerful influence on national issues, social behaviors, attitudes about war and crime, and, ultimately, reaffirmed the already existing values and attitudes in moviegoers. Interestingly, they showed that the influence of the community played an equally important part in overshadowing the negative influence movies had on that community. The studies also found that people were led to conventional behavior just as readily as they were to criminal behavior. Specifically, the influence of motion pictures on our youth and culture was shown to be proportionate to the weakness of the influence from family, neighborhood, school, and church. In other words, when the family, neighborhood, school, and church supports have broken down, movies seem to step in and fill the gaps left by all these groups. Remember, this was in the 1930s, yet the exact thing could be said for our society today.

THE NEW CODE

There was a time in Hollywood when movies were considered to be similar to morality plays. Social behavior, moral values, even political issues associated with the family, church, and government were issues that all religious groups thought movies should contain. Recognizing the dangerous impact these productions were having on society, leaders from the Protestant Film Office and the Roman Catholic Legion of Decency joined together and set up what they called "The Motion Picture Code" or "The 1930s Production Code"[2]—a set of moral guidelines based on the Ten Commandments. Under the threat of a nationwide theater boycott, Hollywood and the MPPDA agreed to adopt the code. Thus began what is referred to as the Golden Age of Hollywood, a period between 1933 and 1966 that produced some of Hollywood's best and most creative films.

In response, William Hays established the Production Code Administration (PCA) to enforce the tenants of the code, and film companies couldn't distribute or exhibit without this PCA seal. During the next few decades, the "code" was a repressive force of censorship that regulated the studios and filmmakers to produce clean movies with statements about our modern culture and religion. Films were morally safe, and family entertainment had become the art of the multitudes. Studios distributed films that promoted an "American culture" that quickly became a national culture and promoted an ideal kind of classless superiority and way of life for the middle class. The "American Dream" was born into our society at this time and blended ethnic heritage with materialism, success, religious beliefs, and ideals that all people were created equal and all were a part of America.[3] The PCA, in essence, kept films morally safe but artistically undeveloped and reflected a reality Hollywood helped to create.

In 1948 the Supreme Court ruled that movie studios were in violation of antitrust laws and ordered studios to dismantle and sell their theater chains.[4] That dismantling gave the industry a new power to carry foreign and independent films that weren't regulated by the PCA.

ARTISTIC FREEDOM

In the 1950s the trend in films was geared toward families. Big-budget movies were aimed at general audiences, and the blockbuster movies were what Hollywood thought everyone wanted. Independent companies, however, catered to younger audiences, and this division of sales and interest started to collapse the Hollywood studio empire.

Between the 1950s and mid-1960s, the moviegoing audience shifted from the middle-aged and middle class to a younger, better-educated, and more affluent audience that had different values and was accepting of controversial themes. In 1968 the MPAA moved to create a ratings system and agreed to submit films to the Code and Rating Administration (CARA) for ratings classification by the rating board. Basically, it put the burden of deciding which movies were appropriate on the audience and left the viewers responsible. With the breakup of the studio monopoly and the Production Code, the establishing of the MPAA ratings system, and a younger, postwar baby boomer generation, Hollywood was changing. For the first time in American history, the majority of teens in America attended school and had a subculture based on entertainment, dating, cars, and social groups. So naturally this was the audience Hollywood appealed to.

Without the moral code or influence of the religious film commissions, filmmakers were free to include just about any type of graphic material they desired. The new rating system encouraged producers to push the envelope in seeing how far they could go in their big-screen depictions of sex, nudity, violence, profanity, and immorality.

War had been declared on biblical values, and freedom of artistic expression was the weapon of choice. That "freedom" from a moral code that once was a standard in Hollywood introduced a counter-culture that has become the norm for entertainment in this country.

Today, there is a liberal, anti-conservative, anti-Judeo-Christian, anti-anything to do with moral-based values mentality that started in a pulpit from Hollywood. It was evident in the presidential election of 2000 as well as in the attitudes of our young people at their schools. It is rampant in our society and saturates the news media, our movies, and TV. Even our national pride, patriotism, and sacrifice that proudly held our country together during WWII have been watered down with "political correctness." "One nation under God" is no longer meaningfully understood. The "American Dream" has been distorted beyond recognition. One of the best films of 2000 was *The Patriot*, which embodied the spirit of the early patriots who fought for this country with faith, family, community, and sacrifice behind them. It was a brilliant epic that the public loved and supported at the box office but was completely snubbed by the Academy and the Hollywood community.

These days the entertainment industry is bombarding our lives with movies, television shows, MTV, and celebrities all pushing their own morality, ethics, values, and belief systems. Family, traditional marriage relationships, Judeo-Christian values, a respect for mankind, morality, ethical principles, and an appreciation of the traditional American lifestyle can be found on only a few TV shows (*7th Heaven, Everybody Loves Raymond, Touched by an Angel, Doc*)—which, coincidentally, are the most popular shows on television.

THE MPAA

Larry Poland, Chairman and CEO of Mastermedia International, states: "The Motion Picture Association of America, contrary to popular belief, is not some objective, well-motivated, independent evaluative agency. The MPAA, which has the rating system with which we're all familiar—the R, PG-13, PG, and G—is really an industry operation run and funded by film studios to get you to go through the door of as many theaters as possible. So what we have is the fox guarding the chickens. And the rating system is driven largely by a set of criteria that are very, very mushy in terms of definition, by a group of raters who remain anonymous. We can't even find out who the people are that come up with these decisions!"[5]

The MPAA is a very strong organization that studios have a relationship with. Directors, producers, and studio heads go to MPAA and actually dialogue and negotiate about the ratings they want for their films. James Cameron went to the ratings board for his movie *Titanic* and convinced them that he had an expensive movie with a big budget and he needed the PG-13 rating to earn back his investment. *Titanic* was rated PG-13 with brief upper nudity, a steamy sexual situation in a car, language that would have certainly shocked people of the Victorian era, a gesture with one finger, and, last but not least, people dying tragic deaths on the boat and in the water. Imagine what it was like *before* he took the R-rated material out! The movie deserved an R because of the intense, emotional plot, but because it got a PG-13, young kids and teenagers flocked to see it over and over again. Basically, Cameron bartered till he got what he wanted and went on to make movie history with one of the top grossing films of all time.

LIBERAL MORALITY

Today, the morality Hollywood preaches from the big and little screen is materialism mixed with secular humanism that is rooted in ethical nihilism. People often refer to Hollywood as "liberal," and it is, but that liberalism begins with darker philosophies that reject a moral America based on traditional values. It is rampant in our society, saturating the news media, movies, television, and the Internet. The traditional values-based American programming that was once commonly seen on television can now only be found on a few networks. The "American Dream," birthed in the '30s and glorified in the '50s for creating a new America, has been raped and pillaged by foreign interests eager to cash in on the wealth they've seen exploited in movies and on television. Hollywood's "morality" has permeated our global culture. Our millennial generation has been raised on this brand of liberal morality. Unfortunately, they have no idea of what old-fashioned American patriotism and morality used to be like— unless, of course, they watch *Nick at Night* or *TV Land*.

There is a consensus of values and politics in Hollywood that's clearly to the left of grass roots America and, in most cases, is out of touch with the mainstream. Is it responsible for all of America's woes? Obviously not. But it has and does play a huge role in influencing and creating some of our cultural woes. One only has to turn on the evening news to determine that.

DECADES OF CHANGE

In the 1960s Hollywood opened the door to new levels of sexual freedom, drug use, violence, rebellion against parents, racial and other social and political issues that drew an onslaught of protests from parents and pastors. During the 1970s studios were once again trying to find their audience, and Hollywood began gearing its films toward a younger generation. *Star Wars, Grease, Superman, Close Encounters of the Third Kind, Jaws,* and *Saturday Night Fever* were just a few movies that proved younger audiences guaranteed box-office success. Directors like Spielberg and Lucas ushered in the return to comic-book serials and matinee genres with the *Star Wars* and *Indiana Jones* series. The 1980s gave us a new breed of American science fiction and special effects with movies like *E.T. the Extraterrestrial, Blade Runner, Raiders of the Lost Ark, Indiana Jones and the Temple of Doom, Indiana Jones and the Last Crusade, Last Starfighter,* and *Alien.* A new breed of heroes emerged with *Die Hard, Lethal Weapon, Beverly Hills Cop,* and *Platoon.* And a new kind of teen flick became popular and lucrative with *Sixteen Candles, Pretty in Pink, Ferris Bueller's Day Off, Footloose,* and *Dirty Dancing.* Studios discovered that baby boomers would support movies for their children, so "family films" began to emerge in the late '80s and continue to be popular today with top box-office successes such as *Home Alone, Toy Story, 101 Dalmatians, A Bug's Life, Mrs. Doubtfire, The Grinch,* and many more.

Through the years Hollywood has been a pervasive media influence on all of our lives. Contemporary American culture and much of the world's culture reflects Hollywood's standards. For the past fifty years, much of what our culture has become is in direct response to what it has been fed from an industry that has maintained a level of autonomy from religious, political, and social institutions. Sadly, the church has greatly diminished in its own cultural influence, while Hollywood has created its own brand of religion by promoting violence, foul language, sex, promiscuity, abnormal behavior, parental rebellion, negative religious stereotypes, drugs, smoking, drinking, alternate lifestyles, mass marketing, hype, and religions such as witch-craft. Parents who don't want these values ingrained in their children's impressionable minds are finding it increasingly difficult.

KID STUFF

One dynamic that makes a parent's job of protecting his child especially hard is Hollywood's powerful marketing strategies. The pres-sure on kids, tweens, and even teens to buy media products because they are being hyped everywhere makes it very difficult for parents to say no to their child. I've heard countless exasperated parents talk about taking their kids to the popular hamburger places, and the "kiddie prize" happens to be an action figure or toy from a PG-13 movie that is not acceptable for younger children (Will Smith's *Wild, Wild West* comes to mind). All that propaganda is designed to make them want to go see the movie.

GOD, THE DEVIL, AND HOLLYWOOD

Director Ingmar Bergman once claimed that "movies were the church of the twentieth century," but the church is doing better than that.

The good news: According to the *Public Perspective*, there are nearly 500,000 churches in America representing about 2,000 denomina-tions. They maintain that the way to reach the American people is through their house of worship, since 60% of the populace can be found attending any given month.[6]

The bad news: In one small recent survey put out by Public Agenda, a nonpartisan New York-based policy research agency, they discovered that the "old-time religion" of denominational teaching, church atten-dance, and a belief in God has been replaced with a "commitment to per-sonal ethics and morality." Fifty-three percent of the 1,507 adults sur-veyed said that being religious means making sure one's behavior and day-to-day actions match one's faith. Fifty-eight percent stated that it's not necessary to believe in God to be moral and have good values.[7]

In the late '90s, The Princeton Religious Research Center did a survey of the "religious" temperature in this country. They found that:

+ 96% of American people believe in God.
+ 95% say they believe their prayers will be answered.
+ 84% believe Jesus Christ is God or the Son of God.
+ 79% believe in miracles.
+ 69% claim membership in a church, synagogue, or other religious body.

So what about the people who have a standard of faith and have received religious teaching? Do they go to the movies? You bet they do! A poll by *USA Today* reported that Christians spend $7 out of every $100 on entertainment.[8]

Sadly, there's a whole generation of young people with parents who have turned away from or have never even been introduced to a religious heritage. We now have a generation of kids and teens who have never read or even seen a Bible or Torah, or have received any other kind of religious teaching. A whole generation of Gen-Xers and millennials who have no idea what godly principles and values we once held as a standard for this nation. In fact, they don't even know what a traditional belief in God is. But in many ways, they are searching.

RELIGIOUSLY INCORRECT

Many times the media will portray those who have Christian values as the enemy. Often we see Christian characters set forth as bigoted, narrow-minded, intellectually challenged with an anti-Christian vice. The media promotes this denigrating mentality, and it is further promoted in universities and public schools. If there's one group in our society that can be mocked, attacked, and demoralized for their belief system, it is evangelical Christians. It seems odd that in a nation founded upon religious principles and values, those very beliefs are under constant barrage from the political left. Hollywood has continued to undermine the biblical God in general (they rarely bash gods of other religions) and malign Christians or people of the Judeo-Christian faith in particular. Today, more than two-thirds of all media portrayals of Christians are negative. Religious people are usually depicted as social misfits, outcasts, fools, liars, racists, hypocrites, sadists, adulterers, perverts, rapists, child molesters, murders, or even cannibals. A few movies that reinforce this point are *Cape Fear, The Rapture, Alien 3, Leap of Faith, The Seventh Seal, The Witches of Eastwick, Cruel Intentions, Seven, Stigmata, End of Days, Dogma, Quills,* and, unfortunately, many more.

Christian activist Pat Robertson claims, "For many years, there has been a vendetta against religious values in the public arena. We have been under assault by differing groups who have tried their best to strip from our public square every vestige of our Christian heritage, every vestige of biblical truth and biblical morality, and to take from us the religious heritage that has made America great."[9] He adds that many of those assaults are being repelled as Christians become more politically active.

HURRAY FOR HOLLYWOOD!

How do films that feature a pro-Judeo-Christian message fare at the box office? "Religious" movies have proven to be popular and often profitable for Hollywood. In 1927 Cecil B. De Mille came out with a silent version of *The King of Kings.* In the '50s both MGM and Paramount were on the verge of bankruptcy, but their studios were saved as a result of the success of films like *Ben Hur* and the master of cinematic spectacles, *The Ten Commandments,* produced by Cecil B. De Mille.

Up to that point, several wonderful films had been made, such as *David and Bathsheba, Samson and Delilah,* and *The Robe,* but after the popularity of De Milles's venture, others followed. A string of successful films were released with big names vying to star in them. Films like *King of Kings, Spartacus, The Greatest Story Ever Told, The Story of Ruth, Esther and the King, Barabbas,* and *The Bible* were big hits with the public and sent the message to Hollywood that "if you build it they will come!"

Since then, studios have tried to hit that popular vein again with movies such as *The Cross and the Switchblade, Jesus of Nazareth,* and a string of '90s productions, including *Abraham, Jacob, Joseph, Moses, Samson and Delilah,* and *David.* Hollywood started to get creative when it introduced films with a spiritual or religious aspect that included quality actors, diverse circumstances, interesting, well-written scripts, and sometimes just a subtle undertone such as in *Chariots of Fire, The Shawshank Redemption, Dead Man Walking, Braveheart, The Apostle,* and many more. Recently in films such as *Gladiator, The Patriot, All the Pretty Horses,* and even in comedies like *Bedazzled,* there's still a message of good versus bad, but more blatantly, God versus the devil.

THE TOLERANCE MESSAGE

Among the latest political messages coming out of Hollywood these days is the message of "tolerance" and anything having to do with "hate crimes." I have debated this topic several times on *Politically Incorrect* and see this topic trickling down from the media into legislation from local governments. Hate crimes in many cases are hard to define and are a matter of opinion in most cases. This controversial issue is going to become more prevalent and affect our lives in surprising ways. We have seen the media pounce on this theme and blast it across our television sets on the nightly news. Nowhere has it been more defined or pronounced than with issues concerning and dealing with race and homosexuals.

In the spring of 2001, MTV recently staged an eighteen-hour continual airing of "hate crimes" that not only referred to homosexual hate crimes but also listed others as well. At the end of each segment, a toll-free number was given for an organization called "Fight for Your Rights," which encouraged young people to call in and report hate crimes. MTV vowed to run their campaign for a year and encourage young people to contact their political representatives and "send a message to Washington" to endorse hate crime legislation.

Essentially, our schools are being blackmailed to introduce this program to students in exchange for taxpayer funds. So now our schools become a source of monitoring morality, forcing the teaching of "tolerance" for different ethnic, cultural, and sexual backgrounds. Students are being taught to sponsor a "Day of Diversity" and consider how homophobia and racism impact on the life of an African-American gay man. "Diversity panels" are being presented to allow those of various races, religions, and sexual orientations the chance to talk about their experiences and suggest changes to promote equality.

How does this relate to entertainment? The very fact that MTV is skewing its program to young people at the same time programs are being introduced in schools shows how close the entertainment, media, and academia world are blending together and taking on the role of "parent" in teaching and educating your children on the topic.

I find it ironic and despicable that MTV is endorsing the very program that should cite them as the worst example in our culture today. MTV, via its music videos, is the single largest perpetrator of violence, racism, verbal degradation, sexual perversion, bigotry, and abuse against women, gays, minorities, and even against children. The hypocrisy should be embarrassingly obvious.

HOLLYWOOD AND POLITICS

On Feb. 8, 1915, D. W. Griffith's Civil War epic, The Birth of a Nation, *opens at a White House screening. President Wilson calls it "like writing history with lightning."*[10]

Hollywood has had a long love affair with politicians. At every political convention a celebrity endorsement of a candidate is coveted. Inaugural balls and Washington events have been the place where the entertainment and political worlds blend. These days, politicians are being criticized for attaining celebrity-like status and influencing voters. After the Clinton scandals rocked our homes with daily telecasts about Monica Lewinsky, oral sex, and definitions of "is," this country clearly suffered the repercussions of the trickle-down disregard for morality and the office of the presidency.

The history-making 2000 elections between George W. Bush and Al Gore set precedence for much more than just creative politicking. The close election became the battlefield for our nation's conservatives and liberals, and a line was definitely drawn in the sand. After years of God, morals, and family values being maligned by the press, mocked by the president, and ridiculed in Hollywood, presidential contenders laid definitive claims to God and stood on a platform of morals and American values. Bush won, partly because of the backlash on Bill Clinton, but surely because of his political stance and a much-too-long silent minority taking a stand.

THE NOT-SO-HIDDEN AGENDA

Hollywood's agenda is not so hidden anymore. It began gloriously with the Golden Age of Hollywood and was remembered for movies with a moral, cultural, and social message that perpetuated the American Dream. It continued in the '30s when Americans first started to think of themselves as an "American" culture and on through the post-World War II victory period when our nation was healing from the wounds of the Depression. Hollywood restored this nation's confidence in America as a forerunner of a new age, and the "pursuit of happiness" was more than a national ideal; it was a principle and program for social change. The idealistic post-Vietnam War generation became disillusioned, and Hollywood reached a new level of artistic maturity with violent imagery confronting the dark realities of human life. Sex became a culturally depersonalized preoccupation and an obsession of Hollywood. In the '80s and '90s we went through many phases, trends, and new technologies that have made the movie industry exciting and always interesting!

Today, moviegoing remains popular among our youth, who are lavishly catered to by our culture. The not-so-hidden agenda of the entertainment industry blatantly and constantly strives to seduce the seventy-nine million or more of them. Our children are the industry's bread and butter. But it's the graying seventy-eight million baby boomers who are returning to the movies (post child-rearing) who may help determine the future of Hollywood and have a say in the direction it takes.[11] They can remember the good old days of the "Golden Age," through the decades to now, and have entered the new millennium with eager anticipation of what technology can and will bring.

In truth, there's nothing hidden about the entertainment community. Hollywood is brazen, bold, and sometimes radical in the approach they take to influence and entertain us, but we've seen their *M.O.* and have allowed it to thrive. We understand the nature of the beast, and those who want to see change in Hollywood need to get involved in the industry with protest letters or phone calls, or simply vote your opinion at the box office. What Hollywood can get away with is wrapped in the approval they seek at the box office. Ultimately, that's the meter for how Hollywood's "agenda" is judged, and you get to decide that with your ticket.

ALL OF LIFE'S RIDDLES

are answered in the movies.

—STEVE MARTIN in the Movie *Grand Canyon*

Movies

L ights! Camera! Action!" Most people think that filmmaking began in sunny Southern California on holy ground called Hollywood, but it didn't. In fact, you might be surprised to discover that the infamous "Hollywood" sign that has become synonymous with the movie industry itself was originally built and dedicated in 1923 to promote sales of homes in Beachwood Canyon. It just goes to show that when it comes to Hollywood, what you see is not always what it seems.

The movie industry, which has become larger than life, sweeps us up into a fantasyland of entertainment that profoundly influences our daily lives. What began so simply at the turn of the twentieth century has seen incredible growth and phenomenal changes over the past one hundred years and has become one of this country's largest and most profitable exports. Where did it all begin? How did Hollywood become so powerful?

A CENTURY OF MOVIE MAGIC

On January 1, 1900, French film pioneer Charles Pathe released the first historical reenactment entitled the *Episodes of the Transvaal War*, which began a journey in film that has captured the hearts and souls of people worldwide. Movies and their filmmakers have not only experimented, changed, and evolved since those first days of the twentieth century, but they have captured our histories, cultures, wars, triumphs, and tragedies. Filmmaking has done something no human can do on their own—capture a moment in time, a story to be told, temporarily stopping and preserving it for future generations.

The movie industry has had a fascinating history with its beginnings taking place internationally and eventually settling more prominently and permanently in Hollywood. In the early days, filmmakers at the Pan-American Exposition in Buffalo, New York, first captured images of an American President, William McKinley, September 5, 1901, one day before his assassination. By 1906 the first feature-length (seventy-minute) motion picture, *The Story of the Kelly Gang*, was released in Melbourne, Australia. Technically, sometimes accidentally, and always creatively, the film industry was born out of a passion to be the "first" in an excitingly new, burgeoning adventure.

The first two decades of the 1900s created many firsts in this unexplored industry that began producing silent movies for the masses, and it was a time that exploded with technological advances:

✦ Thomas Edison formed The Motion Picture Patents Company (MPPC), a first for production and distribution control.

✦ Wilbur Wright took a cameraman into the skies over France for the first film footage shot from an airplane.

✦ The first film studio was constructed in the Los Angeles area.

✦ The first feature-length film produced in the United States was *Les Misérables*.

✦ Freeze frame was first used for dramatic effect in *A Corner in Wheat*.

✦ The first horror film was *Frankenstein*.

✦ America's first cowboy star was actor G. M. Anderson as "Broncho Billy."

✦ John Bunny was the first to try comedy, debuting in *Jack Fat and Jim Slim at Coney Island*.

✦ The nation's first newsreel was *Pathes Weekly*.

✦ The first film studio rented on Sunset Boulevard went for $40 a month.

✦ Sarah Bernhardt starred in *Queen Elizabeth* and first gave a new respectability to motion pictures.

✦ On February 18, 1913, The Edison Film Company introduced the synchronized film-phonograph Kinetoscope process for "sound films."

◆   The first feature-length western was made.

◆   Less than two years after the sinking of the Titanic, the disaster comes to the screen as *Atlantis.*

Just before the 1920s, the movie industry was booming with films such as *Little Tramp* and the first film score for an American feature titled *Civilization.* The major studios such as Paramount, Warner Brothers, Columbia, MGM, RKO Radio Pictures, and even Walt Disney were starting to make names for themselves and producing new technology which affirmed that a new era of the "talkies" was about to change movie history.

The film industry went to a new commercial level with Warner Brothers introducing the first few minutes of sound with the "talkie" *The Jazz Singer,* starring Al Jolson in 1927. The next year, the first all-talking picture, *Lights of New York,* was released by Warner Brothers. The now famous Grauman's Chinese Theater opened its doors in 1927, and the first to leave their marks in cement were Mary Pickford, Douglas Fairbanks, and Norma Talmadge in what would end up becoming a long-standing Hollywood tradition.

By 1933 feature films started to replace the silent pictures with newer, more innovative forms of sound and film technology, and the Golden Age of Hollywood began. Stars started to emerge with John Barrymore, Katherine Hepburn, Errol Flynn, Hedy Lamarr, Fred Astaire, and others. On June 6, 1933, the first drive-in theater opened in Camden, New Jersey, and began a moviegoing tradition that attracted almost every teenager with a car for the next sixty years. By the mid '30s a Depression-weary American public was ready to see Frank Capra's comedy *It Happened One Night,* starring two very popular stars, Claudette Colbert and Clarke Gable. Shirley Temple charmed the socks off devoted audiences, The Three Stooges hit the big screen with *Woman Haters, The Thin Man* series launched the beginning of six films, and the Marx brothers' first feature, *A Night at the Opera,* became a smashing success.

By the late '30s premieres started attracting huge crowds, celebrities such as Judy Garland and Lana Turner were being groomed by Mayer, and Roy Rogers was starring in his first western released by Republic Pictures. Warner Brothers started to get in on the family action by introducing a duck named Daffy and a bunny named Bugs. Clark

Gable and Myrna Loy were crowned "King and Queen of Hollywood." *Gone With the Wind* started filming on December 10, 1938, with the burning of Atlanta sequence using sets that were once the Skull Island wall from *King Kong*. The huge casting search with Clark Gable as Rhett Butler continued after Christmas, and in January Vivien Leigh signed on to play Scarlett O'Hara. John Wayne rode into stardom when he appeared as the Ringo Kid in John Ford's *Stagecoach*. And in 1939 the first Sherlock Holmes' movie featured Basil Rathbone and Nigel Bruce in *The Hound of the Baskervilles*. Hollywood's Golden Age of the '30s ended with the passing of Douglas Fairbanks from a heart attack at the age of fifty-six, and two days later on December 14, 1939, Atlanta held the world premiere of *Gone With the Wind*, which captured nine Oscars two months later.

The '40s ushered in comedy with road movies from Bob Hope and Bing Crosby, Mel Blanc as the voice for WB's characters, and Abbott and Costello bantered their way to the big screen in *One Night in the Tropics*. Katharine Hepburn and Spencer Tracy teamed up for the first time in *Woman of the Year*, and James Cagney sang and danced the extravaganza *Yankee Doodle Dandy*. Sexy starlets were also emerging, causing controversy with their sex appeal. Rita Hayworth got steamy in *Gilda*; Esther Williams made a splash in her singing-dancing-swimming musical, *Bathing Beauty*; Betty Grable was a pinup queen; Jane Russell was discovered by Howard Hughes and debuted in *The Outlaw*; and Lauren Bacall taught Humphrey Bogart how to whistle in *To Have and Have Not*.

The Christmas of 1946 made history with Frank Capra's holiday classic *It's a Wonderful Life*, opening to mixed reviews. By the late '40s, McCarthyism politics was rearing its ugly head, and ten Hollywood writers and producers were cited for contempt of Congress and banished from the film community.

The '50s brought new ideas that stretched the studios, but at the same time, stricter moral codes were practiced. In 1952 the U.S. Supreme Court declared movies a form of free speech, and a talking mule named Francis spoke out in a series of films. The medium of TV was growing in popularity, Marlon Brando burst on the scene, Gary Cooper, Humphrey Bogart, Audrey Hepburn, and Frank Sinatra won Academy Awards, and popular starlet Marilyn Monroe became the first cover girl and centerfold for Hugh Hefner's *Playboy* magazine. Disney opened a theme park. Musicals were starting to be released, such as Rodgers and Hammerstein's *Oklahoma!* Charlton Heston parted the sea as Moses in *The Ten Commandments. Around the World in 80 Days* made a hit as one of the first movies filled with "cameo roles." *The Wizard of Oz* made its TV debut on CBS, and a young rock star named Elvis Presley began a film career by starring in *Love Me Tender*.

The early '60s brought a new crop of stars: Gregory Peck, Paul Newman, Warren Beatty, Peter O'Toole, Jerry Lewis, Natalie Wood, Elizabeth Taylor, and Richard Burton. Musicals came of age with *West Side Story, My Fair Lady, Mary Poppins,* and perhaps the most memorable of them all, *The Sound of Music.*

But by the mid '60s many of the Hollywood legends (and those who were a part of the Golden Age) were aging and dropping out of sight. Movies were changing with the times. Beatlemania had erupted, and the fab four made *A Hard Day's Night.* Clint Eastwood made spaghetti westerns popular in *A Fistful of Dollars.* In the late '60s Adam West made his first film appearance since 1943 as *Batman,* Patty Duke starred in the camp classic *Valley of the Dolls,* Dustin Hoffman grew up in *The Graduate,* and Charlton Heston starred in *Planet of the Apes,* which spawned four sequels, including a newly revised version in 2001. In 1966 screen actor and guild president Ronald Reagan was elected governor of California, in 1968 Stanley Kubrick's *2001: A Space Odyssey* was launched, *Airport* began the disaster films, and Barbra Streisand made her film debut in *Funny Girl. Greetings,* starring Robert De Niro in 1969, was launched as the first X-rated movie, and *Easy Rider,* starring Jack Nicholson, Peter Fonda, and Dennis Hopper, rolled across America, liberating a host of copycats and becoming a cult classic for future generations.

The '70s brought message films, whether it was about war in *The Deer Hunter* or *Patton,* homosexuality in *The Boys in the Band,* love in *Love Story,* the devil with *The Exorcist,* the Mafia in *The Godfather,* a meltdown in *The China Syndrome,* irreverent fun poked at westerns in *Blazing Saddles,* a perfect woman in *10,* a good-bye to innocence with a star-studded cast in *American Graffiti,* and a bizarre tale of war in Altman's *MASH.* IMAX made a giant debut and brought us a whole new way of filmmaking. *Dirty Harry* movies became a big hit. The second X-rated film, *A Clockwork Orange*, debuted with controversy, as did *Carnal Knowledge*, *Deep Throat*, and *Last Tango in Paris*. Marlon Brando turned down an Oscar and sent an Indian with a message to tell us so.

The '70s also ushered in a new kind of escapism with *The Poseidon Adventure*, *Superman*, *Star Trek: The Motion Picture*, *One Flew Over the Cuckoo's Nest*, *Jaws*, *Rocky*, *Close Encounters of the Third Kind*, and *Alien*. John Travolta and the Bee Gees moved a nation to disco in the musical *Saturday Night Fever*. And I was truly saddened in 1979 by the passing of my hero and a veteran of two hundred films, John Wayne, at age seventy-two.

The '80s were filled with Reagan in the White House, more technically advanced movies with incredible special effects, stories with powerful messages, and heroes were popular again. Only this time, they came in all shapes, sizes, and species: *The Empire Strikes Back*, *Raiders of the Lost Ark*, *Star Trek II: Wrath of Khan*, *The Twilight Zone*, *Return of the Jedi*, *The Terminator*, *The Color Purple*, *Crocodile Dundee*, *Die Hard*, *Batman*, and *Big*. *E. T. the Extraterrestrial* became one of the highest grossing films of all time, and *When Harry Met Sally* defined America's single life with humor and truth.

The '90s gave us a wide assortment of memorable films: *Pretty Woman*, *City Slickers*, *Sleepless in Seattle*, *There's Something About Mary*, one of my favorite westerns of all time, *Dances With Wolves*, incredible thrillers like *Terminator 2: Judgment Day*, *Basic Instinct*, *The Crying Game*, *Jurassic Park*, and *Pulp Fiction*, and just plain cool: *Speed* and *The Matrix*. And the finishing touch to the '90s and a century of filmmaking ended with profound films like *Schindler's List*, *Forrest Gump*, *Saving Private Ryan*, *The Usual Suspects*, *LA Confidential*, and romantic winners, *Shakespeare in Love* and *Titanic*.

Obviously I couldn't include all of the great films, stars, and trends that have graced the big screen, but you can get an idea of just how far we've come and the magnitude of change the industry has gone through in the last 100 years.

HOLLYWOOD
IS NOT HOLYWOOD

After a century of epics and sagas handed down from directors, writers, and producers, moviegoers seem surprised when they go to a movie and find that Hollywood is no moral compass. Rather, they discover a collection of secular views, worldly ideals, and standards very different from their own, sometimes shockingly so.

The simple fact is that Hollywood basically dispenses entertainment . . . and that's all. Some of it is powerful and often profound, occasionally it's life changing, much of it is shallow, and rarely is it redeeming. But it's that desire of wanting to believe that those mixed messages that are delivered in the dark on a big screen contain a window to our souls. That is what is so compelling and so addicting.

Movies basically reflect what's going on (or in some cases what's "about" to go on) in our society. Whether we see them on the big screen or at home on our VCR, movies send messages on how to meet and fall in love (usually instantaneously), commit murder in various bizarre ways, succeed at committing crimes, manipulate men and women in relationships, walk away from marriage, family, and friends, idolize materialism, embrace irreverence, worship hedonism, destroy life without guilt, use profanity as a second language, live with pain, treat dysfunction as normal, and much more.

The truth is that Hollywood has become a powerful force both domestically and internationally. Movies and television have more of a daily influence on our society than all of the churches in America combined. They have elevated celebrities and stars to a godlike status and created an addicted society that just can't get enough of them. We have a public that feeds off the tabloid news, is hooked on voyeurism, worships fame, and secretly dreams of their own "fifteen minutes." But for all of the brokenhearted, disappointed, hopeless masses who turn to Hollywood to believe in its many messages through film, even more will be disillusioned by it.

For anyone who looks to Hollywood to be anything more than what it is, stop fooling yourselves and change your expectations. Hollywood is not a god; we just treat it like one. Especially our kids and teenagers. This is where parents have to step in and clarify what message your kids are getting from movies these days. The sooner you can get a fix on what your kids and teens think is "morally" acceptable and where they look to be "inspired" for guidance, the better adjusted your family will be.

LET'S GO TO THE MOVIES!

People of all ages enjoy sitting back in a comfortable chair, immersed in darkness, losing themselves in a good story, and feeling sort of disengaged from the outside world. Going to the movies is fantasy in its most vivid form, and that fantasy provides a welcomed escape from our busy lives and daily problems. Going to the movies used to be an occasional social treat, but not anymore.

Americans love to go to the movies! Hollywood is elated that 79 million millennial kids and 40 million Gen-Xers are the marketing products of a culture raised on movies, television, video games, and videos.[1] These millennials not only have an insatiable appetite to constantly be entertained, but more importantly they have the money to buy it! But teenagers aren't the only ones going to the movies. Americans spent $7.45 billion at the movies in 2000 according to AC Nielsen EDI, a box-office tracking firm.[2] That was more money spent on movie entertainment than in any previous year. And apparently it's not stopping there. Global ticket sales are expected to rise to $21.4 billion in 2003.[3]

When Hollywood studios, producers, and investors see that kind of revenue spent at the box office, they realize the public is willing to spend good money on good entertainment. Unfortunately, much of what Hollywood gives the moviegoing public is not considered "good" entertainment.

The fact that the entertainment industry is America's largest export and trade to other countries makes the messages that it conveys that much more important and relevant to our ever-changing world. We are seeing an explosion of global changes in cultures around the world, beginning with the ability to access the Internet and continuing with the growing interest in the entertainment industry. For all of the good that has come out of the industry, there has been an overwhelming fallout from the bad, which has equally been culturally devastating.

THE SECRET TO THE SUCCESS

Out of the approximate two hundred fifty to three hundred fifty films released each year, most of us can probably only remember a handful that we would deem as "good entertainment." For example, take a few of the top box-office films from 2000 that appealed to the moviegoing public: *Gladiator; The Patriot; The Perfect Storm; The Grinch; Mission Impossible: 2; Crouching Tiger, Hidden Dragon; Meet the Parents; Erin Brockovich; Cast Away,* and others. The reason these films were so successful was because of the star power attached to each of them (Russell Crowe, Mel Gibson, George Clooney, Jim Carey, Tom Cruise, director Ang Lee, Robert De Niro, Julia Roberts, and Tom Hanks), a good choice of co-stars, and the fact that each was an interesting story.

Those stars were the secret to a successful 2000 box office, creating movie magic with the highest revenues ever. Ratings, star power, lots of PG-13 movies, 5,000 new movie screens in megaplexes that gave viewers more options, and the Internet have all contributed to that success. But what's proven to be the biggest box-office king for Hollywood is the PG-13 rating. Out of the above mentioned box-office successes, the PG-13 rating helped make most of those movies hits. G, PG, and PG-13 rated movies have proven to be the most successful moneymakers for Hollywood and the most popular with audiences as well.

SUMMER FUN

Memorial Day weekend used to be the traditional "kick-off" weekend for summer fun and movies. In 1975 Steven Spielberg opened the season with *Jaws,* and the summer blockbuster was born! Every year it seems as though summer movies are inching back weekend by weekend. *Gladiator* kicked off the summer of 2000 with a strong bang in early May that earned it Oscar recognition and made it one of the most successful movies of 2000. *Mission Impossible: 2* was also a huge success and helped Memorial Day weekend 2000 bring in $184.8 million,[4] the largest take for a three-day weekend in movie history. Summertime is traditionally the season when studios release their action/adventure movies, teen flicks, and a couple of kid-friendly choices aimed at the munchkins out of school. There can be anywhere from sixty to ninety films released between Memorial Day and Labor Day weekend, all with high hopes of hitting the big box office.

HAPPY HOLIDAY
BOX OFFICE

Traditionally the holiday season has represented the big year-end box office for Hollywood with the week between Christmas and New Year's as the biggest moviegoing time of the year. Family-friendly movies are intentionally positioned between Thanksgiving and Christmas to lure kids who are home on vacation, visiting relatives and parents, or escaping the hustle and bustle of shopping. From the beginning of November to the time you celebrate New Year's Eve, anywhere from sixty to ninety films can be released. All these come with the hopes that you and your loved ones will take a break from the holidays and see a movie, maybe even twice!

The holiday season for 2000 proved to be the best ever. Thanksgiving weekend was one of the biggest weekends (thanks to *The Grinch*) with $176.8 million.[5] During the four-day New Year's holiday, moviegoers spent $183 million,[6] making it the second-biggest weekend in movie history, just $3 million shy of the record set over Memorial Day weekend that same year. The who-larious Jim Carey in *Dr. Seuss' How the Grinch Stole Christmas* saved the year with a whopping $270 million.[7] That means 2000 ushered in the new millennium as Hollywood's best year ever with box-office sales totaling $7.45 billion,[8] selling an estimated 1,294 billion tickets![9] Now you can see why audiences are targeted at this time of year. Needless to say, the average adult could use a wise old man in a red suit with a white beard, twinkling eyes, and eight really savvy reindeer to guide them through their holiday movie choices. But if you don't happen to have one, use my family friendly reviews at www.hollymcclure.com to help.

Here are a few of the top box-office holiday movies in years past that were winners with young and old alike:

+ *The Grinch* (2000)—$270 million
+ *Unbreakable* (2000)—$90 million
+ *Toy Story 2* (1999)—$245.9 million
+ *A Bug's Life* (1998)—$162.8 million
+ *101 Dalmatians* (1996)—$136.2 million
+ *Toy Story* (1995)—$91.8 million[10]

WHAT OSCARS MEAN TO MOVIES

In January 1927, during a dinner at his villa, Louis B. Mayer, director Fred Niblo, actor Conrad Nagel, and Fred Beetson conceived the idea of issuing film awards to people in the industry. And on May 11, 1927, The Academy of Motion Pictures Arts and Sciences was founded by thirty-six members and presided over by Douglas Fairbanks. On May 16, 1929, The Academy of Motion Picture Arts and Sciences held the first Academy Awards ceremony at Hollywood's Roosevelt Hotel, where statuettes designed by art director Cedric Gibbons were handed out for technical merits but not for performers. On March 13, 1934, Walt Disney accepted his award for *The Three Little Pigs* and was the first winner to refer to the gold statuette as an "Oscar." The race has been on for that coveted piece of "Oscar" gold ever since.

It wasn't until March 23, 1950, that Mercedes McCambridge became the first performer ever to win an Academy Award. The Academy Awards weren't televised until March 19, 1953, with Bob Hope hosting. The only times the Academy Awards have been delayed or postponed was on April 10, 1968, for two days due to the assassination of Martin Luther King, and again on March 31, 1981, when President Reagan was shot.

The "art" of positioning a movie at a certain time of year, pouring out the marketing dollars, and sending screeners to everyone in the industry has given new meaning to "winning" an Oscar. Most studios unveil their lesser quality movies in the early part of each year because they save their "quality" productions for the final quarter in order to be eligible for nominations for an Academy Award. Movie execs hope their strategically marketed "best bets" will get public recognition and, more importantly, Oscar nods.

Why is a nomination so important? Those coveted Oscar nominations mean bigger box office and more favorable public recognition long after the holidays and well into the next year. In fact, it can mean as much as $40 million to some movies in free publicity and extra ticket sales.

So what does the Hollywood Oscar hype have to do with you? Well, not only is there a deluge of commercials for these new films, but there's also an abundance of marketing. Fast-food meals, action figures, cute toys, stocking stuffers with movie themes, and *lots* of trailers are aimed at enticing you and your family to the cineplex to support the movie.

TEENAGERS HAVE THEIR SEASON TOO!

Moviegoers between the ages of twelve and twenty-four make up 38% of the domestic box office, so it's no wonder that Hollywood pays a lot of attention in marketing movies meant just for them. What you may not realize is that teenagers have also become an important calendar target for film marketers.

January and February are profitable months to attract high school and college kids to theaters. In January 1999 the football movie *Varsity Blues* scored a touchdown at the box office, grossing $17.5 million its first weekend and continuing on to make $52.9 million. In January 2001 *Save the Last Dance*, a "hip-hop meets *Dirty Dancing*" movie about an interracial couple, boogied to the tune of $60 million[11] by the end of January and still hadn't hit the foreign market.

Why are these two months so popular right after the holidays? First, there is a lot of vacation time. Between Martin Luther King Day (box office during the King holiday weekend has jumped 63% in the last decade), Presidents Day weekend, early spring breaks, and post-final mini-breaks, these two months have proven to be profitable for the movie industry. Second, films that have no hope in vying for an Oscar or competing with the lag time between the New Year and Oscar night are also introduced at this time of year.

THE INFLUENCE OF MOVIES

The financial data and dueling moguls stuff is sharper than ever, but Hollywood is not so much driven by cold, hard financial calculations as by personal relationships—by hatreds, rivalries, egos, sins and crimes; coverage of that seedy, gothic, sometimes criminal reality of the business has deteriorated massively over the years. . . . Most editors would rather have the quick hit of celebrity profiles and clever pseudo-analyses.

—Michael Cieply, West Coast editorial director for www.inside.com[12]

With the use of enticing images, likable celebrities, and dramatic stories, movies have the ability to manipulate our emotions and change our lives. Lighting, makeup, editing, rehearsed dialogue, music, and special effects combine to create an alternative world of make-believe that sometimes seems very real. The choice of camera angle forces us to focus our attention on exactly what the director wants us to see, to the exclusion of surrounding areas. The larger-than-life screen, the darkened theater, the Dolby surround sound system, all contribute to a heightened sense of awareness, thus making the moviegoing experience one of the most influential and popular forms of entertainment today.

Over the past years movies have transcended the movie theaters and are now seen in homes on VCRs, cable, DVDs, laptops, and, depending on when you read this book, other new techno-toys flooding the market. Technology has opened the world of entertainment so that it's not just for the big screen but every kind of screen you can imagine. Through the world of technology, the many movies that are now available to anyone, anywhere, anytime, which stream into our everyday lives, can blur the line of fantasy and reality.

When watching a movie, most people believe they're simply being entertained, and for the most part, they are. But filmmaking has become such an art form that almost any idea conceived in the imagination stage can easily be translated onto the big screen, and that's where the problems begin for many people, especially children. Is the world of movies real? Just because it's very convincing on the big screen doesn't mean it represents reality, or does it?

When *Superman* debuted on December 15, 1978, more than one person reportedly believed that Christopher Reeve could actually fly because of the convincing special effects. Hollywood would love to have you easily convinced about many things if they could. In fact, I bet there are many things you take for granted because you've always seen them done in the movies.

Here are a few examples of "real life" in Hollywood:

1. When people turn off the lights in a room, everything will still be visible, only with a slight bluish tint or powerful moonlight beaming through the window.
2. It doesn't matter if you are heavily outnumbered in a fight, particularly in battle scenes, martial arts fights, gang fights, or war. Your enemies will

patiently wait to attack you one by one, dancing around in a threatening manner until you have knocked out or killed their colleagues.

3. If you decide to start dancing in the street, everyone around you will automatically be able to mirror all the steps you come up with and hear the music in your head. If you choose to burst into song, others around you will join in, and all parts will be sung in perfect harmony. Except if you're in New York, then they'll just ignore you.

4. When women with dark or glossy lipstick kiss a man, none of it rubs off on his face or gets on his shirt.

5. A man can take a beating and show no pain, but when a woman tries to clean his wounds, he'll wince.

6. People can jump out of two-story windows, roll, get up, and keep running without a scratch on them.

7. If you break into a car chase because someone is after you, you will: (1) Never hit another car; (2) Maneuver your car through rush-hour traffic without getting stuck; (3) Drive like a pro; (4) If you're in San Francisco, launch off at least three hills and continue driving down steep winding roads without stopping once.

HOLLYWOOD'S VALUES AND WORLDVIEW

In Hollywood there is a consensus of opinions that have become values, which puts it mostly out of touch with typical Americans. As a rule of thumb, the leaders of the film and television industry are twice as likely, statistically, to approve things that the average moviegoer (especially parents) feels are wrong. For instance, Hollywood is very accepting of adultery, pornography, homosexuality, sex (especially among teenagers), and other moral issues many parents object to.

It's this condition of heart that motivates the writers, directors, and producers to include the material in their films, scripts, productions, and television shows. Because the media's values are very much out of step with the American people, the values tend to come through and become actual propaganda messages in the movies that are being produced.

These strong subliminal messages have a profound influence on vulnerable audiences who desire to be accepted and loved. Younger members of society especially want to be accepted, want to be "in," and want to be part of that fashionable, stylish thought process. That's why so much of what parents see on the screen (clothing and hair styles, drinking, smoking, casual sex, language, crude behavior) is imitated and carried out off the screen at home or in social circles. These days parents are finding it hard to find movies with scripts that portray a healthy family life, traditional marriage relationships, spiritual values, a respect for humanity, and an appreciation of life in general, or if they are in the script, they are watered down considerably.

IT'S ONLY MAKE-BELIEVE

When you were little, did you believe in Santa Claus? The Tooth Fairy? The Easter Bunny? Did you grow up believing that what you saw on TV was real? Did you ever want to live in "the Beaver's" neighborhood, spend the night with the Brady Bunch, visit Big Bird, imagine yourself taking a spin with David Hasselhof in his cool car "K.I.T.T.," or go to school with the *Saved by the Bell* gang? When you watched movies, did you believe what you saw really happened? Be honest! I bet you can remember something you believed was real, only to learn with disappointment later that it wasn't.

I remember as a child traveling in the car from Oklahoma City to Dallas and asking my dad when we were going to see some "cowboys and Indians" like the ones we "saw on TV." I recall in junior high wanting to move to California because I thought everyone had a golden tan, was beautiful, and wore swimsuits all the time. I'm embarrassed to say that my naiveté didn't stop as a child. When I moved to Southern California in 1989, I almost didn't bring any winter clothes because I thought the weather was tropical all year long.

Obviously, we are all shaped by the experiences we go through and what we observe. Whether from watching television or going to the movies, the media impacts all of our lives. Research indicates that some movies and media images can so closely imitate our lives that it's easy to get swept up in the story, relate with the characters, and over-look the obvious. And if *we* can do that as adults, imagine what happens to children when *they* watch a movie that relates with their world. Imagine what their perception of reality is? That's why it's so important to monitor the movies your children watch. Your child's inability to discern what's real and what's not is much higher than yours. Younger children up to about the age of six or seven are unable to discern the difference between reality and fantasy. They are more frightened by dangerous or larger-than-life characters rather than a scary threat. Children from the ages of seven to twelve are more apt to focus on the behavior of a character rather than the plot behind the action or what motivates the character to the action.

When kids see "fake" violence portrayed in a movie, they are more likely to imitate that violence immediately. Go to a screening of a children's movie with an abundance of pratfalls, Three Stooges type violence, or martial arts (remember *Power Rangers* and *Teenage Mutant Ninja Turtles?*). When kids walk out of those types of movies, they are hyper, stimulated, and ready to imitate everything they've just seen.

The minds of our children and teenagers are so overloaded and overflowing with movies and television programs, they can actually confuse them with reality and actual events. Imagine all of the information you've collected in your brain to this point in your life. Occasionally our brain gets confused as to what has been real and what is simply an image of something we've watched or briefly seen.

Bottom line: Your children are like sponges and soak up whatever they are impressed by or exposed to long enough. Here are some areas your children may be struggling with because of what they've seen in movies or programs on TV that contain adult themes.

1. Violence is acceptable and the only way to deal with anger.
2. Sex outside of marriage is normal and everyone does it.
3. Religion is usually kooky or weird.
4. Money is the ultimate status symbol.
5. Kids need material things to make them happy.

Kids learn their values of life based on what they absorb, experience, and see on a daily basis. If you as a parent aren't there to step in and decipher Hollywood's ethics and moral code, you may see more and more of the world's standards and behavior exemplified in your child.

READ THE MOVIE

There's only one thing that can kill the movies, and that's education.

—Will Rogers

I've noticed a trend in the last few years that I think is a positive one: Reading in movies. Since we're seeing an influx of international films, independent filmmakers, and creative directors, more and more movies are being released that require you to read the subtitles and, in many cases, the entire movie.

Traditionally audiences seem to shy away from films that require reading subtitles. A *USA Today* poll found that 35% of people will watch a film with subtitles if it's really good; 34% feel subtitles pose no problem; and 31% won't watch a movie if they have to read their way through.[13] But analysts believe today that audiences are getting more sophisticated and educated and will go to see a good movie that is directed well. Tom Bernard, co-president of Sony Pictures Classics, says, "What we've found is that the style of direction plays a much greater role. That's what provides a mainstream moviegoing experience. So much so, that the fact the film has subtitles quickly fades from memory."[14]

Ang Lee's *Crouching Tiger, Hidden Dragon* exemplifies the best in this category so far. As the winner of the Oscar for Best Foreign Film of 2000, there has never been an international film with this level of special effects, direction, and stunning visual photography. Truly, it is such a remarkable approach to filmmaking, you forget you're even reading subtitles. I encouraged my fourteen-year-old son to go see it with his friend, and it was interesting enough to hold his attention (even though subtitles aren't his favorite). Matt Damon required audiences to translate his Spanish in *All the Pretty Horses*. Oscar favorite *Traffic* likewise had several scenes that needed Spanish interpretation. Even Brendan Fraser had a hilarious scene in *Bedazzled* where he fluently rattled off beautiful Spanish in several scenes.

As our American culture embraces larger Hispanic and Asian demographics, we will also need to accept the new directions films may go and different styles of movies being made that more than likely will include more subtitles. This new trend is a prime example of the future of movies and how they will reflect our changing culture and entertainment needs, as well as influencing the audiences who attend them. Making the average moviegoer read to keep up with the plot happens to be one trend I'm all for!

MOVIES TEACH SCHOOL

October Sky is a movie based on the autobiographical book *Rocket Boys: A Memoir*. It's about Homer Hickman Jr. and his seven friends who were encouraged by their teacher to build a rocket and enter a national science fair to achieve their dream of getting out of their mining town. They win the science fair, and Homer receives a college scholarship that eventually leads him to fulfill his dream of working as a NASA engineer. I chose *October Sky* as one of the best family films of 2000 because of its inspiring message, and I'm encouraged that teachers all over the country have shown it in classrooms to inspire students and encourage them to follow their dream. Both the book and movie show young people how trigonometry, calculus, and physics are connected to the outside world in a real way.

However, some teachers are teaching the wrong message and showing R-rated movies in their classroom. (Both my son and daughter have had this happen in their high school classes.)

Most parents wouldn't choose to have their teenager sit through an R-rated movie or even some controversial PG-13s in a classroom of peers for a school assignment.

THE YEAR MOVIES CHANGED

Nineteen ninety-nine was the year that changed Hollywood and movies forever. It was a year when a new generation of directors hit the screen with unusual films and unheard-of special effects that changed the concept of moviemaking and made movies "cool" again. The narrative film was declared "dead" by R.E.M.'s Michael Stipe (*Being John Malkovich*), and it was feared that the limits of traditional filmmaking had become too "perfectionistic."

This was the year when characters slid into John Malkovich's head. Ghosts, Satan, the anti-Christ, witchcraft, and a female god were popular. And a small project that jerked in and out of focus throughout the entire movie was called *The Blair Witch Project* and became the cult movie of the summer. Another popular movie called *The Matrix* earned $171 million[15] at the box office and has since become the best-selling movie ever in DVD format. With its incredible special effects and futuristic style of dart and weave, it dramatically changed the way a typical gun battle between the good and bad guys could be filmed and turned violence into an artful bullet ballet with bad guys morphing at will into other characters.

It was as though a generation of filmmakers raised on cut-and-paste laptops took a visual art form of storytelling and created a new visual breed of film for eager fans who had been raised on billions and billions of images. The bombardment of PlayStation, the Internet, video games, advertising, and even hip-hop music has influenced these young filmmakers who are on the cutting edge of changing the way we will watch movies in the future. They don't worry if their audience will keep up because they know they have a generation of channel flippers who are used to the quick styles. But more important than that, they paved the way for movies to be different and to be accepted by a younger generation who "gets them."

Movies such as *Run Lola Run, Being John Malkovich, The Limey, Go,* and *Fight Club* took violence to a bloody new level and brought the macabre and strange to a tolerant, almost rational zone. Films exploring the dark side were a huge success. One summer sleeper took a suspenseful blow-your-mind spook flick with a child uttering a line no one would forget, an ending everyone would remember, a supernatural writer/director everyone talked about, a new way to see dead people, and turned *The Sixth Sense* into the twelfth highest domestic grossing film of all time. *Magnolia* and *American Beauty* were edgy, dark satires on life, love, and a twisted version of family that broke away from stringent, ideological restrictions. All of these films earned attention from critics and Hollywood alike.

"At the time we made 2001*, I don't think I saw the fact that it was filled with so many metaphors. Until recently, I had no idea that when the ape man throws the bone, it becomes a nuclear weapon in what is the longest flash forward (4 million years) in the history of filmmaking."*

—Keir Dullea (Dr. Dave Bowman, the astronaut who unplugs Hal)[16]

CAN MOVIES PREDICT THE FUTURE?

Perhaps you remember that when the science-fiction film *2001: A Space Odyssey* was launched in 1968, the media had a field day predicting how many of Arthur C. Clarke's predictions about the future would come true. The year 2001 came, and although the Space Station Mir and Pan Am no longer exist, many things have progressed, including our movies. Much of what you see at the theaters incorporates technology that soon may be a part of our daily lives. Scripts are more intelligent, and imaginative devices are created by teams that work hand-in-hand with scientists, technology, and innovative industry. As the audiences become more sophisticated, it forces the writers, technology, and screenplays to stay current with trends and future ideas. In many cases, movies are a reflection of what's to come in our society, and some movies are simply showing you what's already here.

Have you ever noticed how a movie comes out, and then within days, weeks, or months, life seems to imitate it? Most of the time we think it's just a quirky coincidence or twist of fate. But sometimes writers appear to have a supernatural connection, because some stories too eerily reflect real life. Even though they were written months, sometimes years, before. I have a friend who writes sitcoms and once told me that he knew a writer who allowed himself to be used by a spirit that would literally "write his scripts for him." And when you think about it, the demonic ghouls, beasts, and monstrous-looking creatures you see on many of the TV shows and in movies could be inspired but from no other place than one who has seen this kind of evil up close.

For instance, in 1979 *The China Syndrome* depicted a nuclear power plant accident that was played out in real life at the Chernobyl power plant in the Ukraine in 1986. The 1995 movie *Outbreak* was about a virus outbreak in the U.S. that came from an African monkey. Soon after, the same kind of virus broke out in South Africa. Foreshadowing President Clinton's affair with Monica Lewinsky was the 1997 *Wag the Dog* movie, in which a Whitehouse staff, eager to fend off bad publicity about the president's sexual improprieties, staged a nonexistent war to distract the public. The 2000 hit *Proof of Life* centered on the rescue of an American kidnapped and kept in a Colombian mountain prison by guerrilla fighters who wanted to collect a large ransom. In

December 2000, a report came out from the Free Country Foundation (a private group that tracks abductions in Columbia) that stated at least 3,029 people were kidnapped through November 2000 to be ransomed. Most were Colombian, but thirty-six were foreigners. In 1998 *Armageddon* portrayed Bruce Willis and his crew landing on an asteroid headed for Earth, and although one wasn't threatening our planet, NASA accomplished the same feat in February 2001.

Sometimes movies predict the future, and sometimes they eerily coincide with history being made.

MOVIE ART IMITATES SCIENCE

Today writers can start coming up with an incredible science-fiction plot, and before the movie is finished, scientists have already found a way to create it. For example, if you have seen the Arnold Schwarzenegger science-fiction film *The 6th Day*, you may have noticed some inventions that are already here and some that are in the not-so-distant future. Self-driving prototype GM trucks (they exist), cloned pets (we have sheep, pigs, and who knows what's brewing in a petri dish), a "virtual" girlfriend who caters to a man's desires (that one is also debatable), and jet helicopters that fly by themselves (who knows what the government is hiding!), but the biggest thing we may soon have that the movie introduces is cloned humans.

Cormac and Marianne Wibberley, the husband and wife team who wrote the movie, say they knew nothing of cloning at the time. "We had the science fiction before the science fact," Cormac says. "Honestly, it was just us making stuff up," Marianne says. "We're big science-fiction fans. We just wanted to make a big popcorn movie." The film's director, Roger Spottiswoode, says the production began *before* the announcement that Ian Wilmut and colleagues in Scotland had cloned Dolly the sheep in 1997. It was a classic case of art imitating science, and the film couldn't have asked for better publicity. In the film, right-to-life-type of religious people fight cloning, feeling that man is taking God's work into his own hands. "That I understand," Schwarzenegger says, "because if you claim God created man, obviously, if man can create himself, it gets a little bit confusing." I'm guessing Arnold just wants to be able to say, "I'll be back!" and mean it . . . forever.[17]

SEQUELS, WAR, AND FANTASY

The rule of thumb is that a sequel makes about 60% of the original movie's gross, so why is Hollywood continuing to deliver them? Sequels have a built-in audience with a proven track record, and studios love them! If the original made $150 million, then the sequel is called a "tent-pole" movie because it already has an audience that will flock to see the next one. *Hannibal* was the first film of 2001 that was a long-awaited sequel (ten years) to *Silence of the Lambs.* But take a look at sequels, and you'll see a "safe" pattern of "safe" sequels whose originals have proven themselves to be big box-office hits. It's a security blanket for Hollywood.

It's nice to see war movies (especially of the epic kind—my favorite!) making a comeback thanks to *Gladiator* and *Saving Private Ryan,* which paved the way. World War II movies experienced a major comeback in 2001 with several films: *Pearl Harbor, Enemy at the Gates, Windtalkers,* and *Hart's War.*

Fantasy was also big in 2001 with high-profile movies such as *Harry Potter and the Sorcerer's Stone, Lord of the Rings, A.I. Artificial Intelligence, Planet of the Apes, Final Fantasy: The Spirits Within,* and *Atlantis.* Fantasy is easier to sell to broader audiences, namely the pre-teens and teenagers who'll spend their money to see several of them more than once. And close behind fantasy comes animated movies: *Monsters, Inc.* (from the *Toy Story* team), *Shrek* from DreamWorks, and Paramount's *Jimmy Neutron: Boy Genius.*

THE FAMILY

The depiction of the American family has perhaps changed the most in recent years and come under severe attack from the movie industry. Hollywood used to make movies that lauded the family as a strong unit, a solid foundation of love, comfort, and parental wisdom, and built story lines around the members that kept the respect for family intact. Now families are portrayed as dysfunctional, stupid, redefined, or just plain strange. Recent films took that pain and dysfunction one step further in *American Beauty* and *Nutty Professor II: The Klumps.* In these movies parents act like fools, children act like the parents, and family members disrespect one another with irreverence, mockery, and sarcasm. Supposedly this is a reflection of the dysfunctional family of the twenty-first century, but that mockery has only succeeded in tearing down the strength of the traditional family, not defining it.

"THE TOKEN GAY"

For years the homosexual movement has succeeded in pushing their tolerance agenda onto the big screen via gay writers, directors, producers, actors, and actresses. Sometimes the movies awkwardly use subplots featuring gay characters just for the sake of political correctness (*Sweet November, American Beauty, Wonder Boys, Lucky Numbers, Dr. T and the Women, Bounce, Best in Show, The Mexican*) rather than an element that moves the plot. Movies portraying fathers in a gay role (*American Beauty*), cross-dressing (*Mrs. Doubtfire*), or taking on single-parenting (*The Next Best Thing*), and other scenarios are beginning to emerge in more movies today. "Token gay" is Hollywood slang for a movie featuring a character who's gay, just for the sake of having one in the movie. These characters have been used so much and done in such exaggerated ways it has turned more people off to the misuse of gay characters than endear the moviegoing public to the gay agenda.

SINGLE PARENTS

Parental roles have drastically changed, and now the theme of single parents occupies a lot of screen time, story lines, and scripts, reflecting what's culturally becoming an accepted norm. These story lines sometimes paint fathers out of the picture completely (*Erin Brockovich, Big Momma's House*) and focus on the woman overcoming her difficult circumstances for a new life. Or many times the fathers become the catalyst for the plot (*Frequency, Billy Elliot, Unbreakable, Rugrats in Paris, Big Daddy, Disney's The Kid, Me, Myself, & Irene*) and, in some way, struggle or even fight to keep their family together (*The Patriot, Romeo Must Die*).

What Hollywood discovered is that if you remove the male influence necessary for balance, you don't have an interesting movie. So gradually we are seeing the pendulum swing back, and movies focused on parents and the strength of family (however defined) are making a comeback (*October Sky, Remember the Titans, My Dog Skip, Meet the Parents, Snow Day*).

It's important and imperative for Hollywood to recognize the value and importance of family. What is portrayed as either elevating or demeaning on the big screen is emulated by society in our culture (especially through the youth). The power of Hollywood's influence ultimately comes from its audience. That's why it's important to recognize the studios that produce positive movies about family and, even more importantly, to support them by going to see their movies. The only way we are going to see more quality family entertainment produced in Hollywood is if the public supports their effort.

MINORITY INTERESTS

- January 1912—Bill Foster's chase comedy, *The Railroad Porter,* is the first film with an "all black" cast.
- 1926—The Charlie Chan character was a popular serial in movies, with Japanese actor George Kuwa playing the first Chinese detective Charlie Chan in the movie *House Without a Key.*
- May 1929—Fox Film releases *Hearts in Dixie,* starring Stepin Fetchit, the first "all black" musical by a major studio.
- April 13, 1964—Sidney Poitier becomes the first African-American to win the Best Actor Academy Award for *Lilies of the Field.* And on June 23, 1967, Poitier becomes the first black performer to leave his hand and footprint at Grauman's Chinese Theater for his work in the controversial *Guess Who's Coming to Dinner?*
- August 6, 1969—the first mainstream movie (*The Learning Tree*) directed by an African-American (Gordon Parks) hits the theaters.

Many people may not realize it, but the African-American or black community (as well as other ethnic groups) has been a part of Hollywood from the early years of films' inception to today. We've seen incredible performances from Hattie Daniels, Lena Horne, Sidney Poitier, and Sammy Davis Jr. to present-day favorites such as Halley Berry, Eddie Murphy, Denzel Washington, Morgan Freeman, Will Smith, Whoopi Goldberg and the list could go on and on with talent. Although people like producer/director Spike Lee complain about black representation in Hollywood, simply take a look at the movies playing in theaters today.

In the fall of 2000 there were complaints from the Hispanic and Asian communities, as well as other minorities, against television producers about how much preferential treatment the homosexual community was getting on television shows. Apparently, more gays were on the television than writers knew what to do with, and the imbalance was obviously felt. The groups made a point of distinguishing themselves as "true minorities," not polarized "special interest groups," and they raised the question of "equal representation" on TV and in movies. Studio execs heard their cries, and today the diversity of characters and story lines mixed with different racial groups is appearing across the networks.

Although it may not seem like enough representation to many, today that perception is rapidly changing, and Hollywood is definitely creating a multiethnic and cultural talent pool.

BLACK FILMS ARE BIG BOX OFFICE

Martin Luther King Jr.'s holiday weekend has proven to be a big box-office weekend for releasing teen films, particularly ones aimed at blacks. In 2000 Ice Cube released *Next Friday*, and it did extremely well. In 2001 MTV pumped up *Save the Last Dance*, and it brought in a phenomenal $27 million[18] over the four-day weekend, proving that teenagers are ready to support a good movie when studios least expect it.

INTERRACIAL DATING

The interesting thing about *Save the Last Dance* (2001) is that it tackles the controversial topic of interracial dating from a black perspective. The movie is about a young white teenage girl who moves into a mostly black neighborhood, attends a mostly black school, and begins dating a college-bound black man who wants to be a doctor. Several issues are dealt with (primarily focusing on the black community), and while it may not provide all the answers to the complex questions it raises, it does bring to light the whole topic of racism, including reverse discrimination.

A 1997 *USA Today/Gallup* poll found that 57% of teens who date have gone out with a person of another race or ethnic group.[19] Obviously our younger generation doesn't seem to have a problem with interracial dating. As many of these young people grow older and eventually intermarry, their tolerance will hopefully change the intolerance and prejudice toward interracial dating and mixed marriages that still reside in this country. This is true for any race, whether it is African-American, Asian, Hispanic, or any growing minority. The youth of today will demand that we face this issue in the future and what better place to start to face it than in the movies.

CAMEOS MAKE A MOVIE

It has become popular for stars to pop up in surprise appearances or roles in movies. Directors insist cameos should only be used to help a plot along, but since we are a celebrity-worshiping society, when we find out stars have made an appearance it tends to validate the movie.

Cameos first got their big start in 1956 when producer Mike Todd got an all-star cast to appear in *Around the World in 80 Days*. Now it's considered a box-office boost for movies, and the fun part is that it can be anyone these days—an actor, actress, model, sports figure, chef, politician, news anchor, even appearances by Jay Leno, Larry King, and David Letterman add that reality late-night touch to story lines. In 2001, *Saving Silverman* featured Neil Diamond in a cameo role because the story line used him as a major plot point.

WHO ARE OUR HEROES?

From the death of Rudolph Valentino, America's first beloved screen idol who died in 1926 at the young age of thirty-one, to the present, fans have had a fascination with screen idols as heroes. Heroes used to be bigger than life on both the big screen and the little one when I was growing up. In the early days of TV and movies, western figures such as John Wayne, Roy Rogers, Will Rogers, Gene Autry, Gary Cooper, Randolph Scott, Zorro, and the Lone Ranger were characters kids looked up to and wanted to emulate. They had screen roles that were always for good and always protective.

Many times actors had another job, talent, or hobby that enabled them to be known for something besides their movie roles. Some actors were real-life heroes. Audie Murphy came back from war and took on a Hollywood persona, starring in several war and western movies. Harold Russell, who lost both hands in a WWII grenade explosion, went on to win two Oscars for his role in *The Best Years of Our Lives*. Lieutenant Clark Gable was awarded the Distinguished Flying Cross and Air Medal after taking part in five combat missions, and even Jimmy Stewart and Elvis Presley served their country. Charlton Heston earned his popularity from several wonderful roles, including *Ben Hur*, but it was his performance as Moses in *The Ten Commandments* that endeared him to the Christian community. Sports heroes such as Babe Ruth, Mickey Mantle, Muhammad Ali, and cowboys such as Gene Autry and Roy Rogers were the kind of role models kids wanted to be, or at least meet.

It's not that these men were moral giants. They weren't. But the public wasn't privileged to a lot of details about movie stars or actors in those days. The fact that most of their personal lives didn't get exploited in tabloids served their status and reputation well. Studios presented the image they wanted you to have of their stars, and that allowed kids to have heroes the public revered.

When I was growing up, John Wayne, Roy Rogers, Jimmy Stewart, and Charlton Heston were a few of my heroes. Each of them was bigger than life, and in their own way they fought for truth and justice, and represented all that was good about America, passing that persona on to everyone who watched them. How many stars and celebrities could live up to that standard today?

My point is this. Today's kids don't have movie heroes like those they used to. Oh, they've got Madonna, The Rock, Tiger Woods, or maybe even an 'NSync favorite, or Julia Roberts' crush. But where are the heroes born from a war, a heroic deed, a situation where they've proven to be a leader? The closest thing we've had to movie heroes in the last ten years are Arnold Schwarzenegger, Bruce Willis, Sylvester Stallone, Chuck Norris, and probably a few others. The only qualifications for heroes today seem to be celebrities who get movie roles as heroes and who get their picture taken a lot. It is not for what they knowingly stand for. To be a hero or role model has become a popularity contest, and nothing more.

A survey of junior high and high school students found that 36% choose actors as their top heroes. Musicians finished second with

19%, and comedians and athletes tied for third with 11% each.[20] Why don't kids have heroes today? What kind of hero does your child or teen idolize?

ARE VILLAINS OUR NEW HEROES?

Hollywood's "anti-heroes" were born in 1967 with Warren Beatty and Faye Dunaway in *Bonnie and Clyde*. It was the first time many people felt guilty for rooting for the bad guys. These days, the audience is sometimes forced to root for killers, and the bad guys become good, while the good guys become the bad guys.

Teen slasher movies create bad guys such as Freddie, Jason, or the masked killer in *Scream* to be the anti-heroes. These guys almost always get away with the murders or crimes committed and have the audiences cheering for them to kill people.

It was interesting to see the publicity Anthony Hopkins recently received for his role in *Hannibal.* As audiences nervously watched their hero Hannibal chew his way through the script and characters, he safely escapes once again, missing the clutches of the law and emerging as a sort of hero for the disturbed. These kinds of "enemies" are emerging in more and more films. The problem is that their characters are then idolized, popularized, and emulated by impressionable young teens. When the bad guys become the good guys, we have a serious societal problem.

WHO ARE OUR HEROINES?

Sadly, women don't seem to have a lot of roles written for them to be the heroines these days. Good stories like *Erin Brockovich* and *The Contender* are rare. In fact, Julia Roberts cashed in with *Pretty Woman* and influenced a generation of young women to think that hitting the streets as a hooker just might pay off with a handsome prince/customer who will marry you. These days, leading female roles are shifting to accommodate stronger characters, looser morals, and a story line that features new and younger female roles.

Top box-office actresses such as Julia Roberts, Gwyneth Paltrow, Sandra Bullock, Charlize Theron, Helen Hunt, Cameron Diaz, Drew Barrymore, and others don't usually get prime roles or scripts that focus primarily on them. As likable as Julia Roberts is, Erin Brockovich was a brassy, abrasive, in-your-face-woman who fought her way to the top. And face it, there's just not a real high demand for that kind of independent, free-thinking woman in Hollywood, or the real world for that matter.

HOLLYWOOD DADS AND MOMS

Dads had a fair treatment with Kevin Bacon as the overprotective dad in *My Dog Skip*, and Mel Gibson was the ultimate all-around single dad who loves his kids in *The Patriot*. *Frequency* was a great father/son movie with Dennis Quaid fathering his future son Jim Cavaziel. In *Disney's the Kid*, Bruce Willis played the most unusual role of his career . . . finding his little boy self in order to go on and become his father self.

Today moms are required to pretty much just be a mom. But occasionally they get a chance to really shine in a role where a mother is required to help the child deal with his father (*My Dog Skip, October Sky*), or in some cases protect the child from the father (*Traffic, Pay It Forward*), or protect the child from the bad guys (*Gladiator*), be the cheerleader when they need encouragement (*Bring It On, Finding Forrester*), keep the home under control (*The Amati Girls*), find a husband to make a home (*The Perfect Storm*), and, in some cases, leave altogether so the mayhem can happen (*Home Alone I & II, Spot the Dog*). Although the mother gets to be a strong support for the story, rarely does a mother role come along (such as in *Little Women*) where the story revolves around the mom being a mom.

CELEBRITIES AND YOUR FIFTEEN MINUTES

"God takes care of the worst idiots, and he certainly takes care of me."
—Mel Gibson

On March 28, 1920, Douglas Fairbanks presented bride Mary Pickford with the twenty-two-room "Pickfair." The royal Hollywood couple had established the first social capital of the movie world, and those who were in the industry flocked to see it. What is the lure and magic that makes being a celebrity a sought-after occupation by most

kids today? How did we get to this point in the entertainment industry when being famous is all anyone wants to be? What started out as
Andy Warhol's cynical statement about our society and culture (everyone wants their "fifteen minutes" of fame) ended up being a prophetic
utterance over the youth of our society today. But it's not just kids
who want to cash in on fame and get on TV or in the news. Parents
and adults are just as guilty.

In January 1915, Theodosia Goodman became Theda Barr and
was Hollywood's first fabricated movie star in *A Fool There Was*. Soon
the fledgling studios and agents realized there was money to be made
with a public that was interested in not only seeing their movie stars
but fantasizing about being one too. In those days, contracts were
signed, then the grooming process began with hair, makeup, clothing,
weight checks, arranged dating relationships—basically, an actor or
actress sold their soul to the studio in exchange for fame.

Times and studios have changed over the years, and studios no
longer "own" their stars. That independence has worked wonders with
certain stars who bring in big office for a movie because they can now
demand top dollars for what they do. Bruce Willis is one of the top
movie stars today, followed by Tom Hanks, Julia Roberts, and Mel
Gibson, according to www.castmaker.com. Although all celebrities
don't receive the same preferential treatment, many are catered and
pandered to on and off the set. I've heard many "horror stories" you
wouldn't believe from people on the set about some of the requests for
personal trailers, certain exercise equipment, nannies, jets, bizarre
foods, pets, clothing, Jacuzzi tubs, cars, etc. The list goes on, but the
patience in Hollywood doesn't. Many stars and celebrities find that
their "star" quality needs bumping up a notch or two, and that's where
a good role and adoring fans can make or break a star.

Unfortunately, one area that celebrities can't be protected from is
the biting press that hounds them when their marriage breaks up or
personal tragedy hits. With high-profile couples representing the
Hollywood glitzy, glamour, and fantasy life, a solid marriage is hard to
make and keep. Tom Cruise and Nicole Kidman are recent victims.
Bruce Willis and Demi Moore, Meg Ryan and Dennis Quaid, Helen
Hunt, Harrison Ford, Mick Jagger, and unfortunately many more.

The world's fascination with celebrities, movie stars, sports figures, musicians, TV stars, and whoever else earns that title has to recognize that they are only people. Their lives may be one of privilege because of money and fame, but in the end they want and need the same things out of life that you and I do. Their fantasy world off the screen and in their own arena becomes a test of living life the best way they can, the same as you or I would.

TALK IS NOT CHEAP

You've heard the expression "word of mouth" used in the film industry to describe the buzz around movie openings and big movie weekends? Industry experts gauge what moviegoers are saying about a movie by how steeply the box office drops after opening day. The bigger the drop, the worse the "word of mouth." Anything less than 25% is considered good; any film that drops more than 60% is considered disastrous.

By spreading the word on bad movies, audiences can ruin expensive ad campaigns and destroy the box-office rush that studios were hoping to attract. For instance, in the year 2000 audiences trashed *Pokémon the Movie*, which crashed at 68% in its second week; *Battlefield Earth* (which I personally voted the worst movie of 2000) dropped to 66%; both *Titan A.E.* and *Godzilla 2000* dropped to 60%, according to box-office tracking firm ACNielson EDI.[21]

Despite critics' thumbs up or down, movies getting good notices from viewers can add to their box office for the next weekend. The Internet has also helped to spread the word with numerous sites for people to read and chat about the movies they have seen. An ACNielson EDI analysis in 2000 showed that major releases are dropping off faster, an average of 46% in the second weekend, which is 5% more than in '98 and '99. But that's not necessarily because people like the movies less. Movies are raking in more during the first weekend, so there's more distance to fall. Studios are aiming for big debuts, spending large amounts of money to build a "what to see" buzz before a movie opens. And there are more theater screens than ever, so few moviegoers are shut out the first weekend.

Tom Sherak, the distribution head at Twentieth Century Fox, says word of mouth still matters. "This is a business that is built on

DEATH BY ENTERTAINMENT　　　　　　　　　　78

word of mouth. It's the main way people know what to see and what not to see."[22]

FADE TO BLACK

The world's first multiplex theater was owned by Durwood, Inc. (now AMC Theaters) in Kansas City, Missouri, and opened in 1963, showing *The Great Escape* on two screens. Since that day, movie theaters have never been the same. In fact, the race to build as many multiscreen theaters as possible has created a financial crisis in the movie industry of America and may eventually affect the audience at the box office.

Movie theaters across America are in trouble and closing, as major chains are in bankruptcy court. AMC, Loews, Edwards, United, and others are closing thousands (maybe as many as 15,000 of the 36,448 U.S. screens)[23] because of the self-inflicted greed the theaters put on the market. The major chains competitively built new and trendy megaplexes to keep up with one another, but in the wake of expansion, they had to hang on to smaller, less profitable, and older theaters. Despite a banner year of ticket sales, the theaters are citing declining attendance at their older theaters, causing a serious problem for the industry.

One of the reasons these chains are having trouble with unsatisfied customers is due to greed and indifference. Gouging prices have required heads of families, dates, and teenagers to practically take out a loan before going to the movies. When entertainment starts to average around forty dollars by the time you're seated, many moviegoers are beginning to reconsider.

JAMES CAMERON PRODUCED, WROTE, AND DIRECTED *TITANIC*, which was rumored to have cost over $200 million. When Cameron appealed to the ratings board to give him a PG-13 rating instead of an R, he made it clear he had to have this rating to recover the expensive costs. So a few scenes were cut out, and the rating then allowed audiences of all ages to buy a ticket. If *Titanic* had been given the R rating it deserved, it originally never would have been the number one box-office movie in the world. Hollywood learned a big lesson from *Titanic*'s success and realized if they make more movies with this rating, it assures bigger box-office success. In fact, we're already seeing it in the box office because Hollywood is giving us more PG-13 films than ever before.

The Ratings Game

From 1933 to 1968, most films produced for theatrical release were the equivalent of a G or PG rating. The first film ever released with a label stating "suggested for mature audiences" was *Georgy Girl* in 1966.[1] It was not until November 1, 1968, that the Motion Picture Association of America's self-imposed ratings system went into effect. From 1968 to 1990, over 60% of the movies Hollywood produced for theatrical release were R-rated.[2] Statistics started to prove in the '90s that a good G, PG, or PG-13 movie can be a big moneymaker for Hollywood, and a shift in focus took place.[3] After the high school shootings at Columbine in 1999, then-President Clinton issued a statement that asked the movie industry to "reevaluate" its rating system and appeal to young people to ease up on the violence.

Hollywood's rating system has long been under fire from parents who think it's too broad and vague in description. For parents who use it as a literal barometer for what is or isn't acceptable, the PG-13 category has proven far too liberal and adult-oriented, promoting movies with content that used to be R-rated. Rather than swing more conservatively toward discretion and protection for impressionable children who can buy tickets for these movies, Hollywood has discovered the PG-13 rating equals more box-office dollars and has become a "soft R" minefield. A survey by the national PTAs showed that 80% of parents want to know how much sex, language, violence, and adult behavior is in a movie and not just what age group the industry officials think should be watching.

Many parents feel ratings are only marginally helpful. For example, the movie *Dinosaur* was rated PG for animated violence. When I reviewed it in my column, parents asked me what qualified as "animated violence"? The fact that there were a couple deaths of two main characters and that the action was computer-animated technology is what gave the movie its PG rating and caused kids to squirm. When the T-Rex closes in for the kill, the scene is intense and could cause nightmares for some children.

THE MPAA & THE MPA

It's hard to grasp the magnitude of our movie industry and its influence, but American movies are shown in over 150 countries worldwide, and American television programs are broadcast in over 125 international markets.[4] Our film industry provides the majority of movies seen in millions of homes around the world and is regulated domestically by the Motion Picture Association of America (MPAA). This group gives the movies their ratings and determines what's appropriate and what's not. The organization that oversees it internationally is the Motion Picture Association (MPA). Our movie, home video, and television industries depend on the MPAA and the MPA to be their voice as well as do producers and distributors of entertainment programming for television, cable, and home video.

Founded in 1922 as the trade association of the American film industry, the MPAA has broadened its mandate over the years. Back in the days of silent films and when motion pictures' first talkies began appearing on public screens, the association was developed initially to "clean up" the motion picture business and give it a more favorable public image. It did an adequate job until the '60s, when Hollywood's movies started to change. The cultural revolution and spirit of change that rolled across America affected everything from our music to our movies. A more liberal style of filmmaking erupted and caused havoc with the MPAA and the Hollywood community.

On March 18, 1964, after scenes had to be cut from *The Americanization of Emily*, producer Martin Ransohoff went to the MPAA and asked them to lift its ban on nudity in Hollywood films.

On December 7, 1964, director Sam Peckinpah was fired by the producer of *The Cincinnati Kid* for shooting nude scenes that were not written in the script. Then on April 20, 1965, Sidney Lumet's *The Pawnbroker,* starring Rod Steiger, took its place in Hollywood history as the first mainstream film to include female frontal nudity. The war on decency in Hollywood was quickly sliding down the slippery slope of no return, and morality, modesty, and movies were forever changed.

The MPA was formed in 1945 and was originally called the MPEAA (Motion Picture Export Association of America). The name was changed in 1994 to more accurately reflect the global nature of today's international entertainment marketplace. The MPA, often referred to as "a little State Department," covers a wide range of diplomatic, economic, and political arenas internationally.

These days the MPAA is having to defend the work that comes out of Hollywood and counter the criticism from Washington aimed at the producers, directors, advertisers, marketers, and the movie and television industry itself.

If you aren't familiar with the ratings system and what the symbols stand for, here's a quick look at the MPAA ratings code.

MPAA RATINGS

G = General Audiences—Acceptable for all ages or general audiences.

PG = Parental Guidance Suggested—Some material may not be suited for children under thirteen and may require parental guidance due to some profanity, obscenity, or violence that isn't strong but still may be too adult or offensive for younger children.

PG-13 = Parents Strongly Cautioned—Some material may be inappropriate for children under thirteen, such as bathroom humor, crude dialogue, offensive language, religious profanities, partial nudity, scenes of characters in underwear, implied sexual situations, crude sexual dialogue, drug use, adult themes and issues. May be a movie appropriate for adults only despite this rating.

R = Restricted—Under seventeen requires accompanying parent or adult guardian because of strong language, strong religious profanity, nudity, graphic sexual situations, graphic violence, horror, adult themes and issues.

NC-17—No one under seventeen admitted because of adult language, graphic sex, and sadistic or explicit violence. Adult themes too extreme for children and teens. This rating replaced the X rating on September 26, 1990.

PG KIDDIE MOVIES REPLACING THE G?

Most parents know that the only real "safe" rating for younger children (ages four to ten) is the G rating. For years Disney has been the hallmark and main supplier for the G market with kid-friendly family films and animated entertainment. A few years ago, parents started to complain about the questionable and mature content and adult sexual-theme messages that were found in G-rated story lines in movies such as *The Hunchback of Notre Dame, Hercules, Pocahontas*, and others. Their complaints were that the animated children's stories were either too mature, scary, or sexually suggestive for children.

About that time a better selection of family films started to be produced by other studios competing for Disney's audience. Adventurous studios such as DreamWorks, WB, Paramount, and Pixar rose to the challenge and invaded Disney's magic kingdom, introducing creative family entertainment geared for the adults as well as children. Quality movies such as *The Prince of Egypt, Babe, A Little Princess, Anastasia, Antz, The Iron Giant,* and *Chicken Run* were created by studios willing to trespass Disney's sacred territory and take a share of the dominated market for family entertainment.

But Disney paid attention as well. Their G-rated films *Tarzan* and *The Emperor's New Groove* connected with all ages and proved to be box-office hits. Clearly, Disney is aiming for winning formulas that will rebuild parents' trust and renew its leading status in family entertainment.

Gradually, with more selections and films geared to please adults as well as kids, parents have started taking their younger children to PG movies without any reservation despite the caution attached with the rating. Two of the top box-office family hits in 2000 were the PG-rated movies *Dinosaur* and *The Grinch*. Both were rated for some intense scenes and mature themes, but that didn't stop the films from becoming two of the most successful family movies that year.

Still, a PG rating on a kid's movie should cause parents to ask what the caution in the rating is for. Many parents complained to me about *The Grinch* and said their little ones were "creeped out" by the mean one's green makeup, close-up camera angles, and the scary faces Jim Carey made. Despite the ratings and scenes that might cause bad dreams or night-lights to be left on, it's clear parents are gravitating toward the PG movies that will hold their interest while entertaining the kids.

THE R-RATED PG-13

When *Indiana Jones and the Temple of Doom* and *Gremlins* were released in 1984, their PG rating caused a huge protest from angry parents upset about the graphic violence and mature themes contained in the story lines. The graphic scenes in both movies were too mature for children and parents conditioned to a softer rating, so the PG-13 rating was created in July 1984 to warn parents of questionable content but still allow kids to purchase tickets. With theaters cracking down on kids and teens sneaking into R-rated movies, the PG-13 rating was an important and liberating step to bring in more revenue for the movie industry and, over the past decade, became essential for big-time box-office success.[5]

The PG rating is considered to be "childlike" and "less mature" than PG-13 films and can be deadly to a movie targeted at teenagers because of that perception. Over the years I've witnessed a gradual leniency and change in the PG and PG-13 ratings. The PG-13 rating has become a powerful weapon in the hands of the MPAA, the studios, and marketing people. In some cases that rating has become a weapon, waging an all-out assault on teenagers and kids to get them to use their money and ability to buy a ticket for that particular movie. The largest moviegoing group is still the heavy spending twelve- to twenty-four-year-olds who make up 39% of audiences.[6]

Within the parameters of a PG-13 rating is a plethora of questionable material ranging from mild language and violence or even mild sexual innuendoes to an abundance of vulgar language, crude dialogue, sexually suggestive situations with nudity, an abundance of violence, and a variety of crude or questionable behaviors (drinking, drug use, a shot of someone throwing up, people using the bathroom, etc.).

The umbrella of the PG-13 rating has the ability to hide many movies that most parents would rate R. Hollywood has found a convenient way to dance around the R rating and pass horrendous movies filled with adult material under the PG-13 protection. What's a parent to do? How can a parent possibly look at the rating and determine what elements in a movie make it too adult for their kids? They can't, which is the flaw in the ratings system.

Here's the real story. The MPAA is the lobbying organization for the major movie studios. President Jack Valenti is paid by those studios, and the ratings the MPAA gives vary, depending on the tastes and tolerances of the eight to thirteen parents who constitute the board. The organization does not exist to serve the public or concerned parents. Rather, the ratings board serves as a smokescreen that stands between the studios and disillusioned parents. In other words, if we have a complaint against what Hollywood is giving us, we can't shoot the messenger.

Since the PG-13 was created in July 1984, over twenty-two films have grossed more than $200 million.[7] This impressive list serves to point out that the moviegoing public will flock to good movies with a decent rating more than R-rated movies loaded with adult themes:

1. *Titanic*
2. *Dr. Seuss' How the Grinch Stole Christmas*
3. *Mission Impossible: 2*
4. *The Perfect Storm*
5. *Star Wars, Episode I: The Phantom Menace*
6. *Jurassic Park*
7. *Forrest Gump*
8. *Independence Day*
9. *X-Men*
10. *The Sixth Sense*

In fact, the box-office grosses for PG-13 films jumped 26% in 2000 to $3.1 billion![8]

THE PG-13 DECEPTION

It is nearly impossible for parents to decipher which PG-13 movies are acceptable for their kids. Without having specific reviews like mine to consult, many parents feel as though they're playing

Russian roulette with their child's mind every time they make a decision about what movie the child can or cannot go to see. Many PG-13 movies appear acceptable because the trailers feature a family, cute kids, romance, or tame-looking scenes. But far too often looks are deceiving, and what you end up with is a story line too adult for children and occasionally even too adult for young teens.

How is it possible that the religious movie *Left Behind* or Tom Hank's movie *Cast Away* received the same rating as the political thriller *Thirteen Days*? Or take the comically irreverent *O Brother, Where Art Thou?* or the even more disgustingly irreverent *Saving Silverman* and compare those to the hilarious *Shanghai Noon*. How can the raunchy, oversexed teen flick *Sugar & Spice* and the sweet, simple love story in *The Wedding Planner* be in the same category? *The Family Man, Meet the Parents, Mission: I, 2,* and *Remember the Titans* all have completely different target audiences, yet all shared the same PG-13 rating.

I have seen many PG-13 movies that should have been rated R listed right next to a fairly innocuous PG-13 movie that might contain only mild language, yet both carry the same rating. It's enough to drive parents crazy, but as a critic, it's even harder to evaluate. I try to rate films on the basis of the targeted market audience. If it's an adult PG-13, I say so. If it's aimed at teens, I tell why and list the ages. I am "age appropriate specific" in my reviews, which is what a parent wants and needs to make a well-informed judgment about a particular movie.

So why the increase in PG-13 movies containing R-rated material? Jack Valenti acknowledges that the criteria for PG-13 have become more lenient. But he claims it's a function of current culture, not his ratings board. "The society isn't what it used to be. The worst thing that can happen in a democracy is rigidity and an unwillingness to change. The same can be said for the ratings system."[9]

LUCKY #13

It used to be that filmmakers signed contracts promising their movies would get an R rating, but that has changed. Aware of what's at stake, Hollywood understands the young adolescent and teen market extremely well. Studios, producers, directors, and especially the ratings board know that if a movie can pass with a PG-13 rating, it signals repeat business from older kids and young teens without tempting them to sneak into R-rated movies. When all ages can buy tickets, the movies have the potential to make more money and reach a broader audience. Parents will be more inclined to attend a PG-13 movie with their family in tow, so socially it's a better draw for the theater as well.

Over the past decade the PG-13 film has almost become the essential ingredient for a studio to achieve box-office success. Studios can discharge marketing costs by teaming up with corporate tie-ins and cross-promotional media blitzes. But many companies won't even consider sponsoring an R-rated movie unless it carries a big name that will promote the product. Remember *The Grinch* who almost stole the reason for the 2000 Christmas season? It was wildly profitable beyond even director Ron Howard's wildest dreams and sold everything from cookies to household items with the mean green one's face plastered on them. The amount of products sold because of tie-ins was mind-boggling.

Another example of this kind of marketing was MGM's *The World Is Not Enough* (1999). It was the fourth consecutive James Bond movie released with a PG-13 rating to attract the 60% male audience under twenty-five, and it became one of the largest opening films in MGM's history. MGM had agreements with BMW and Omega watches (among others) as well as a pact to advertise worldwide on MTV. That deal would have been difficult had it been an R-rated movie. But there's yet another benefit to the PG-13 strategy that studios have recently learned to appreciate in a titanic way.

A TITANIC EXAMPLE

The movie *Titanic* was a PG-13 movie that earned a staggering 22% return rate (a typical movie will have 3-5% of its viewers return to see it) because of the appeal of the leading actors Leonardo DiCaprio and Kate Winslet, as well as the romantic/dramatic story. The combination appealed to young adolescents and teenagers who saw this three-hour movie—many went back four to ten times. *Titanic* became the highest grossing film of all time mainly because of seven- to twelve-year-olds going to see this movie multiple times.

But many parents brought children under thirteen, thinking *Titanic* was a historical story about the famous ship, and were shocked to hear an abundance of offensive language and watch the lead actress defiantly flash the sign of the finger, appalled to see female frontal nudity, and offended by the sexual situation of two teenagers in the back of a car. There were obviously adult themes in this movie that weren't meant for eight- to thirteen-year-olds, but many parents believe the "family-friendly" PG-13 rating means the movie is OK.

James Cameron produced, wrote, and directed *Titanic*, which was rumored to have cost over $200 million. When Cameron appealed to the ratings board to give him a PG-13 rating instead of an R, he made it clear he had to have this rating to recover the expensive costs. So a few scenes were cut out, and the rating then allowed audiences of all ages to buy a ticket. If *Titanic* had been given an R rating it deserved, it never would have been the number one box-office movie in the world.

Hollywood learned a big lesson from *Titanic*'s success and realized if they make more movies with this rating, it assures bigger box-office success. In fact, we're already seeing it in the box office, because Hollywood is giving us more PG-13 films than ever before.

THE R RATING

The R rating is another tricky one. In some movies it is simply the language that gives the movie its adult-only code (*The Milagro Beanfield War*, for instance). Other movies have received it because of violence in the context with an adult story (*Saving Private Ryan, The Patriot, Gladiator*). But for the most part, it is the combination of sexual situations, nudity, or even implied sexual acts mixed with a combination of language, violence, and adult situations that usually earns a movie its R rating. Because of its vast range, the R rating has confused not just parents but other moviegoers as well.

How is the typical moviegoer to know what material might be in an R movie? *Hannibal* and *Quills* both deal with cult heroes who are criminals with a high intelligence—one is a cannibal, the other is an author of pornography. Both have a perverted obsession and approach to sex, both observe or participate in ghastly murderous rituals, both gloat with cynical pride throughout the story, and one ends up escaping. Compare those dark characters and themes of perversion, murder, and mayhem with *The Patriot* or *Gladiator*. These stories feature heroes who have high ideals, a love for their country, government, family, and moral responsibility to their fellow man. Except for the violence that is in keeping with the time period and the situations rendered against these two men, there's no other reason for the R rating. These two movies should be in completely different categories due to completely different R-rated material.

The NC-17 rating has had such a negative effect on the public that after the failure of *Showgirls* and the negative press it generated, studios won't let that rating get attached to their projects for fear of box-office failure. So what we have on the market is an abundance of R-rated movies such as *Hannibal, Quills, Scary Movie*, and others that deserve a hard R but don't quite fit into the NC-17.

I am in the process of proposing a new R rating for movies with excessive violence, sex, and material simply not suited for children under seventeen. If there was an *R-17* rating that would represent movies like the ones mentioned above, studios could make more movies for "adults" to enjoy without fear of children seeing them. Legally, children could be kept out of the theater, and ultimately it would solve the problem of children seeing these kinds of movies in the first place. Parents could better monitor the kind of R-rated movie their teenager wants to see, theaters could better monitor children and young teens from sneaking in, and fellow moviegoers and theater owners could politely and legally ask the mindless parents who self-ishly bring their young child to a movie like *Hannibal* to leave. If you support my cause, write me and let me know.

R MOVIES AIMED AT KIDS

It's become apparent that violence isn't the only issue Washington needs to be concerned about. Sexual matter has to be high on the list of concerns for parents. Sex is being sold on a daily basis in alarming proportions to children, preteens, and teens through various forms of the media. Hollywood has become the instructor for kids and teens on not only "how to" have sex but also how to define it. We marvel at a younger generation that seems to have grown up too fast, bypassing innocence and youth, and replacing it with adult behaviors. When did society's moral bar lower to allow adult material to be sold to impressionable twelve- to sixteen-year-olds?

Today's millennials are viewing more sex, violence, and R-rated movies than ever before. In fact, 80% of R-rated movies are targeted to kids under eighteen![10] Hollywood has often tested the patience of parents, and lately of Washington, with the marketing of R-rated films to teenagers under seventeen, and in most cases to kids twelve to sixteen. Today's adolescents and teens view any movie in the theater as fair game. Gone are the days when adult-rated movies were considered strictly for adults and taboo for kids.

Mini-malls and multiplexes have changed the way we go to movies and purposefully make most R-rated films available to whoever can walk in and sit down. It's no wonder kids have seen so many R-rated movies. They assume they can walk in to see an R-rated movie anytime they want, because it's usually uncontested. No one is really monitoring the law or punishing violators who sneak in. The "importance" lies mostly with the under-seventeen crowd, because it's still a big deal to kids, a social "rite of passage" that proves they are old enough to watch an R-rated movie with their peers.

As a society, we are offended at sexual crimes committed against our children. Pedophiles, child abusers, child pornographers, and those who exploit children for their own financial gain are deemed disgusting to us as a society and morally insulting to our sense of decency. Yet when we have people in Hollywood blatantly targeting their R-rated smut directly at our children and young impressionable teenagers, strictly for the purpose of making money and exploiting them, no one seems to be offended.

MORE PARENTS ARE TAKING THEIR KIDS TO SEE R-RATED MOVIES

Caught somewhere between Washington and Hollywood in the battle zone over how violence in the media is affecting children are the parents of the kids who are being targeted. Some parents are greatly concerned and appreciate everything a senator, president, or politician will do to change what's coming out of Hollywood. Others don't think Washington is going to do much to change the current trend of movies, so they do the best they can to ensure their child or teen is protected from deceiving ratings and violent or sexual movies. And then there are parents who take a surprising approach—they *take* their kids to see R-rated movies.

That's right! For numerous reasons more and more parents are taking their children, preteens, and teens to see R-rated movies. I saw this trend coming a while back, and I believe it's getting worse. Some parents claim the R-rated movies are "no worse than what you see on cable." Many parents let their kids watch R-rated videos at home and see no problem with doing the same at the theater. Still others are too cheap to pay a baby-sitter and instead choose to bring their young child to an adult movie, assuming the child can't follow the story or will go to sleep. Then you have some parents who believe their child is mature for their age and buy the ticket for them. No matter what the reason, experts say taking your preteen to a hard R-rated movie isn't wise.

It's a mixed-up world. Some parents don't even try to find out any information on a movie before they let their kids go see it. Or when they do go, they're upset with the content that shocks both the kids and them. Many parents get offended if told that a certain R-rated movie is too violent for their child to see, and the parents become the problem as theaters push to get tougher on teens getting into R-rated movies. Other parents buy a ticket for a child to get into an R-rated movie, then the parent goes to see a different movie.

Washington and Hollywood can tell us how to market their films, but there's no law or ready cure for regulating bad parenting. Too bad.

THE HORROR OF *HANNIBAL*

When the horror sequel to *Silence of the Lambs* opened at a record-breaking $58 million gross, it became the biggest debut for an R-rated film outside the summer season and the largest debut for MGM. The studio was worried about this movie attracting the younger teen crowd, so it sent a letter stating it was for adults only so reviewers would be specific when talking about the rating and the content.

MGM made it very clear it was not marketing this movie to anyone but adults. I applaud their responsible actions of limiting MTV buys until after 9 P.M., eliminating daytime airings of commercials on MTV, and monitoring radio-promoted screenings. Despite that, theaters were packed the weekend it opened! People flocked to see the cult hero Hannibal literally devour his skeptics and prove he still had what it takes. And apparently he did.

I knew the movie did well, but I was shocked to read how many parents took their kids to see this movie! Even MGM was amazed at the number of parents who showed up with their preteens ready to watch this graphic horror film. *USA Today* wrote an article about it, quoting mothers and kids who ignorantly bragged about it as they left the theater. I was so angry I wrote a long, hot letter to *USA Today* about it. I find it ironic that the closing scene of Hannibal feeding a piece of brain to an innocent child is a perfect metaphor for what those parents did. They fed their children a meal of graphic horror and violence, then assumed those children could digest and process the images in their limited scope of life and reality.

In the Minneapolis *Star Tribune* for February 21, 2001, columnist James Lileks's headline read: "R rating for movies also should stand for Responsibility among kids' guardians." He wrote about what he witnessed at a theater in these words: "We were all here to be scared. We were all here for Hannibal Lecter. The lights faded; darkness slid over the room like a soft black shroud. *Mommmeeeee?* said a small voice behind us. I turned, my wife turned, our friends turned: A 3-year-old girl was staring wide-eyed at the screen. Three. Years. Old."

Parental wisdom to make responsible movie choices for the health and well-being of their child is not an option; it's a moral duty. I encourage you to write your local newspapers, national papers, magazines, and other media venues whenever there is an issue about parenting entertainment. It helps for the news media to see that there are concerned parents who do not approve of other parents exposing their kids to horror and extreme violence. And it should send a message to the studios that pander violence to the youth.

R-RATED AIR TRAVEL

The first airline in-flight movie, *By Love Possessed* starring Lana Turner, was offered by TWA on July 19, 1961. It started a trend that provided relief for long, boring flights, but showing R-rated movies during flights is currently a problem for parents who want to protect their children.

A few years ago I received a letter from a woman who expressed her shock and disdain for a certain airline because they played an R-rated movie on a flight she was taking with her son. She had written the airline and sent them my movie review, clearly showing them they had aired an inappropriate movie for children. The airline apologized, but the woman felt the damage already done to her son couldn't be changed.

As airlines seek to offer more multiple entertainment selections and personal viewing screens, they are showing more theater versions of movies that can include R material and explicit scenes. For years R-rated titles have been offered in first and business classes on many airlines, but in the last few years they've shown up in coach. US Airways became the first domestic carrier to offer an on-demand video system, including R-rated movies in the coach sections of its new Airbus A330-300s to Europe. Airlines are being careful to keep R-rated films out of the unintended sight of children through private screens. The US Airways' system has a "KidView" feature that restricts content to G-rated fare, and a "TeenView" button limits entertainment to PG-rated material for teenagers.[11]

TEST IT ON THE TEENS

Warren Zide, one of the producers of the hit *American Pie*, stated this: "We really feel like some of the funniest things that happen in high school are R-rated, and we felt like the marketplace was shifting and that the audience wanted an R-rated picture."[12] By "the audience" he meant children under seventeen. Obviously, parental concerns or "wants" for their own children are never a consideration. In fact, *American Pie* was so successful that leading star Jason Biggs made another movie directly targeted to the thirteen- to twenty-four-year-old crowds called *Saving Silverman*. It was a mindless mess of offensive language, sexual dialogue, and questionable adult situations. And who do you think they said was their best test audience for the film? You guessed it! Thirteen- to twenty-four-year-olds. That's a big age range! What's acceptable and "OK" for someone over seventeen is not "OK" for a thirteen-year-old. And that's really the problem. Moviemakers don't seem to take into account the vast difference in maturity, impressionability, and discernment between ages.

But the problem has never really been with the seventeen-and-up crowd. Hollywood is deliberately targeting your twelve- to sixteen-year-olds, highly impressionable teens, who most likely aren't ready for the mature sex, violence, and language contained in many of the R-rated movies they want to see. Mike Tollin, the producer of *Varsity Blues,* said he believed that an R rating was necessary for his movie to be realistic. "We felt strongly that for the real issues kids deal with, and the real way they talk in the locker room, it had to have an R rating."[13]

Obviously, producers like Tollin and directors like Zide need a "realistic" check on who has the final word in our teenagers' lives. Hollywood is more than ready to tell you what your teenager's "needs" are and how they can best be met. It's time parents wake up, react, and protect their precious children from mindless entertainment moguls who ultimately only want your money.

BLASTING HOLLYWOOD

In September 2000 the Federal Trade Commission blasted Hollywood for marketing violent fare to children. This is not a new fight. Since the dawn of motion pictures, the Washington-Hollywood connection has often been at odds and highly charged. Weathering an occasional attack has become part of the territory for the industry, but the complaints have stayed consistent and constant. The claim is that the entertainment industry's products—movies, television, popular music, video games—are responsible for the declining morals and rampant criminal acts in our society, influencing the impressionable youth the most.

While Washington puts pressure on the major movie studios to promise they'll watch how they market violent films, companies that released films such as *American Psycho* and *The Blair Witch Project* managed to sidestep the Senate Commerce Committee hearings and the FTC. Only the big studios are feeling the wrath of the FTC, because smaller distributors are not members of the MPAA and are not required to adhere to the twelve-step plan aimed at limiting inappropriate marketing to kids. The plan calls for reviewing marketing and advertising practices for violent R-rated movies and refusing those under age seventeen to preview or test market R-rated movies unless a parent or guardian is present. Independents must follow certain MPM standards to receive a rating, and therefore, the guidelines could be added. For most films a rating is *essential* because major theater chains won't play a film unless it is rated. The major movie studios are promising to watch how they market R-rated or violent films, but ultimately all non-MPAA companies could be forced to support the rules.

MOVIE TRAILERS—TOO ADULT FOR YOUR KIDS?

One of the biggest complaints I hear from parents is about movie trailers. I'm glad to see Hollywood taking some initiative to prohibit R-rated trailers from showing before PG- and PG-13-rated movies and banning underage youths from attending focus groups for R movies. More importantly, I'm encouraged to see the National Association of Theater Owners make a similar promise to ban trailers of R-rated attractions before any G- or PG-rated films

The Senate Commerce Committee was presented initiatives by several studios that show steps aimed at curtailing the marketing of R-rated movies to kids. Here are what a few proposed:

+ Fox and Warner Brothers will not attach *any* R-rated trailers on G or PG movies.

+ Fox and Warner Brothers will not advertise R-rated films on network shows where 35% or more of its audience is under seventeen.

+ Warner Brothers plans to add more information to the R rating logo that will signal parents why it has an R rating: V = violence, S = sex, L = language.

+ Fox TV Network will not accept ads for R-rated films during "Family Programming" or shows likely to have audiences of 35% or more under seventeen.

+ Universal put an end to including underage kids without a parent or guardian in test screenings for films likely to be rated R.[14]

I applaud all of these studios for their efforts to do what they can to protect children and families from the exposure to R-rated adult themes. It may sound like small steps, but it will relieve a lot of parents who objected to the adult trailers flashed in front of their children's eyes before a kid-friendly movie.

ID, PLEASE

These days the National Association of Theater Owners needs to make money. Plain and simple, that is their first concern and desire. The fact that some movie theaters sell tickets to teenagers under seventeen and allow kids to get into their R-rated movies is not a surprise.

In the summer of 1999, as a reaction to the Columbine High School massacre in Colorado, President Clinton tried to force theater owners to prevent under-age teens from buying tickets to R-rated movies. While it proved to be one more self-promoting media tool for the president, in most cases the long-term efforts proved futile. Because of the politics of violence in the media that hangs over Hollywood right now, the MPAA is encouraging theater owners to check IDs and prevent kids from being admitted to R-rated movies.

While the average moviegoing adult sees only six films a year, the average teenager attends at least fifty, with the vast majority of these films being rated PG-13 and R. The R rating was originally designed to restrict children under seventeen from gaining entrance into a theater unless accompanied by a parent. Profit-driven theater owners, however, are not required to uphold this rule. Eighty percent of all children under seventeen in the U.S. have had no trouble at all getting into R-rated films.[15] A recent study by the *New York Times* found that children as young as ten years old were frequenting R-rated films on a regular basis. In case you doubt my statistics, ask a group of kids and they'll tell you.

No matter what efforts are made by your local theater, ultimately it's up to the parents to train their child or teen on what is right and wrong for them. A rating can't teach them that; only a parent can.

As an adult, you can make a difference by starting with your local theater. Get to know your theater manager or managers and thank them for checking teenagers' IDs. Thank them for keeping kids out of R-rated movies. Whether they know you or not, they will realize that there are parents and adults without children who care and are paying attention to the theater's business standards. When you walk into an R-rated movie and see young teens or kids sitting in the audience, quietly go ask for the manager and let that person know there are kids or teens in your theater and you would like the manager to check their IDs.

CAN YOU BELIEVE THE CRITICS?

A common complaint I hear from frustrated parents is that they are misled by the critics. The reviews entice audiences to see what they define as "Brilliant," "The Year's Best Film!," "A Masterpiece," but usually the movie stinks. Face it, most of the critics won't give a movie like *The Wedding Planner* or *Remember the Titans* a good review because it's not "critic worthy" in script or casting. Those movies end up being favorites with the public because they have the cast and story the public enjoys. The sum total of a critic's review is simply a personal opinion. If you take into account the background, religious beliefs, moral and ethical slants from a reviewer, you can have a consistent idea of how they'll review movies.

I try to present my reviews by objectively listing the good, not-so-good, and other elements (such as language, sex, and violence) so that people can make up their own mind. But if it's a really bad movie, I blast it! It doesn't happen often, but when movies such as *Battlefield Earth, Screwed, Sugar & Spice, Valentine,* and others are just so bad, I can't help myself! Check my reviews on www.hollymcclure.com before you make any decisions about a movie and let me help you make wise movie choices!

WE HAVE JUST AN AVALANCHE OF LANGUAGE on the simplest level. And you see, the point that Hollywood always makes in its own defense is, "We just give the pubic what they want." This is a big lie. It's a great big lie. Because if you look at the language, who wants the language? What's the audience? Have you ever heard anyone coming out of a movie theater saying, "Gee, I'm just disappointed because the language in that movie was too clean"?

—MICHAEL MEDVED, Nationally Syndicated Talk Show Host[1]

THE AVERAGE CHILD has witnessed sixteen thousand murders and two hundred thousand other acts of violence on TV alone by the time he reaches the age of eighteen.[2]

Language, Sex, Violence, and Horror in the Movies

LANGUAGE

Profanity is used once every six minutes on network TV and every three minutes in a movie. Culturally bad language exploded during the '60s when swearing became a liberating way to rebel against "the establishment" and show disdain for authority. Whenever there is an increase in swearing, respect for authority declines. Unfortunately, what the baby boomers began, their children are continuing because their parents showed them it was "OK" language to use.

The "F" Word

In the early months of 2000 when the moviegoing public flocked to see Julia Roberts' *Erin Brockovich*, they were not only amused by her character's heart of gold and tacky hooker dress code, but they were also equally shocked by her character's blatant, sailor-mouth barbs, particularly her frequent use of the "F" word. America supported their sweetheart with ticket sales, and the R-rated movie went on to become a crowning achievement for Roberts' career, earning her an Oscar and bringing the "F" word to a new level of "entertainment acceptance."

The question then seems to be, do we as a culture (or you personally) consider foul language entertainment? Clearly, vulgar language was as much a part of Brockovich's character (since she was based on a real person) as her fashion statements, but did it have to be used so often? Lately the "F" word has been slipping into more story lines, dialogue, and social settings in movies than ever before. Even the opening musical number of *South Park: Bigger, Longer & Uncut*, the movie spin-off from the cable cartoon, features the "F" word about thirty times, and that movie was targeted to younger teens and kids under seventeen.

MTV rappers and other musical artists spew the "F" word out twenty-four hours a day, using it as a "second language"—apparently because they never learned a first one. Internet chat rooms banter it around as a "catch phrase" that means everything when no one can spell anything. Comedian Chris Rock made it part of his stand-up routine and even passed it on to his movie roles until studios had a hard time getting a PG-13 from the MPAA, who didn't think his "F" word tirade was kid-friendly funny. Some sports figures and even well-known coaches are notorious for using it. It is no surprise, then, that even the hallways of elementary, junior, and senior high schools are not immune to it.

When did we as a society allow a word that used to be considered profanity of the worst nature to cross over into mainstream America and become a part of our daily dialect? It's obvious that many people, especially the younger generation, think using socially edgy language makes for a cool way to communicate and that profanity more effectively and succinctly (if not eloquently) expresses a person's exasperated thoughts. As one high school senior put it, "Sometimes using the 'F' word simply sums it all up."

Obscenities have become a verbal crutch that limit our capacity to communicate clearly with one another. The "F" word and the "S" word are gradually blending into the fabric of our culture, widely used as broad definitions of a variety of words but ultimately replacing more descriptive words in the English language. Is it really a depiction of our whole society? I view it as part of the "dumbing down" of America, an acceptance of a mind-set and substandard way of speaking that has crossed economic and class barriers with our youth and gained almost universal popularity.

How did it happen? Through movies and music. Unlike network television, these two entertainment industries have had a freedom to make it cool to use the "F" word in public. Charismatic people such as Eminem, Snoop Doggy Dog, Dr. Dre, and others use it in their songs, movie scripts are ladened with it, and even popular celebrities such as Drew Barrymore and Courtney Love use it regularly in interviews on and off camera, promoting the use of these foul words as permissible where they had never been socially acceptable before.

In older circles and the business world, the "F" word remains a sign that a person lacks communicative skills and social etiquette. But as movies and TV keep pushing the envelope with language, it becomes harder to draw the lines in our public lives, schools, and the workplace. Throwing the "F" word around has replaced the need to speak civilly to one another, to adequately converse and communicate clearly, and it's used far too often and too loosely.

Profanity coming from a woman with the stature of Julia Roberts in *Erin Brockovich* was a risky move, and in future roles it might go too far for most people and actually hurt her at the box office. Swearing profanities adds an element of realism to movies and television if the dialogue includes a group that uses it naturally (gangs, the Mafia, adults in a bar, the military, etc.). But when profanity is used gratuitously to replace good dialogue or descriptive writing, then it is considered lazy language and reveals more about the swearer than the subject of the cursing.

Many people swear casually for the fun of it in front of friends or while playing a sport because they can get away with it. But when it becomes a reflex, it's a harder habit to break. Profanity is more intense and is caused by an emotion that flares to anger, frustration, or impatience and definitely indicates hostility.

Don't believe the hype that the "F" word is overcoming the bad reputation it has had for years. The "everybody-does-it" argument doesn't work either, because everybody *doesn't* do it. I'm in contact with people in different walks of life every day, and *nobody* whom I talk with uses that kind of language. The word is still considered by most people as uncouth and socially unacceptable. It can feel good to swear, but it feels much better not to and maintain control of your own mind. There are men and women who have never used this word, and believe it or not, they lead normal, productive lives.

The "N" Word

Do we as a culture consider the word *nigger* entertainment?

MTV and BET continually play music videos that feature black artists singing or rapping this word over and over. Movie scripts feature actors who use it both affectionately and viciously. And comedians seem to favor this word in their stand-up routines.

The dictionary defines the word as "acceptable only in black English; in all other contexts it is now generally regarded as taboo because of the legacy of racial hatred that underlies the history of its use among whites."[3]

I would like to know why is it acceptable in our culture for black people to call themselves a degrading name (and it supposedly is an affectionate term), but when a white person says it, then it's racial hatred? It's obvious why a person shouldn't use that word. But I contend that using the word *at all* sends a mixed message to our young people when they hear that word spoken with laughter, sung seductively, or rapped in sarcasm and anger.

Not only does it send a message that culturally there's a double standard on what you can and can't say if you're a certain color (which is culturally what we're trying to rise above, aren't we?), but it also sends a sad message of self-degradation and low self-esteem, even if it is only spoken within the "inner circle."

My vote would be for that word to be considered "taboo" if spoken by anyone.

SEX

If I had it to do all over again, I wouldn't have had sex when I was a teenager. It wasn't worth it. —Sharon Stone, Actress[4]

My first R-rated movie was an accident. When I was fourteen, my parents dropped my twelve-year-old sister and me off at the local theater. Unfortunately, two out of three movies we would have chosen to see were sold out, so we went to see *The Sailor Who Fell From Grace With the Sea*, having absolutely no idea what it was about. Anyone who has seen this intensely erotic romance based on Yukio Mishima's novel will remember the electrifying love scenes between Kris Kristofferson and Sarah Myles as well as the shocking finale.

My sister and I were overwhelmed by what we saw on screen. Coming from a protective Christian home, Dena and I decided not to tell our parents what we had seen because we knew we would get into trouble. But I wish I had! I wish I had felt comfortable enough to bring it up and discuss what I saw with my parents, because the movie's extremely adult love scenes haunted me for months. From an innocent, sheltered, young teenager's hormonal perspective, I realized that I was in no way ready to see adult movies like that for a long while!

Sex on the Big Screen

For years Hollywood had standards for sex in movies. From the first romantic pairing of Francis X. Bushman and Beverly Bayne in the 1912 movie *The House of Pride,* Hollywood discovered that romance sells and so does sex. The early years of Hollywood produced glimpses of eroticism in 1916 when Annette Kellerman, swimming star turned actress, appeared nude in *A Daughter of the Gods.* Or in 1933 when Hedy Lamarr caused a sensation by swimming in the nude in *Ecstasy.* Those performances were followed in later years by sexy Jane Russell, Marilyn Monroe, Rita Hayworth, Jane Mansfield, and others. And studios started to feel that if they could push the envelope of acceptance on nudity, Hollywood could make more money.

The mid '60s saw an onslaught of producers, directors, and studios pushing the MPAA to lift its ban on nudity in Hollywood films. Sidney Lumet's *The Pawnbroker* became the first mainstream film to include full frontal nudity in April 1965, and it has only spiraled down into a dark, honorless abyss ever since.

Sexual Reality

For years media psychologists, such as Stuart Fischoff at California State University, Los Angeles, have explained that Hollywood's fascination with portraying unmarried sex is for obvious reasons. "It's much more exciting to have people who don't know each other have sex than people who have known each other awhile," states Fischoff. "You're more likely to have novel, error-prone, exciting sex because you're exploring new bodies and new pathways."[5] Passionate "stranger sex" is more dangerous and fantasy filled. Then add into the equation the fact that many screenwriters haven't been married or haven't been married long enough to be creative with married sex, so it's simply going to lack in all the right areas.

Moviemakers are constantly criticized for their portrayals of sex and violence on the big screen as being anything but realistic. And when it comes to sex between married people, the fact that we hardly see any at all is anything but realism. "The existence of sex between married people is almost completely nonexistent in today's movies," says John Mark Dempsey, who with co-researcher Tom Reichert charted every sex scene in the top twenty-five video rentals of 1998. They found that 85% of movie sex is between unmarried people, and on television there are five times as many love scenes between unmarried couples as there are between married couples. If movies made an effort to be more like real life, Dempsey says, "It might be helpful in giving people a better attitude toward marriage and a better feeling about their own marriage."[6]

Add to all of this the fact that any kind of sex doesn't need to be graphically shown or dealt with anyway. There are numerous, healthy ways to portray sex between married people in a way that makes it exciting, passionate, and enviable without making it tawdry, voyeuristic, or a turnoff. In *The Horse Whisperer,* Robert Redford directed himself in a slow dance scene with Kristen Scott Thomas. Using camera angles and the right blend of lighting and music, it is one of the most romantic, erotic dance numbers I've ever seen on screen. Yet there wasn't a word spoken, a stitch of clothing removed, inappropriate touching, none of that. It was just brilliant directing from a gifted director who knows how to capitalize on the art of romance.

If more directors were imaginative in this way, romance and sex in movies would achieve new levels of popularity among discerning moviegoers and possibly create an appreciation in the younger audiences for the old-fashioned art of "less-is-more" in Hollywood. Ultimately, what the audience doesn't see and has to use their imagination for has always been the most attractive lure of romance in movies.

Hollywood, Sex, and Your Children

By now you probably realize that Hollywood is targeting your children and teens with more PG-13 movies than ever before and that many of those movies contain R-rated adult themes. The reality is that most children and teenagers are getting their questions about sex answered from movies, TV, MTV, the Internet, and magazines. Their self-esteem, peer perception, emotional radar, how they interact with peers and dating partners, and how they dress are mostly taken from those sources. Young teenagers study these mediums to gain their self-confidence and awareness on how to act sexy, which increases the popularity of PG-13 movies with heavy sexual themes.

Go straight to the bottom line: the celluloid message your kids are getting is encouraging them to have sex. Not only have sex, but experiment with sex in some form or fashion. Here are some of the ways it's being promoted.

"Hooking Up"

This is a millennial term used by teens and twenty-somethings to describe a free, noncommittal sexual relationship that takes place after meeting someone for the first time on a school campus, in a social setting, or usually in a bar. "Hooking up" is considered to be a safe, pleasurable, and satisfying way to enjoy yourself without any commitment. This is "socially acceptable sex" that's being practiced all over this country, and the serious health risks alone should be alarming for any halfway intelligent man or woman.

Parents, check and see if your preteen or teen knows what this term means and ask them if they know someone who's done it. This is a huge and disturbing lie teenagers and young twenty-somethings have been sold! "Hooking up" isn't "safe" sex, and parents need to explain how insane, crazy, and, not to mention, deadly it can be!

Oral Sex—a New Definition of What "Is"

Here's a paradox that should trouble any parent of a teenager. While the number of teens who say they're sexually abstinent and are virgins is on the rise, so too is the number of those who have had oral sex.

While parents in today's society will have to take responsibility for the moral climate their children have been raised in, Hollywood has been a major forerunner for setting a precedence for this new "definition of sex." For years movies have painted a lusty, sexy image of two people pleasuring and enjoying each other in a "nonsexual" way. Movies targeted at teens such as *Sweet November, Sugar & Spice, Saving Silverman, Valentine, Scream 2 & 3, Scary Movie, American Pie,* and many more contain scenes where the boy or girl slip off camera and oral sex is implied, talked about, or shown as a sex act that's just below kissing.

The Guttmacher Institute periodical, *Family Planning Perspectives*, reports that there has been an increase in oral sex, starting with our youngest teens. Robert Blum, director of the division of general pediatrics and adolescent health at the University of Minnesota, says, "There is a sense that most younger teens, even ten- to twelve-year-olds, and most teens (in general) don't define this as sex." Apparently most of these kids have convinced themselves that sex equals vaginal intercourse, and therefore oral sex is not really sex. Part of the issues, he says, "is that we define sexual behavior in a very narrow way. And we talk about abstinence, but we are never clear what we are abstaining from."[7]

Indicative of the prevalence of society's redefinition of oral sex came through loud and clear in the endless media discussions about what took place between President Clinton and Monica Lewinsky. With references to where, when, and how it occurred, our children listened to that daily rhetoric blasted on every television network and talk radio station right along with their parents. Their innocent minds were filled with a whole new idea of what was socially "expectable," and they witnessed a nation's respect for the office of the president sink to a new low.

Jokes were made on late-night talk shows, parents talked about it in the car and at home, kids discussed the impeachment in their school, television shows (particularly *Saturday Night Live*) made fun of it, and Clinton performed a verbal tap dance with some of the fanciest legal footwork this country has ever seen, introducing a new definition of what "is" is. I appeared on *Politically Incorrect*, *The Charles Grodin Show*, and *Equal Time* to debate the effect Clinton's exposure (forgive my pun) had on our country's moral compass as well as on our children. The conservative outrage I vented over the moral damage done is being played out in our country on a daily basis. In fact, Lynn Ponton, a psychiatrist at the University of California at San Francisco and author of *The Sex Lives of Teenagers*, revealed that she continually hears, "Clinton said oral sex isn't sex. Kids tell me that over and over in my office. The President did it."[8]

In an online sex survey from *Twist* magazine, more than 10,000 girls responded (over half were fourteen and younger). Eighty percent said they are virgins, but 25% had had oral sex. Twenty-seven percent described the act as "something you do with a guy for fun."[9] The consensus in many high schools is that oral sex makes girls popular, whereas intercourse makes them outcasts. Lisa Remez of the Guttmacher Institute says, "Many teenagers perceive oral sex as safer and less intimate than intercourse."[10] In the respect that the risk of pregnancy is not there, that's true, but the risk of STDs has definitely risen.

But what about the psychological problems? What kind of fallout are we going to see surface in our young adults in later years when they attempt intimacy in marriage?

Parents, it's time to talk with your kids about oral sex before it devastates their lives! The next time you see a movie with your teen where a character implies they are having oral sex, talk about it afterward and ask them if they thought that scene was appropriate, embarrassing, or wrong. You will probably have a great discussion and learn something you didn't know about your teenager.

Despite All the Exposure

Recently I was surprised to read a study done that stated U.S. teens are ignorant about the basics of sex. How can teens possibly be so clueless when they have been inundated with sex in all shapes and forms from every aspect of the media from movies to magazines along with some sort of sex education in the classroom?

Despite adolescents' knowledge of hip terms and an "I-know-everything-about-sex" demeanor, for the most part, young teens apparently do not understand the mechanics. Rutgers University sponsors a Web site (www.sxetc.com) at which teenagers can research information about sex. They can go online to take part in polls, read letters from peers, research materials, and ask questions, which are answered by staffed sex educators.

When program manager Danene Sorace spoke to the Society for the Scientific Study of Sexuality, she revealed that teens' questions ranged from wondering if there was a time of the month when pregnancy can't happen to whether you can get a sexually transmitted disease from oral sex. The site shows that kids today want to be responsible by avoiding pregnancy and STDs. But it also reveals a serious lack of communication with parents. Even though many parents feel uncomfortable about talking about sex, if you're relying on sex education in schools to cover it, it's probable your kids don't truly understand.

VIOLENCE

Let's face it, *life is violent!* When you take a look at life through the daily news, it is shocking how much violence is increasing in our schools, neighborhoods, communities, college campuses, the workplace, and even in our churches. We are a violent society with a social structure that seldom values morality or absolutes.

Innocent young children have a natural trust for their surroundings, parental figures, and family, as well as a sense of security in their environment. When that environment is defiled with something shocking, brutal, scary, horrible, intense, or frightening, the memories of that event and their reaction to it stay locked within that child's memories long into adult years. Which is why exposing children (ages four to ten) to adult themes in most PG-13 and R-rated films is so damaging. Younger children have no ability to fully distinguish between reality and fantasy, good from bad, truth from fiction, or genuine innocence from perversion.

How does all of our scary world affect kids' minds? A survey taken at the Universities of Michigan and Wisconsin found that one in four students had some lingering "fright" affect from a movie or TV show they saw as a child or teenager, but particularly from movies. Studies show that is what impacts kids and teens the most. *Ninety percent* said they were scared by a movie they saw in their childhood or their adolescence. *Twenty-six percent* said they still experience residual anxiety.[11] The younger the children were when they were frightened, the longer the reaction lasted.

The FTC ruled that the government should not regulate Hollywood's marketing of movies, music, and the electronic gaming industry. These industries have come under attack by Congress following the release of an FTC report indicating that companies were marketing violent entertainment to children. But the FTC said the government has "significant legal limitations," including First Amendment concerns, to carry out effective law enforcement.

Since the shootings at Columbine High School, Hollywood has toned down the violence in many of its movies and kept some of the graphic blood and gore out. That's not to say there still aren't slasher movies drawing crowds, but the amount of those movies and the level of heavy gore has been reduced to appease Washington and give us a cycle of hope. Movies about heart (*Bagger Vance*), racial differences (*Remember the Titans*), courage (*Cast Away*), aspirations (*Billy Elliot*), achieving dreams (*Finding Forrester*), and the importance of family (*Family Man*) were just a few to fill the kinder, gentler lineup for 2000. They seem to be an indicator that studios are paying attention to what they can socially (and sometimes even morally) get away with.

Violent Movies and Our Youth

Violence in film is nothing new. Since the beginning of film, there has been tension in some form or other to catapult the action and create the drama. Today the difference in violence on TV and in the movies is the gratuitous gore and intensity that can be shown. Television is regulated and mostly censored, whereas movies deliver a larger-than-life version of those themes, and most of it is worse than anything you'll see on TV.

In August 1967 the movie *Bonnie and Clyde* ushered a new wave of screen realism and violence that audiences had never seen before. Watching favorite stars riddled with bullets was graphic but poignant. That was just the beginning. In the '80s violence launched the careers of Schwarzenegger, Willis, Stallone, and Van Damme, making violent action pictures the hot commodity for every major studio. The more bizarre and gratuitous it became, the more teenagers and adult males flocked to see it. They were our heroes in the '80s, our modern gladiators, and the good guys in the ultimate westerns that combined special effects with lots of graphic blood, guts, and gore.

In the '90s violent movies found their target audience of young teenagers by using stars who'd attract that audience. *The Basketball Diaries* with Leonardo DiCaprio, *Natural Born Killers* with Woody Harrelson, *Scream* with its list of well-known actors and directed by *Dawson's Creek* creator Kevin Williamson, and *American History X* with Edward Norton promoted violence and simultaneously sent a powerful message to youth: violence is power and another form of rebellion against society.

After decades of denying that movies influence behavior, 87% of media executives and studio heads now admit that violence in mass media contributes to violence in society. Scientists, parents, teachers, and teenagers themselves know that media violence leads to aggressive behavior because it overstimulates the children. Intense scenes with realistic, scary violence is stored in the memory of your child or teenager and over time will affect the temperament and nature of your child.

Amazingly, three out of four Americans blame the breakdown of family and social values for the increase in youth violence.[12] More than 3,000 serious studies on the subject have made the evidence irrefutable.[13]

Good Ole Summertime Violence

In case you are immune to reports on violence, it might interest you to take a look at what young audiences are exposed to every summer. This is traditionally the time of year when studios bring out their most violent, action-packed movies to attract their target audience, sixteen- to twenty-six-year-old males. And if they happen to have a really good movie, adults will support it too. In the summer of 2000, a list of a few of the films shows how much violence the audience was exposed to: *Gladiator, MI:2, The Patriot, The Perfect Storm, Gone in 60 Seconds, Shaft, Hollow Man, What Lies Beneath, X-Men,* and let's not forget *Scary Movie* with eighteen deaths, including a grandma squashed by a piano. The corpse total was 435 for that summer.[14] It's enough to make you say, "I see dead people!"

Violence in Schools

Coinciding with the violence that has exploded on screen is an evil that is being played out on campuses across the nation. Adolescent boys and teens began a killing spree on campuses from Kentucky to Colorado to California. Schools became the war zones that people watched on the nightly news, and a growing concern and awareness for the effects that violence has on our children began to emerge in churches, schools, and homes. Toward the end of the '90s, shootings on school campuses were eerily becoming commonplace. Films such as *The Matrix,* video games such as "Doom," and the music of Marilyn Manson are believed to have served as the inspiration for the horrific shootings that occurred at Columbine High School.

Violence is not limited to shootings, though. The Bureau of Justice Statistics reported that in 1999, 8.9% of ninth grade students were victims of crime; 8.2% of seventh graders; and 7.6% of eighth graders.[15] Clearly the violence that young teenagers see on television and in the movies still affects the way they interact among their peers.

Copycat Crimes

Young people today are emulating what they see on the screen more than ever before—not only in style of dress and language, but more ominously in the areas of sexuality and violence.

According to national police records, media-inspired crimes are on the rise. Are our kids and young teenagers growing up to be desensitized to violence? In addition to their exposure to violence, more than 90% of children under eighteen have viewed extreme hard-core X-rated materials. Of these, more than 50% say they wanted to copy what they had seen, while 25% actually did so within a few days of viewing the material. Children of all ages, some as young as four years old, have sexually assaulted siblings and neighbors after viewing their parents' pornographic materials.

All of these statistics come as no surprise. Crime occurs ten times more often on television than in real life. Approximately a dozen murders occur every hour during prime time. It's critically important that we realize that whatever we put in our minds is what we and our children become. When we consume something that's violent, we vicariously experience and practice violence. Someone has called this "virtual sin," because sin may be distant from us if someone else does it, but when we constantly play the images of sin, sex, or violence through our minds, we vicariously experience all of that, and it becomes part of our own personal experience and eventually translates into our own action.

Family values and even the family itself are portrayed with nihilism as the pop culture plays up the evil in film and television and frequently incites the audience to real-life violence. This attack is subtle, complicated, and disturbing. The demonic anti-heroes and seductive comic evil of popular culture are not conspicuous weapons in a cultural assault, but rather reactions to the apathy and conformity of American life.

HORROR

Memories of first horror movies are easy to come by. My first horror movie came when I was eight years old and arrived at a theater with a group of friends. The movie we were supposed to see was sold out, and the only other choice was *Dracula*. A very hesitant mother, overpowered by begging, disappointed eight-year-olds, reluctantly agreed to let us go in, even though it was a horror movie. Within a half hour my mother was called and asked to pick up her petrified, teary-eyed, embarrassed daughter who had been peeled from the seat. For weeks I had nightmares about a vampire sneaking into my room and biting my neck.

When I was nine and playing at a girlfriend's house, she turned on the TV and discovered the old *Hunchback of Notre Dame*. This movie was a far cry from the '90s Disney version, and I became hypnotized by the black-and-white 1939 homage to the monster with the hump on his back. The old classic starred Charles Laughton as Quasimodo and Maureen O'Hara as the beautiful gypsy girl. I was petrified at the ending when Quasimodo lies down by the dead gypsy girl and dies by her side. I can still see his body turning into a skeleton and sand blowing over the two bony bodies as they lay in a burial crypt. That visual decomposing image haunted me throughout my childhood years because I saw how I was going to look when I died—a pretty grim reality check for a child of nine.

America's Evil Ways

Americans' pursuit of happiness has always been frustrated by the dark evil forces beyond our control and understanding. Contemporary society seems to be living in a state of spiritual impoverishment where aspirations of a bright future are giving way to youthful frustration and apathy. Our fascination with violence has filtered into our mainstream culture through the encouragement of real-life violence in film and television. The demonic anti-heroes and seductive comic evil of our popular culture are artistic weapons of a conscious nature raised out of a society that worships apathy, conformity, themselves, and, oh yes, entertainment!

Movies of yesteryear's Frank Capra and Cecil B. De Mille celebrated life, the living, and the triumph of good over evil. In the twenty-first century, entrepreneur and do-gooder-hero George Bailey has been replaced by Hannibal "the cannibal" Lecter, who chewed his way to the top box office. Movies with grisly themes have been around for several years now (*The Exorcist, Cape Fear, Silence of the Lambs, Seven, Natural Born Killers, Scream 1, 2, 3, Scary Movie, Titanic, Trainspotting, Pulp Fiction, Lock, Stock and Two Smoking Barrels, Snatch, Hannibal*), revealing a preoccupation with the power of evil.

Box-Office Evil

From the moment young British director Alfred Hitchcock released his first work, *The Pleasure Garden*, in 1925 to a new style of bloody screen horror launched in England in 1957 with *Curse of Frankenstein* and continued in 1968 with George Romero's *Night of the Living Dead*, horror has moved toward gore. Hollywood's horror genre would never be the same.

In 1931 two horror movies were released that forever changed the way we choose to be scared to death. Bela Lugosi debuted as *Dracula*, and Universal Pictures released *Frankenstein*, starring Boris Karloff. On December 12, 1941, Lon Chaney Jr. followed in his father's footsteps and played the title role in *The Wolf Man*, reviving the horror genre. Horror went a little understated in 1942 with RKO's *Cat People*, and in 1948 it took a comedic twist in *Abbott and Costello Meet Frankenstein*. Today's box-office evil comes in sadistic, sick, and twisted messages such as *Scream, Friday the 13th*, or even beautifully packaged movies such as *The Cell*.

Sex + Violence = Teenagers

Scientists have proven that watching violence can stimulate a part of the brain that makes a person believe they are in a life-threatening situation.[16] When this happens, adrenal epinephrine is released into the bloodstream, giving the person an adrenal rush. Watching sexual situations and nudity signals the brain that the body is about to have sex or mate, so the body releases passion hormones that can cause an addictive adrenal rush. When sex and violence are combined in a horror movie, you have teenagers fleeing for their lives. For more effect and fright, they are killed off one by one, and somewhere in the story a couple gets caught romantically in a sexual situation. The sight of peers having suggestive sex and dialogue about it, combined with the abundance of intense bloody violence and quick camera angles, cause young audiences to react with an euphoric, stimulated response, the kind that teenagers enjoy feeling together.

Sex + Violence + Teenagers = Horror

Horror movies have always been popular with teenagers. In the '70s it was *The Exorcist, The Omen, Carrie*, and *I Was a Teenage Werewolf*. The '80s brought a new breed of horror films that appealed to teenagers more than any other demographic group because of the special effects, scary camera angles, bloody gore, and sexual suggestive themes mixed with violence.

Films such as *Hellraiser, Friday the 13th, A Nightmare on Elm Street, Halloween,* and *Prom Night* were all popular beginnings to a long line of sequels that spawned successful moneymaking formulas and introduced gore and violence as it never had been seen before. Writers, producers, and directors found that the more sexual themes they mixed with their violence, the more teenagers flocked to see the movie.

In the late '80s and all through the '90s, Wes Craven, Kevin Williamson, Stephen King, and others took a different path to directing teen gore movies, mixing a more sadistic side with humor. Edgy movies such as *Scream, I Know What You Did Last Summer, I Still Know What You Did Last Summer,* and *Urban Legend* introduced audiences to not only more violence, gore, and special-effect fright (that looked real) but also more suggestive sexual situations mixed in with teen humor.

In the summer of 2000 Miramax had a big surprise with their highest-grossing movie of all time, *Scary Movie.* It cost just $19 million to make, was an R-rated spoof on teen horror films, and brought in $150 million at the box office. This movie had an abundance of foul language, crude dialogue, bathroom humor, half-naked teenagers, lots of shocking sexual situations, dialogue between the couples about having sex, girls talking about losing their virginity and wanting sex with the guys, jokes about characters' deaths, and token lesbian/gay characters thrown in for political correctness—now that's scary!

Besides the blatant sex and violence, what made these movies popular with the '90s teenagers was the edgy dialogue, funny plot twists, sarcastic wit, humor, and jokes on social taboos. Although the movies were scary and usually gory, the humor took the sadistic, evil edge off of it and made it unrealistic.

Fantasy, Witchcraft, and Pokémon Are In

Hollywood's preoccupation with the power of evil spread to the big screen with *Harry Potter and the Sorcerer's Stone* and *Lord of the Rings* making their debuts in 2001. The dark forces seem to have taken over Hollywood with their culturally popular and accepted messages, best-selling books, and planned sequels. Meanwhile our children (the studios' future box-office consumers) are lured with the fantasy that not only promotes offensive language, secular themes, sexual messages, violence, questionable religious teaching, and autonomy to children but also likewise preys on parents' pocketbooks. Fast-food promotions, action figures, games, puzzles, and everything you can think of that children will find hard to resist (and parents will find hard to avoid) came with these movies.

Do Scary Scenes Stay With You?

When I was four years old, my parents took me to see a special screening of *The Wizard of Oz* at our local theater. My mother said I burrowed my face in her arm the entire time, and when the flying monkeys swooped down, grabbed Dorothy, then scooped her into the air with the wicked witch ranting, I went ballistic. I started crying so loud my embarrassed mother must have resembled one of those flying monkeys as she scooped me up and flew to the lobby with me attached to her hip. I have no recollection of that experience at all. But for years afterward, every time I watched *The Wizard of Oz* on TV, those flying monkeys gave me the creeps! Seeing that scary face of the green witch in the crystal ball struck a familiar chord of fear in me that I grew to remember.

Since I have no early recollection of that event, did childhood memories of that fear stay locked away inside my head for years afterward? Did that event mark a psychological turning point in my ability to distinguish fantasy from reality, fiction from truth? Years of research and numerous articles point to the fact that when young children are exposed to frightening movies filled with violence, terror, and horror, they react differently than elementary age children. Younger children are more likely to be frightened by monsters, witches, creatures—the visual, perceptual images. Older children will take in the fantasy and separate the fake from what could be real, and then center on the characters, becoming upset more by evil motives than looks. Just how far-reaching that damage goes is what reports and studies are now discovering.

The Supernatural Thrill

In 1999 the millennium's approach (and Y2K buzz) seemed to trigger a cultural need to "feel" spiritual. Baby boomers were clearly grappling with their mortality, Gen-Xers were searching for religious roots their parents never taught them, and millennials were simply looking for spooky thrills. Movies emerged with foreboding messages of gloom, doom, and Satan's impending power. *Stigmata, Lost Souls, A Stir of Echoes, End of Days,* and *The Ninth Gate* dealt with witchcraft, Satanism, the occult, ghosts, and the anti-Christ. God was either helpless or nowhere to be found, and the power of evil became intriguing as the clock ticked toward the new millennium. A new strain of evil crept into Hollywood under the guise of a psychological thriller and introduced cerebral horror as it had never been done before. *The Blair Witch Project, The Sixth Sense, The Green Mile, Being John Malkovich, Fight Club, American Psycho, Magnolia,* and *The Matrix* joined teen-scream movies like *Halloween, Scream, Sleepy Hollow,* and *I Know What You Did Last Summer* for impressive box-office returns. These movies were created by new directors who delivered unique styles, new technology, revolutionized special effects, and new and unusual ways of showing how violence could impact a movie.

Victims of Violent Movies

The impact of that seductive appeal to the increasing violence in our movies has seemingly caught on with the youth in our society. An increase in unthinkable crimes and murders, ranging from parents being killed, to school shootings, imitated wrestling deaths, and even a teacher assassination, involve young pre-teens and teenagers who grew up on a steady diet of watching violence on television, in video games, and in movies.

In February of 2001, two eleven-year-old boys in Florida went to watch the R-rated horror movie *Valentine.* During the movie, one of the boys fatally stabbed the other in the lobby. The attendants didn't stop the movie, and when patrons exited, they commented on not only the movie's extremely violent tone but also the number of young children (many elementary school-age, and even preschoolers) in attendance with adults who were apparently their parents. Why would parents take young children to see an R-rated horror movie with extreme bloody violence? Are they so callused and immune to that violence that they don't see the significance in sheltering their child's precious mind and innocence from that?

As I pointed out in a previous chapter, the trend of taking children to watch violent, adult movies in order to save a few baby-sitting dollars is a trend of stupidity that will ultimately cost our society. How many more victims will there have to be, how much more blood needs to be shed, before parents wake up and realize the deadly consequences of exposing their impressionable children and pre-teens to endless "entertainment" violence?

TELEVISION IS A PRETTY ACCURATE REFLECTION OF SOCIETY

as a whole, and stereotypes just don't work anymore. Forget offensive—they're just not believable. They don't ring true. Gay stereotypes on TV would be like black stereotypes, nobody would buy it. The world has changed.

—MAX MUTCHNICK, Co-creator of *Will & Grace*[1]

KAREN TELLS JACK, a gay man staying at her place, that her husband "sleepwalks, so if you bump into him in the middle of the night and he puts the moves on you, just go with it. You might get a mink in the morning."

—WILL & GRACE

THIS IS A "REFLECTION OF SOCIETY as a whole" with no stereotypes?

CHAPTER SIX

TV

It's hard to fathom that in just a few decades we've gone from Lucy and Ricky sleeping in twin beds and censored from saying the word "pregnancy" on television to the MTV show *Undressed,* which consists of numerous couples in their twenties, dialoging and swapping sex with numerous partners, including gays and lesbians. It's enough to make you put it on pause, isn't it?

Since the days of censors, we've come a long way, baby! Flick on late-night television, and you will see a bevy of beautiful teenage girls advertising phone sex. Or MTV holding a contest where the contestants can only wear something edible on stage so their partner can eat it off. What about *Buffy the Vampire Slayer* featuring two lesbian witches who practice their spells and love on each other? Or pick any daytime soap—all of them feature passionate couples having steamy sex. Even commercials push sex, sex, sex, with couples passionately embracing or kissing while hawking beer, pizza, and rice. And trashy infomercials offer videos of wild topless girls who "bare it all" on vacation.

If the television censors from the '50s had caught a glimpse of any of that, they would have blown a picture tube! Perhaps no other invention has had more of an impact on family life than the television. In the half century since its introduction into the home, television has mutated from being a champion of moral values to leading the assault against them.

But what hasn't changed over the years are the millions of children who daily sit down to meditate on TV programming. Their innocence is just as precious and pure as ours was when we were children, and it's sad that their innocence will be sacrificed for the sake of today's pleasure and entertainment and money.

FROM THE GOLDEN AGE TO THE TARNISHED AGE

The first time television was introduced to the public was at the 1939 World's Fair. But limited network service did not start until the late '40s, and by the late '50s Americans were gathering around the big brown boxes in their living rooms to watch live programs on a few networks. By 1995, 99% of American households owned a television before they owned a phone, 60% had cable, and more than two-thirds had one or more VCRs.[2]

Over 235 million televisions are in American homes today (one for nearly every viewer), and more than 48% of households have a set in a child's bedroom.[3] With satellite and cable channels exploding across the country, the average household now has ninety-nine channels from which to choose. The quality and content vary, but the selection is a smorgasbord. I love the line that young actor Spencer Breslin said in the Disney movie *The Kid*. "Ninety-nine channels and nothing to watch!"

I DON'T HATE TV

Contrary to what you may think, I don't hate television and I'm not out to demonize all aspects of it. There are many wonderful, educational, and entertaining programs that I enjoy watching—Fox News, CNN, *Hannity and Colmes*, *The O'Reilly Factor*, and Chris Matthew's program, *Hardball*. I have appeared on FOX news, CNN & Co., and "TalkBack," and I greatly appreciate the venue it opens up for a conservative voice to be heard. I enjoy a few sitcoms, tune into entertainment shows for the latest updates, and delight in winding down to an old movie classic. Oh, and my son and I love *The Crocodile Hunter*!

I would be remiss if I didn't mention my loyalty to *Politically Incorrect*. Bill Maher has taken a forum unique to late-night network television and crafted it into a stimulating, challenging, amusing, usually irreverent, and often frustrating (to conservatives) half-hour show. I have had the privilege of appearing on *P.I.* over twenty times in the last four years and enjoyed every single time. I'm grateful for the many opportunities Bill has given me to voice my conservative opinions and be a part of his show. It's one of the few forums on network television where conservatives and religious people are asked to represent "the other side" in the midst of a group of liberals.

THE POWER OF TV

In the twentieth century, television was only around for about the last fifty years. Television began as essentially a storytelling medium. The networks have constantly tried to come up with imaginative and creative ways to tell these stories, whether it's in the form of a sitcom, drama, or movie of the week. But it has eventually morphed into so much more than its creators ever dreamed it would be. At the helm of the new millennium, television has become an all-encompassing influence not only on our country but on the whole world. Can you imagine your world without it?

Television has dramatically changed social, leisure, and family habits for almost everyone in this country. Even the medium of TV is slowly changing with companies investing in high-definition television, consumer satellite services, and interactive media. In fact, the latest trend in new home building is to add a "media" or "entertainment" room with the latest interactive technologies to link to a person's telephones, computers, and televisions. Digital Satellite TV programming, movies, shopping, video games, music, and sporting events are all at our fingertips and found in the comfort of our own home.

Television is a seductive dream machine that parades in front of you what you don't have but what marketers hope you soon think you'll need. It gives you what you're not ready or asking for. It wears you down with what you cannot stand until you accept it, and then it skews the definition of reality with its own moral and ethical code. TV has corrupted our children, seduced our teens, and anesthetized adults to the point that they are just as indifferent and desensitized to the harmful influences.

Baby boomers grew up on TV and seemed to turn out "OK." Gen-Xers were a little harder hit with the sex, violence, and materialism and were neglected in the values and morality department. In turn, their skepticism and cynicism have produced a generation that focuses on the material world. Claiming to be workaholics driven to attain "the good life," they live to work instead of work to live.

But it's the millennials of today who are a direct reflection of the product-driven, grown-up world they've absorbed through television all of their lives. They have grown up to be the most prosperous and materialistic group, hotly pursued by advertisers who pander to their every desire. TV has been their baby-sitter, friend, psychotherapist, teacher, sex counselor, and often the parent they never had.

WE ARE THE FROG IN HOLLYWOOD'S KETTLE

Obviously, there are numerous shows that rise to the standard of quality programming. Shows that raise our social awareness, educate us, give us insight into ourselves and our issues, entertain and humor us, take us to faraway lands where we could never go, stimulate interesting discussions, steer us politically, and remind us that we are emotional human beings with a soft spot for love and romance. My concerns are not aimed at that kind of programming.

My specific problem is with the pervasive influence and bombardment of sex, violence, vulgar language, and immorality on our children and teenagers. Questionable programming has sucked the imagination out of our youth, stripped them of their modesty, flagrantly flaunted base behavior as normal, pushed the envelope of parental reasoning further than it should go, and rammed acceptance (under the umbrella of tolerance) down our throats.

I'm talking about the numerous predictable sitcoms, dramas, or shows that demean decency, tear down the family, portray parents as out-of-touch idiots, distance siblings, worship sex, praise sexual experimentation, condone adultery, exploit violence as if it's a routine part of a child's day, elevate aliens to a revered position over man, and mock and degrade religion and religious people.

I am appalled at the parade of people on Jerry Springer, Ricki Lake, Jenny Jones, and Sally Jesse Raphael who willingly mortify and degrade themselves for the sake of a few minutes of fame and a little money. They do more harm to the image of American culture abroad than any other televised export, and we as a nation should be embarrassed.

Our society seems to have tuned out much of what is truly offensive material on TV and just ignores it. I'd like to think it's because no one is watching the boob tube to begin with, but the statistics prove different. We have become the frogs in Hollywood's kettle! If you're not careful, Hollywood will seduce you and your children into accepting their standards, morality, and agenda. And if you're not good parents, Hollywood will gladly step in and take over for you, raising your children to be just like them!

THE OLD FAMILY HOUR

The rise in the amount of sex and profanity and violence during the "family hour" does American families a tremendous disservice. The continued and accelerating degradation of network television in all these areas has a powerful cumulative impact on thinking and behavior, especially among children. Let's take a look at some of the influences that affect our society (especially our children) and survey the damage.

Before television was the dominant entertainment of families, the outside world was brought into homes by the power of radio, and listening to favorite programs featuring Abbott and Costello, Fanny Bryce, and Will Rogers was a family event. In a time when this country was focused on war, work, and rebuilding America, the family unit was strong, united, and fairly sheltered from outside influences. Divorce was rare, most moms were home, siblings helped raise siblings, and parents were the gatekeepers of their children's innocence.

As television was introduced in the '50s and its popularity grew, so grew the amount of time that families spent in front of the television. Variety shows such as *The Red Skelton Show* and *The Lawrence Welk Show,* and family formats such as *Disney's Wonderful World of Color, Bonanza, Lassie, Father Knows Best, Leave It to Beaver, The Ozzie and Harriet Show, The Donna Reed Show,* and others entertained millions and set a precedence for family-friendly programming. When programming increased during the '60s and '70s, parents were concerned about their children watching objectionable material during the time when the family gathered around the TV in the evening. So the networks were asked to reserve the 8 to 9 P.M. time slot for family-oriented programming, and the term "family hour" was born.

MY CHILDHOOD FAMILY HOUR

I grew up the oldest of four girls with both parents working, and I watched a lot of TV every day until my parents came home. When my mom would drag in around 5 P.M., exhausted from teaching school all day, my sister Dena and I would think of creative ways to prepare dinners for our family of six. After the meal was cooked, we would all sit around the table, one of us would say a prayer, and then we proceeded to laugh, tell jokes, eat our dinner, and reminisce about our day. It was the only time each day when we all connected as a family. Afterward, during dishes duty, Dena, Amy, Kelly, and I would sing songs in harmony from all of our favorite musicals. Those dinner stories, the hearty laughter, and memories of dinner preparation and songs are some of my favorite youthful recollections of my family hour.

Over time my sisters and I convinced my parents that people were watching TV and eating dinner together. No longer were we required to sit around the table and have our conversations. Instead, we lined our trays up in front of the TV and ate our dinner in silence. We were victims of our own lust for entertainment, and we filled that addictive need in a lazy way that stole precious time from our family. We thought it was fun and called what we watched "family" entertainment—such as *The Sonny and Cher Show* and *Laugh-In* (convincing my mom we wouldn't go to hell if we saw Cher's navel or Goldie Hawn's bikini).

Did all of that TV time bruise or scar me for life? No. But the programs we watched twenty years ago didn't contain the insulting story lines, offensive language, sexual situations, or graphic violence that blankets the family hour today. What I do regret, however, is the fact that our family dinners were never the same again. Those precious moments of laughter, song, and tales of the day were replaced by passive group time. Although we were all together, the lack of stimulating conversation, exchange of ideas, and interaction with one another robbed our family of time and love.

THE NEW FAMILY HOUR

Seventy percent of today's households say they sit down to dinner together at least five times a week. Nearly half of the families spend forty-five minutes preparing dinner, but only thirty minutes eating together. A survey by the research firm of Yankelovich Partners for Kraft Foods found that 40% of households have the TV on while eating dinner, but they're not necessarily enjoying "quality family time."[4]

It's clear the choices for family viewing are dwindling. I'm talking about being able to sit down and not have to worry about what's being heard or viewed by children and young teenagers. According to a 1999 Parents Television Council report, objectionable content during family hour rose 75% since 1989, a rate of nearly 7 incidences per hour of programming. Only 9 out of 37 family hour shows are deemed acceptable during prime time. Foul language is up 58%, violent content is up 68%, and cable and satellite stations have made the family hour a thing of the past.[5]

FOCUSED TIME

For the first year after my divorce, I had a hard time sitting at the family table with my three kids for a meal without getting melancholy about not being a family anymore. So we started doing what a lot of single parents and their kids do. We went out to eat. It became a time I really enjoyed with my children. While we waited, the kids talked about their day, and the four of us were a family. My kids had my full attention without phones, TV, or neighborhood kids, and those meals began to be a highlight in my day instead of a dread. I called it focused time because I could focus in on my kids.

Now, years later, I have two teenagers with their own school and work schedules who can't always eat a meal with their younger brother and me. But when we do, it's focused time, and we cherish the moments we have together. For those of you who haven't tried this, give it a chance the next time you go to a restaurant. Focus on your child (children) and make it a special family time away from TV, friends, the phone, and work. You can create a sharing experience and memory you will treasure and your child will appreciate for years.

VIEWING HABITS

Today's shows that air in the earliest prime-time hour to the evening news usually contain mature content with sexually suggestive dialogue, situations, crude and vulgar jokes, or violence. But it's not just kids or teenagers who are glued to the boob tube. Most college students own a set, and at least half of them have a VCR or cable. TV time accounts for 40% of free time for women and 50% for men.[6]

In 1998 Nielsen Media Research concluded that the average household watched seven and a quarter hours of television daily.

Women spent four and a half hours in front of a set and men nearly four hours a day. Teens and children averaged three hours a day.[7] Adults spend more time with television than with any other medium and almost as much as with all other media combined. Sadly, most children spend more time with the television set before the age of six than they will spend with their fathers *during their entire lives*. If you're a dad, think about that one.

True, many families watch television together in the evenings or on weekends. But for the most part, the family hour has given way to kids and teens retreating to their rooms. Over half the kids in this country have a television in their room that they view by themselves, and only a third watch with the rest of the family. With bedtime for many preteens and teenagers extending to 11 P.M., kids entertain themselves by talking with friends on their phone, doing homework, playing video games, surfing the Internet, or . . . you guessed it, watching TV, all in the privacy of their own sanctuary.

VIEWING TRENDS IN THE '90S

A recent *USA Today/CNN/Gallup* poll of 65,000 viewers found that 96% are concerned about sexual content on television, 97% are concerned about violence, and 65% felt the entertainment industry was completely out of touch with the values of Americans.[8]

Television has trends just as the movies do. In true Hollywood style, what works for one network will usually get copied in some other form on another network. Sitcoms have always been a mainstay for selling a supposed slice of American life to the public, and these days there are a variety on the boob tube. What you see on the screen is usually a reflection of a group of writers who brainstorm about what they think will work.

There also are trends in Hollywood programming according to what's popular. Right now that would be reality shows, because they are cheap, easy to produce, popular, devoid of moody or snooty "stars" to work with. They're just real people making real mistakes, and that's always popular with the masses.

But the '90s had a variety of talent hit the little screen, and some of them have stayed for a while. Comedies using real-life comedians were popular, so networks brought them off the stage (Ellen DeGeneres,

Jerry Seinfeld, and Jeff Foxworthy) and gave them their own show. Then came sitcoms about families in all forms—couples living the married life (*Dharma and Greg*), funny families (*Third Rock From the Sun, Everybody Loves Raymond*), a family of faith (*7th Heaven, Moesha, Touched by an Angel*). The WB catered to teens who believe in spooks (*Buffy the Vampire Slayer, Angel, Charmed, Sabrina the Teenage Witch*), singles living their professional and personal life onscreen (*Frasier, Will & Grace, Ally McBeal*), and perhaps the sitcom people will remember the most, endured the longest, and brought the highest paid salaries of a million each to the cast, *Friends*.

Intrigue with the afterlife, aliens, and higher intelligence brought *Roswell, The X-Files, Pretender, Profiler,* and *Millennium*. Reality TV sort of entered through the back door with shows such as *Real World* on MTV but broke new territory in the late '90s and right on into the millennium with *Who Wants to Be a Millionaire, Who Wants to Marry a Millionaire, Survivor I & II, Temptation Island, The Mole,* and probably many more.

RATINGS

In the past decade, the broadcast networks' standards have obviously relaxed to embrace the ever-changing culture and younger generation. The three broadcast networks (ABC, CBS, and NBC) still command 35.7% of the viewing audience and set the standards for the entire entertainment industry.[9] Some movies, cable, music CDs, the Internet, videos, and video games have ratings, but none are as restricted in content as the television. The industry puts a rating on each program, and they are supposedly devised to help parents know what material their teen or child is viewing. This rating gives the viewer the option of changing the channel, but I contend nobody really reads or abides by the rating.

TV RATINGS DEFINITIONS

97% of All-American households own at least one television set—which is more than those possessing indoor plumbing or refrigerators.

For Children

TV-Y—Suitable for children of all ages. Programming that is "kiddy-friendly," such as animated cartoons, live-action shows, and storytelling programming. The themes and elements in this program are specifically designed for a very young audience (ages 2-6), so there's no need for parents to worry. (*Winnie the Pooh*, ABC)

TV-Y-7—Suitable for children seven and older. May contain material that includes mild physical or comedic violence and may frighten or disturb children who have not acquired the developmental skills needed to distinguish between fantasy and reality. Some children may not be mature enough to handle some of the material. For those programs where fantasy violence may be more intense or more combative than other programs in this category, such programs will be designated TV-Y7-FV. (*Goosebumps*, Fox)

Older Audiences

TV-G—Suitable for all ages. It contains little or no violence, no strong language, and little or no sexual dialogue or situations. Most parents would find this program suitable for all ages, although this rating does not signify a program designed specifically for children. Most parents may let younger children watch this program unattended. (*Touched by an Angel*, CBS)

TV-PG—Parental guidance is suggested. Programs may contain crude or uncouth language, some violence and suggestive sexual dialogue, and inappropriate situations for younger children to see. Many parents may want to watch it with their younger children. The theme itself may call for parental guidance, and/or the program contains one or more of the following: moderate violence (V), some sexual situations (S), infrequent coarse language (L), or some suggestive dialogue (D). (*Friends*, NBC)

TV-14—This program contains some material that many parents would find unsuitable for children under fourteen. Parents are strongly urged to exercise greater care in monitoring this program and are cautioned against letting children under the age of fourteen watch unattended. This program contains one or more of the following: intense violence (V), intense sexual situations (S), strong coarse language (L), or intensely suggestive dialogue (D). (*NYPD Blue*, ABC)

TV-M—Definitely for adults and mature audiences who can discern reality from fiction or reenactment. Probably will contain language, realistic violence, sexual situations, partial or implied nudity. Adult issues and themes. This program is specifically designed to be viewed by adults and therefore may be unsuitable for children under seventeen. This program contains one or more of the following: graphic violence (V), explicit sexual activity (S), or crude indecent language (L). (Cable movies)

PRIME-TIME LANGUAGE, SEX, AND VIOLENCE

Kelso after missing a basketball free throw: "Damn!"
Hyde: "I believe that's H-O-R—"
Fez: "Ah, you are a whore."
Kelso: "No, the game is Horse."
Fez: "Make that shot, whore."
Hyde: "... He's screwed."
Donna: "... You lucky bastard."
Eric: "You guys suck. Just, thank God for Donna, that bitch."

—That '70s Show

Remember when words such as "damn" and "hell" were considered bad words? Do you realize that just fifteen years ago the word "butt" wasn't even allowed by censors on prime time TV? Today those words are as common as commercials and have crept into our daily conversation at work and in social settings. Indeed, these words have no "shock value" anymore and are not counted as foul language by many.

By the mid '90s it became clear to anyone who watched television that sexual material, foul language, and violence were becoming increasingly prevalent. Not only at the 9 and 10 P.M. evening hour, but also during the 8 P.M. family hour. The family audience found it increasingly hard to watch programming without questionable filth in it. A tolerant mentality has introduced an open mind-set to accept whatever we see on TV as "OK." Our kids are bombarded with this message every day in subtle advertising and not-so-subtle programming. We adults get our fair share of propaganda about tolerance as well with political rhetoric, bias news hours, and liberal adult dramas depicting the "agenda" of the week. All politically correct, of course!

LANGUAGE

"Jen, damn it! You're such an ass!"   *—Dawson's Creek*

When I was growing up and a child used profanity, mothers washed their mouths out with soap. Early on we learned our lessons about what was socially acceptable and what wasn't. Boy, have things changed! These days language has been stretched, tested, and pushed to new levels of "offensive" on any network, at any time. Try watching your television for one whole day and see if you don't hear a single bad or offensive word . . . it can't be done. Sadly, most children have easy access to profanity through the TV.

The story of sex and foul language on prime time is one of repeated envelope pushing. That process began sooner for sex than for language. Television's sexual revolution started in the '70s, whereas it wasn't until the '90s that parents truly had to worry about their children being exposed to cursing as well. What would have been considered intolerable at one point is now routinely found in sitcom scripts.

"Screw you. You rotten son of a bitch."
                                   —Pacey to his father on *Dawson's Creek*
"You stupid, worthless bitch!"   —*Buffy the Vampire Slayer*

How has language on television changed over a ten-year period? The Parents Television Counsel did a study that concluded that in 1989 "hell" and "damn" were the most commonly used curse words. A decade later, each word was used far more often, but other words have now crept into the "frequently used" zone. The use of "shit" has become a common trend along with "ass," which was rarely uttered on TV in 1989. "Bitch" is another word that has eased into regular slang used in describing female characters, and on comedies with gay characters, it has become a standard catch-phrase to get laughs. Throw in what's considered "mild" language these days ("crap," "son of a bitch," "bastard," "sucks," and various obscure and euphemistic forms of the "F" word) and you get an idea of why children and teens speak the way they do.

When we allow children and preteens to absorb the language, cynicism, crude slang, and sarcastic humor of TV, it is no surprise that those words are repeated in their dialogue? Kids may be fully aware of what's considered taboo in their home, but the temptation to repeat those forbidden words outside in the "real" world enables them with a sort of power. It's called rebellion, and most kids have tried it at least once. Just ask them.

AND MORE BAD LANGUAGE

Profanity is used once every six minutes on prime-time network, every two minutes on premium cable, and every three minutes in major motion pictures, according to a study by the Center for Media and Public Affairs.10

So let me ask you this: Do you use profanity that much? Well, neither do I, and neither do most of the people you probably deal with on a daily basis. I don't know anyone who uses profanity that much. In fact, I know people who *never* use it at all! So why do we get it fed to us as if it is the norm? Who are these statistics skewing to? Who's the audience that wants all of this language?

When cable stations started using profanity and getting away with it, the networks started pushing the boundaries until now your basic garden variety cursing is no longer shocking.

We used to have a standard of civility, social manners, and a basic grasp of the English language in our culture. So when did it become "taboo" to speak proper English? Or a crime to respect decent behavior? When did it become cool and acceptable to dehumanize and degrade one another? To watch television these days, you'd think rudeness, disrespect, and street slang have become the norm for our society.

Only in the past few years has objectionable material become common on the broadcast networks between 8 and 9 P.M. Before then, virtually all shows airing prior to 9 P.M. had been suitable for parents and children to watch together. How sad that a simple guideline of decency, once removed, has destroyed a protected time for families to watch TV together. And on a deeper level, it has paved the way for a downward spiral of verbal etiquette in our country. No wonder foreigners think we are "rude Americans."

SEX

Dawson, a teenage boy: "What are you suggesting?"

Eve, a teenage girl: "Only the obvious. A night of scorching hot, unbridled, mind-altering sex."

Dawson: "Just like that? No first date, no months of getting to know each other?"

*Eve: "Those are small-town rituals for small-town girls. Face it, Dawson,
we're hot for each other."*
                                                        —*Dawson's Creek*

In 1999 the Parent Television Counsel conducted a study and found that sexual content has increased dramatically.[11] Our children and teenagers are getting a daily dose of sexual messages every time they turn on a television, go to a movie, play a CD, open a magazine, glance at a billboard, or go on the Internet. Sex permeates our society, and it is *everywhere!* Yet when your teenagers are viewing sex on TV, the risks and results of physical diseases, pregnancy, and emotional turmoil are rarely explored. Abstinence is not even presented as an alternative.

Television exposes children and teens to adult behaviors at early ages by showing characters (especially teen or twenty-somethings) in mature sexual situations where these actions are considered "normal" and "risk-free" without moral or personal responsibility. Being sexually active is portrayed as a popular thing to do, and many times there are several characters on the show talking about sex (*Buffy the Vampire Slayer, Ally McBeal*). Because sex happens so often on TV, the overall subliminal message is that having sex makes you "grown up" and "everybody does it."

A study conducted by *US News and World Report* finds that a sexual act or reference to sex occurred on average every four minutes in prime time television. By the age of seventeen most children will have viewed at least 400,000 sexual acts on television, primarily between non-married couples.[12] Beyond sexual activity taking place in high school, we're now seeing oral sex rampantly being used among junior high school students. What once was the unthinkable parading in front of the camera during prime-time is now the norm.

*"The foundation for any friendship between a man and a woman is based
on his wanting to sleep with her, unless he's gay. Then it's shopping."*
                                                        —*Ally McBeal*

TV STATS

That same 1999 Parents Television Council report found that there was a 77% rise in the average sexual content of family hour programming since 1989. FOX had the most offensive material overall, and NBC was second. The depictions of sex on television today are markedly different from those of a decade ago. The overall number of sexual references per hour during prime time went up more than any time in television history, and references to sex acts during the family hour have increased dramatically. Teen-oriented shows refer to sex 25% of the time, although I would say that's climbing and changing on a seasonal basis (with more liberal shows being aired). Sixty-eight percent of shows in the family hour contained sexual material.[13]

Dialogues, jokes, and references to sex are not just on shows for adults, but teenagers have sex or talk about sex with other teenagers on most of the network programming. Teenage shows on UPN and WB Network such as *Buffy the Vampire Slayer* don't attract many people over thirty-five, but for the teenagers who watch, two lesbian characters in the main story line routinely talk about their relationship when they aren't experimenting. Buffy is seen in bed with boyfriends, and other characters talk about their sexual exploits. Sex seems as casual and as much a part of their weekly plot as the demons she kills.

HOW DOES SEX INFLUENCE OUR KIDS

Professional organizations such as the American Academy of Pediatrics have drawn links between television's depictions of sexuality and real-life behaviors. A 1995 poll of ten- to sixteen-year-olds showed that children recognize that "what they see on television encourages them to take part in sexual activity too soon, to show disrespect for their parents, to lie, and to engage in aggressive behavior." More than two-thirds said they are influenced by television; 77% said TV shows too much sex before marriage; and 62% said sex on television and in movies influences their peers to have sexual relations when they are too young. Two-thirds also cited certain programs featuring dysfunctional families as encouraging disrespect toward parents.[14]

And it's not just younger children who are influenced. A University of Michigan study found that young women who view just twenty-two hours of prime-time TV on a monthly basis have more permissive views of casual sex than before the viewing.

Drew pulls his girlfriend, a handywoman, aside and asks her to explain a matchbook, hotel key, and condom in her possession.

She responds, "I am working on a restaurant which is in a hotel."
"And the condom?"
"I thought you'd want to put it on your penis when you thank me for the
    big-screen TV."   —The Drew Carey Show

I'm saddened by shows geared to the teenage audience (*Dawson's Creek, Roswell, Popular, Buffy the Vampire Slayer, Undressed,* and a dozen more) that perpetuate sexual immorality, gender experimentation, and sexual promiscuity as the "normal" way of life. They promote what many parents view as "immoral" and story lines that demean values parents are trying to instill in their children. Despite this, many of the shows report that parents haven't complained at all about their content nor have they received sponsor complaints. Amazingly, either the parents don't care, or they don't watch these shows to realize what their kids are being influenced by. If the networks don't receive complaints or comments, they are not going to change their liberal story lines.

Faith: "I'm about ready to pop. Are you up?"
Xander: "I'm suddenly very up."
Faith: "Just relax and take your pants off."
Faith rips Xander's shirt off, and they begin to kiss. They get into bed and have sex. Faith's body is seen on top of Xander in the reflection of the TV.
                                            —Buffy the Vampire Slayer

A straight male character who wants to be gay remarks, "Maybe one day I'll be able to lie naked . . . and stroke another man like a pussycat."
                                                    —Ladies Man

A HYPOCRITICAL MESSAGE

I find it interesting that the blatant sexual messages in most of the television shows slanted to young people are coming from the very community who are the biggest proponents of AIDS awareness. People in the industry wear their AIDS ribbons to every event and awards show, promoting a cure for AIDS and a message of compassion and love. Their cause to find a cure for AIDS and prevent more people from dying from it is a loving and just one. No one should or would find fault with that.

Ironically, the same community turns right around and preaches a message of sexual promiscuity. They write, direct, and produce exploitive, seductive scripts that encourage kids and teens to think about, joke about, and experiment with sex. Many TV characters use popular sexual rhetoric, trendy story lines, cool music, and clothing to entice twelve- to eighteen-year-olds to do the very thing that could get them killed. There is never any follow-up dialogue on being responsible by using protection or about abstaining in the first place! Sadly, most of the messages encourage *unprotected sex,* which is the very thing that spreads the disease the stars staunchly fight against.

Television story lines that encourage kids to experiment sexually before they are ready to understand the consequences should be unthinkable in our society. We should be smarter than that. It is hypocritical, irresponsible, and highly selfish on Hollywood's part to promote that message.

"Don't you ever sweat, or is that a gay thing?"
"Yes, Norris, that's a gay thing. We gays like to save our sweating for the gay sex."
                                                                            —*Oh Grow Up*

A VALID COMPLAINT

Parents have the right to protest gay-themed story lines or shows on television. It is not "mean-spirited," "homophobic," or "intolerant" for parents to disagree with what is being presented to their children. Gays protest bias whenever it occurs against their cause (the 2001 Grammy nomination of Eminem and his appearance with Elton John was heavily protested by GLADD), and they feel they are discriminated against by people "outside" of the entertainment industry. The same privilege and voice should be tolerated and given to people who don't practice the homosexual lifestyle and are on the "outside" of the industry looking in. Tolerance is about tolerating *both* opinions from two different sides. Every person, gay or straight, has the right to choose how he or she wants to live and who (or what) he or she wants to believe in. But there are laws created to make sure those individual opinions don't suppress the rights of the rest of us in the process. Respect and regard for the laws protecting our children and their innocence are slowly disappearing because of our self-absorbed, anything-goes, sex-saturated society.

On one of my appearances on *Politically Incorrect*, I was accused of being "homophobic" by writer/actor Bruce Vilanch. Bruce has had a wife and children, but he professes to be gay and is very active in the gay Hollywood community. I stated that "gay writers in Hollywood are influencing the sexual practices of young people by writing story lines that contain gay characters, especially teenagers, in relationships. I contend that those story lines influence some teenagers to experiment with the gay lifestyle." Bruce then lashed out by calling me "homophobic" for suggesting that the gay lifestyle could be "taught or learned" by watching TV. I replied, "I'm not homophobic, and don't call me that. Just because I have a different opinion than you doesn't make me homophobic. It just means I believe differently than you do." That defensive and intolerant mind-set is unfortunately the norm for much of the "creative" writers in Hollywood.

Parents, you need to understand this. If you have an opinion that differs from the homosexual community on their lifestyle or agenda, and you state that opinion to your child, or publicly, without hate or malice, that opinion doesn't make you homophobic or intolerant. Do not allow that intolerant word to have a silencing power over your fundamental beliefs. If you speak out, your child or teen will learn that they too have an opinion that should count.

VIOLENCE

Buffy, Angel, and Giles go to a warehouse and fight a cult. They behead, stake, and spar with them. Buffy kills Balthazar by electrocuting him.
—Buffy the Vampire Slayer

How many people have witnessed a crime being committed or watched a person being murdered? How many have aimed a gun at someone in anger, been shot, stabbed, or violently attacked? Most people would say no to all of these. But if you or your children have watched television, you're one of the statistics who has seen unending murders and violence carried out in your living room. Approximately a dozen murders occur every hour during prime time.

Violence in movies and television has been linked to influencing violent behavior in young people. In fact, violence on television has become so problematic that even Washington has become involved in campaigns to limit it. With more and more children watching television in their bedrooms and spending unsupervised time absorbing its violent content and messages, violence has increased steadily among our youth.

Research on the link between TV violence and real-life violence has been largely ignored over the years. Both formal and informal studies have been conducted and have proven the direct relationship between them. The percentage of violent content rose faster than any other category, nearly doubling from what it used to be in the late '90s. Most of the violence on TV goes unpunished, and almost half of all violent interactions show no harm to the victims.

The Good, The Bad, or Both

Another trend that's hard to ignore is the lack of distinction between the good guys and the bad guys. More and more story lines blur the distinction between heroes and villains using violence. The roles of good and bad, right and wrong, are crossed with characters who carry out violence for a "good" cause but aren't necessarily all good. *Buffy the Vampire Slayer, Angel,* and *Charmed* use graphic violence as a staple for their story lines, and occult violence is readily accepted as "fantasy." I'm not just talking about gunfights or a few fistfights. It's about serial killers, thugs, henchmen, drug smugglers, sadism, torture, occult violence (driving a stake through creatures' hearts), dismemberment, slow-motion death, etc.

Does All This Violence Really Affect Our Kids?

You bet it does! That our children and teens imitate what they see in the world around them is proven in the statistics from violence on television. And it's not just our country that's feeling the effects of television violence. Research on foreign countries where television has just recently been introduced shows the murder rates there have doubled, while literacy rates, or reading skills, have declined. Studies of various countries show that after the countries adopted television into their culture, the homicide rates doubled in ten to fifteen years.[15]

The rise in teen violence (especially on school campuses) and among younger children has been closely linked with children who are raised with television. Fear of crime and violence has also taken a twisted turn. Increasing exposure to media violence often results in what's being called the "mean world syndrome," causing children to fear for their own safety. The several school shootings that have horrendously marred a generation of kids who can't go to school without fear are a prime example of that mentality all across our country today.

Fantasy or Reality

At the age of three, children do not understand the difference between reality and fantasy, commercials, or regular programming. And between the ages of six and ten, children believe most of what they see on television to be true.

By the time a child finishes elementary school, the average child will have seen 8,000 televised murders and 100,000 acts of violence. By the time a child finishes high school, those numbers will have doubled.[16] Are we surprised kids can't differentiate between what's real and what's fantasy? When TV legitimizes and popularizes certain realities, the kids who watch the programs grow up to accept and act out what they see on TV.

In the Columbine school shootings of 1999, many of the teens said they thought the two gunmen were fake and the whole thing was staged. In another shooting in Dallas at a Baptist church, teenagers once again said they thought the gunman was part of a skit that was being performed for their youth night. These similar reports are in keeping with the desensitizing our children have experienced from all the media violence they have been exposed to.

My own children and I were on the way to the airport when we suddenly found ourselves caught between a motorist and an airport security officer who had pulled his gun on the man. I looked up and we were staring down the barrel of that gun! Years before I would have been petrified and shoved the kids out of the way, but it didn't register. None of us were immediately afraid. We were all so desensitized to seeing a man hold a gun on another man that none of us had the good sense to run or even fall to the ground. Seeing a real-life drama unfold on the streets of the real world simply looks like a TV show to us. That was a wake-up call for me as a parent.

TV Violence Can Be Reversed!

Did you know that overexposure to even nonviolent media can make kids more aggressive? "The theory is plausible because children who watch lots of TV or video games spend less time interacting with others and thus have fewer social skills," says Dr. Katherine Kaufer

Christoffel, a children's violence expert and professor of pediatrics and preventive medicine at Northwestern University.[17]

Past research has linked exposure to media violence with increased aggression and bad behavior in children. That information was eye-opening, helpful, and often obvious, but hardly encouraging. Books have been advising parents how to reverse the behavior for several years now, but few tests had been run to prove the reverse theory could work until recently.

A study was conducted by the Stanford University Medical School in which a third and fourth grade class from two different schools in San Jose, California, were involved. Over a period of six months of being supervised by trained, regular classroom teachers, the 120 participants at one school received no intervention or training, while 105 children at the other school received 18 lessons, each 30 to 50 minutes long, on reducing the use of television, videotapes, and video games.

At the outset the youngsters reported an average of about 15 hours of television a week, 5 hours of videos, and 3 hours of video games. The children were then challenged to abstain for 10 days, watching no more than 7 hours a week. The households involved had their televisions hooked up to a device that could prevent the set from being turned on if the child exceeded the established limit.

At the beginning of the study, peer reports of aggression were similar. By the end of the course, the kids who received the training cut their TV use by almost one-third (9 hours of television viewing, 3 hours of videos, and 1 hour of video games) and were less verbally abusive than the students at the other school. It found that grade-school children were less aggressive when their television and video game time were reduced, proving that the relationship between media exposure and childhood behavior is modifiable.[18]

What hope! What promise! If parents could only do this kind of monitoring and enforced abstaining with each family member, we might see results like these on a national level. Even more importantly, we could see a generation of children and young teens regain their imagination, intelligence, discernment, understanding of fantasy and reality, respect for moral values in their social arena, regard for life, for their parents, for themselves, and for their fellow man.

OF THE 100 MILLION U.S. HOUSE-HOLDS WITH TVS, about 65 million subscribe to cable and 15 million have satellite. This access to a variety of programming choices forced the major networks to get creative in order to gain back a dwindling audience. But it also forced them to be competitive with a ratings free market that isn't under close scrutiny. That is why the lid on language, sex and violence has been blown clean off. In our sex-saturated society, cable has done more to deliver sex in R-rated and X-rated forms of entertainment into the home than any other medium.

—BECKY YERAK, *USA Today*[1]

TV Trivia

HOW DO THE NETWORKS RATE?

The Parents Television Council (PTC) has conducted numerous surveys,[2] rating each prime-time network by how family-friendly their programs are. The NetWork Report Card was created so that you can log on to their Web site or receive their newsletter and stay updated on what the networks are airing and which ones look family-friendly. The results are discouraging—not one network received above a C+ grade. The worst was FOX, rating an F.[3] The networks' poor performances are an indicator of the state of prime-time television today.

Are there any family-safe broadcast networks left? On cable there are many options with admirable specials, movies, and programming for all ages (Odyssey, FOX Family, Disney, ESPN, Toon channel, TV Land).

WHICH NETWORK OFFENDS THE MOST?

WWF Smackdown! was responsible for more than 11% of the combined sex, cursing, and violence in 1999, according to a report by the PTC.[4] UPN aired more offensive content on a per-hour basis than any other network, but it is FOX that had the most offensive material overall, with eleven incidents per hour. Because of the violence on all the wrestling shows, it almost requires a separate rating system all its own.

CABLE

Probably no greater ingredient has contributed to the explosion of language, sex, and violence on television today than cable TV. Cable has expanded into homes with phone lines, extensive service, and satellite dishes, opening a Pandora's box of programming choices delivered in about 100 channels. Of the 100 million U.S. households with TVs, about 65 million have cable, and 15 million have satellite service.[5]

This access to a variety of programming choices forced the major networks to get creative in order to gain back the adult crowd of viewers who had flocked to cable TV. But it also forced the networks to be competitive with a ratings free market that isn't under close scrutiny, resulting in more adult programming filtering into family viewing time. In our sex-saturated society, cable TV has done more to deliver sex in R-rated and X-rated forms into the home than any other medium.

NEW NEWS

News has been a very competitive area of the media, but the mainstream media tends to focus on biased news stories and vast amounts of fluff pieces, disregarding tremendous stories they don't deem important to air. When people come home and turn on the nightly news, they're looking for an overview of what happened that day, but when they see stories on the latest fashion craze or a local restaurant piece, they're lulled into believing that nothing of importance is happening. Viewers want stories that are crucial and important. That's why you'll find more and more people switching to the alternative media on cable and the Internet.

Nowhere did this play out stronger than during the 2000 presidential election. Cable news networks such as MSNBC, FOX NEWS, CNBC, and CNN soared in their ratings. FOX NEWS, however, rose above the rest with its well-rounded coverage that wasn't as biased or one-sided as the traditional network news stations. FOX has single-handedly changed the look of cable news networks, and because of their growing popularity and tenacity, they have caused CNN and others to reformat and take a new look at their programming.

REALITY TV

Toward the end of the twentieth century, network television was uninspiring, dull, and practically dying in the competition against cable, the Internet, MTV, and whatever else entertained us. So the time was ripe for something new to step forward.

America's Funniest Home Videos began a trend that fueled the advent of personal video cameras by encouraging people to become their own subjects in shorts who competed for prize money. This "reality caught on camera is funny" interest caught on quickly, and a rash of copycat video shows sprang up everywhere. The trend for a more sophisticated reality TV seemed to start on a smaller scale with shows such as MTV's *Real World, Road Rules,* and Internet voyeurism. But the show that launched a new direction in reality programming and proved a nation would watch was *Who Wants to Marry a Millionaire.* The show featured two total strangers who met and married, then got it annulled afterward. It was reviled as the low point of reality television. Yet something about that show sparked a change in reality shows on television. It set a precedence for other types of reality shows to follow.

Who Wants to Be a Millionaire? became a surprise sensation on ABC, proving television's power to captivate a nation's acceptance of prime-time game shows. With *Millionaire's* success averaging nearly twenty-eight million viewers each week, the networks scrambled to come up with unique reality-type-format shows that had already caught on in popularity all over the world. When CBS launched *Survivor,* it took our nation by storm, reaching twenty-four million viewers with its blend of exotic survival games, sinister elimination tactics, and gross theatrics. It also cemented viewers' new fascination with reality TV on a prime-time network.

That fascination led to a new level of reality television that has offended our decorum with FOX introducing "spectacle TV" in the form of *Temptation Island.* Four "committed" but unmarried couples with 1-5 year relationships were sent to a tropical paradise to test the "strength" of their commitments. They were separated from their partners, tempted with attractive singles of the opposite sex, and followed to see what they would do and ultimately to see who would stay together.

By the success of these shows, is the American public voting that they'd rather see reality TV than traditional sitcoms, dramas, and movies? Although not generating revenue from syndicated reruns, the average hour-long reality show costs networks about $400,000 to produce—

a third as much as a typical new drama and a fraction of the price paid for top-rated shows like *ER* or *Ally McBeal.*

IS TV BABY-SITTING YOUR CHILD?

A question in most parents' minds about what their children are doing in day-care centers was answered in a study that revealed TV an important part of child-care professional activities. In day-care centers nearly seven out of ten reported that watching television is among the activities on a typical day for children at their facilities. The survey revealed that 91% have one or more TVs.[6] Pediatricians are now recommending that total television time be limited to no more than one to two hours a day, and that children under two should not even watch TV.

THE FADING TV FATHER

If you weren't born yet or can't remember, then maybe you've watched *Nick at Night* or *TV Land* and caught *The Donna Reed Show, Ozzie and Harriet, Father Knows Best,* or *Leave It to Beaver*? Besides being too good to be true (I wanted my dad to call me "kitten" as Robert Young did, but he wouldn't buy it), these shows all had strong father figures.

Try to name even a few sitcoms today that have a strong father figure or shows that have a father at all! An unusual minority called "fathers" rarely shows up on television these days. When they do, they are "eight times more likely to be portrayed negatively compared with mothers," says Wade Horn of the National Fatherhood Initiative, a research and resource organization that promotes responsible fatherhood.[7] The traditional role model that once was held in high esteem and prominence by our society in the '50s and '60s is outdated, outnumbered, and just plain left out. Considering 40% of the men and women making movies today grew up in homes without fathers, it is understandable that it must be hard to write about something they've never known.

NICHE TELEVISION
Nickelodeon

Nickelodeon is designed for children ages two to eleven and has expanded from a small cable company into a prime-time company vying for the younger audience. "Kids love the repetition," says Cheryl Chase, the voice of Angelica on the *Rugrats*. "They like to see it over and over and over." Since networks have mostly given up the family hour and go after the teen audience, cable has the ability to serve a niche audience and discover the children who are ready and willing to become faithful viewers. Children's programming has grown in the last few years, partly because *Rugrats* has been so popular on Nickelodeon since 1991. The *Rugrats* have their own star on the Hollywood walk of fame, they have twenty-seven million weekly viewers, and the show runs up to thirty times a week. How did it become so successful? As the audience from major networks started to splinter off and discover cable, Nickelodeon became more popular, and their technology advanced in the animation department. They even have a Nick Jr. preschool program.

PBS

Where Nickelodeon has excelled with targeting the niche for kids and family, PBS stepped in with educational programming and for years has set a standard of excellence in making learning fun. The show has become a national treasure, and the company has bought extra morning time for young mothers with fascinated little ones who sit, watch, and learn. PBS pioneered the idea of educational programming and opened the doors for other learning channels such as the *History* and *Discovery* channels. America is a nation that loves to learn, and we're intrigued with shows that teach and expand our knowledge. Educational programming has raised the Gen-Xers, and now the Millennials are being introduced to shows such as *Sesame Street* and *Teletubbies*. Although credit has to be given to Barney as a leader in the stuffed character division, who would ever have known that weird-looking overstuffed characters like Tinky Winky, Laa Laa, Dipsy, and Po could excite babies and grab a young market who can't even talk yet?

WB, FX, UPN, USA—Teen Driven

Carmen e-mails a friend about what happened during preparations for a high school play: "Miss Ross made Samantha sit on Josh Ford's lap at rehearsal this morning. And JF sprung a major pup tent."   —*Popular*

These networks, for the most part, cater to the teenagers and twenty-somethings who have spending and viewing power, but they try to appeal to the male audience in particular. WB has traditionally gone after the male and female "tween" audience with shows such as *Dawson's Creek, Buffy the Vampire Slayer, Angel, Charmed, Roswell,* and *Popular.* But perhaps their most successful show is one that is "cross-generational" and extremely family-friendly, *7th Heaven.* FX caters to the young adult male with a variety of shows such as *The X Show, The X-Files,* and *Son of a Beach* that are all sexually enticing and borderline R-rated on any given day. *Loveline* is a teen sex show answering and discussing provocative sexual situations and issues. UPN went straight for the boys with an abundance of wrestling shows, including the popular *WWF Smackdown!* And it would appear that comedies are also being aimed at these young men with shows that include more sketches mixed in with the wrestling. USA also aims for the male crowd with *Baywatch* and *Nikita.*

For Women Only

Women are becoming a niche for smaller markets as well as bigger ones because they are home more often than men and make an estimated 80% of the family purchases. So in the quest to attain that niche of viewers, a new cable channel is being marketed to women that's called *WE: Women's Entertainment.* The service will offer classic romance and tear-jerker favorites and also feature original series, specials, and films. Even though the channel is relatively small, it plans to reach thirty million homes in three years and expand into a wide range of services for women.

It seems odd that there haven't been more channels dedicated to women. *Lifetime* has been around for several years and reaches about seventy-eight million homes, and *Oxygen* reaches about thirteen million. But I shouldn't overlook the *Home Shopping Network* or *QVC,* who depend largely on women and their purchasing power!

Minorities

Minorities have had their seasons in television. It isn't that there haven't been a number of shows featuring actors of different ethnicity and cultural backgrounds, but lately the typecasting of characters and farcical sitcoms have softened a bit to give way to more realistic portrayals such as *Moesha* or unusual shows such as Eddie Murphy's satire *The PJs.* For years the stereotyping of blacks featured pimp-hoods, hookers, and oversexed characters who exaggerated the worst in human behavior, which has brought criticism from the black community. WB, UPN, and BET are the stations where you can find most of the shows that cater to black audiences. In the fall of 1999, *The Parkers* brought an 80% black audience share despite ranking 126th among whites.[8] The good news is there are more black actors in lead roles in network television today. The bad news is there are no significant roles for Latinos, Asian-Americans, or American Indians. Latino advocates have chastised the networks and called for more work for minorities.

THE PRIME-TIME NEOPAGAN MOVEMENT

A vampire has Buffy's mom tied up and gagged. He tells her that he wants to eat and torture her. —Buffy the Vampire Slayer

Witchcraft and the occult are piped into homes every day. And because of the onslaught of popularity with Harry Potter, a growing fascination with the neopagan and supernatural movement is alive and well in movies and on TV. Sorcery, witchcraft, and alternative religions are woven into everything from children's cartoons to teen sitcoms and even in daytime soap operas. These shows contain graphic violence with ghouls, demons, and vamps being reduced to toast across prime time.

WB is presently the main network encouraging this kind of programming, but FOX is reportedly interested in *Buffy* as well. Which proves the neopagan popularity will soon spread to the major networks. In fact, *Buffy* is one of the top-rated shows among teens, with *Angel* and *Charmed* following close behind. Detailed instructions in the casting of spells and the use of items needed for ritual magic are frequently woven into the story lines. You'll find it on *Buffy the Vampire Slayer, Angel, Charmed,* and to a lighter degree on *Sabrina the Teenage Witch.* They all teach and lure your children and teenagers into the attractive Hollywood world of the occult. It's no surprise that teens are flocking to buy books on spells in order to gain a supernatural power or force, and *empowerment* seems to be the key to the fascination that drives them.

Of course, a sexual situation is a "given" element in almost every story. The shows fly off the charts with it. Surprisingly, parents don't seem to be complaining. Not even when Willow, the lesbian character on *Buffy*, made seductive, sensual moves on her college friend. Nothing. Not a peep from parents! When the lesbian theme was first introduced on this show, the writers were braced for complaints. But instead they received letters encouraging Willow to be "more gay."

Either parents don't care, don't think it's an issue, or simply don't understand the destructive influence it is having on the youth of America. I admit *Buffy* is one of the best-looking shows on TV. It's well produced, has an appealing cast, funny dialogue, good writing, and witty "Buffyisms" that teens relate to. Sarah Michelle Gellar is a trend-setter. It's hip, unique, trendy, and highly appealing. Would (or will) your child choose this program over most others at that time? Probably.

So What? It's Just Pretend!

Do these occult shows affect kids or teenagers in real life? A fifteen-year-old girl in Tulsa, Oklahoma, was suspended from school for putting a hex on her teacher. The school had previously suspended her after confiscating short stories she had written, including one that described a shooting on a school bus. So what did she do? She is suing the school in federal court. The American Civil Liberties Union says officials of Union Public School Independent District No. 9 violated Brandi Blackbear's right to due process when they accused her of casting a spell that made a teacher ill and suspended her for fifteen days. School system lawyer Jerry Richardson denied that Blackbear was sanctioned for a hex but would not give details, citing confidentiality rules.

WWF & THE WRESTLING RAGE

A pimp character offers a wrestler his "choice of any one of these fine hos [whores] for the whole night." The wrestler says, "I don't do hos. You got any farm animals? No, no, no, hey, don't look at me like I'm a freak. They're not alive."   —WWF Smackdown!

It is violence of the worst nature, cruel perversion of the worst kind, an insult to the word *sport,* and the equivalent to twenty-first-century gladiators performing near death spectacles to please the cheering crowds. It is fury unleashed, rewarding those who jeer the loudest with a bloody victim, a public pummeling, and a beaten and battered body. The whole ordeal is extremely degrading to the human spirit. It is sexual exhibition of the most disgusting kind, man's defilement of man, and woman's debasement of other females. Worst of all, it is only a click away from your children.

It is believed that much of the violent content attributed to teen violence in youth today is brought to you by the World Wrestling Federation program *WWF Smackdown!* The WWF is viewed weekly by around 1.5 million children, ages 2-11, and another 1.5 million teens under 18.[9] The violence, language, and sexual humiliation of men and women have never been more graphically abused than what we see on *WWF Smackdown!* and other wrestling shows like it. Statistic after statistic is being stacked against these shows as reports come in from across the country about copycat wrestling matches taking place in backyards, murders being committed, and accidents claiming the lives of children who were imitating wrestler/actor moves.

Ask most junior high boys who "Stone Cold" Steve Austin, The Rock, or Goldberg are, and they can probably tell you. Kids watching *WWF Smackdown!* have not only propelled the popularity of wrestling but have empowered their financial power as well.

The two major pro outfits—World Wrestling Federation and World Championship Wrestling—insist they are not responsible for the violence that's taking place among young children and teens in backyards and homes across America. The critics, however, are loud, concerned, and strongly appealing to these organizations to change their ways. The response has been an ad campaign with a gruff-looking WWF wrestler saying, "Don't try this at home. Leave the danger to us."

Right! What kid is going to pay attention to that? In fact, backyard wrestling is more popular than ever, and more and more deaths and accidents are being reported, giving credit or blame to kids mimicking the pros.

Road Dogg pulls Mankind's arm between his legs, then goes behind him and simulates anal sex.   —*WWF Smackdown!*

DON'T TRY THIS AT HOME!

The November 1999 *Insider* reported on a seven-year-old Dallas boy who killed his three-year-old brother by performing a "clothesline" move "that he had seen his wrestling heroes perform on TV."

In Broward County, Florida, twelve-year-old Lionel Tate was charged with first-degree murder in the death of a playmate, six-year-old Tiffany Eunick. According to the *Fort Lauderdale Sun-Sentinel,* Tate told psychiatrist Joel Klass that he had been copying wrestling moves he had seen on TV. Tate's lawyer said the boy was practicing a ring maneuver when he accidentally threw the forty-eight-pound girl into a steel staircase instead of the couch. "He didn't mean to hurt her," said lawyer Jim Lewis. "The child was watching wrestling, and then he was acting it out."[10]

Responding to doubts about this defense, Lewis responds, "Well, I think what you've got to do is turn on wrestling as we know it today. Turn on the WWF and the WCW. See how they market to children. See how they expose the children to violence, what I call 'violence without consequences,' where these guys beat up on each other, and when the match is over they simply get up and walk away. Children can't always understand that. . . . I've had people from all over this country . . . call me and tell me at day-care centers they have little kids body-slamming each other from what they saw on television."[11]

In Hudson County, Georgia, a four-year-old child jumped up and down on a fifteen-month-old baby and killed him after their baby-sitter left to go buy some cigarettes. The baby-sitter had put on a WWF video to entertain the children while he was gone. According to *Court TV,* the prosecutor believes the four-year-old was mimicking what he saw on the wrestling video, and also believes the child thought he could do what he was doing without permanently harming the baby.

In Yakima, Washington, twelve-year-old Jason Whala, an avid wrestling fan, killed his nineteen-month-old cousin William Sweet with a "Jackknife Power Bomb" (what the move is now referred to by the WWF) when he wouldn't stop crying. The move involved Jason picking William up over his head, turning the little child toward him, and slamming him to the ground. Jason was convicted of second-degree felony murder. Jason's attorney, Adam Moore, says, "Parents should wake up. This is a wake-up call. Don't let your little boys watch that [wrestling] or do so at grave risk."[12]

With all of the denials that are made, the truth is still evident—the WWF and other violent shows like it have influenced the killing of our children!

One wrestler throws another into the wall several times. The second hits the first over the head with a metal pail, then in the neck with a metal pole.
—*WWF Smackdown!*

Backyard Fun

Whatever happened to a friendly neighborhood game of softball, basketball, or football? Today's "extreme" kids and teenagers, who want to taste the blood of the sport for themselves, are engaging in "backyard wrestling"—an elaborate parody of TV's pro-wrestling extravaganzas, only with all of the dangers and risks.

Jersey All-Pro Wrestling director Frank Shapiro says he's trained for years to fall in just the right way. "This may sound funny," he says, "but you have to practice being hit with a chair. These kids don't know what they're doing, and it's a serious problem."[13]

Backyard Wrestling Incorporated compiles "best of videos from clubs nationwide." "It's physical, but it's good because it allows kids to role-play and be outrageous characters. It's all entertainment," insists Rick Mahr, who owns the company. "You just want to imitate it, like a little kid wants to imitate action heroes," says one of Extreme Hardcores's wrestlers. "It's just something to do," chimes in his sixteen-year-old ring mate, Jarid Konowski. "For us, it's just fun, man!" But "BYW,"[14] as aficionados affectionately call it, is increasingly becoming a blood sport. For example, members of Extreme Hardcore increased the gore factor by lining the ring with barbed wire, forcing themselves to bleed all over the ring for dramatic effect.

In suburbs across America, teenage boys have converted their backyards into makeshift wrestling rings. Armed with chairs, tables, barbed wire, even staple guns, and razor blades hidden in their gloves, they battle for supremacy, mimicking the moves of their superstar heroes. But it's a definition of "fun" that calls for beating the living daylights out of one another, with points awarded for creativity. Throwing chairs, leaping off garage roofs, and "pile-driving" opponents into the ground headfirst are some of the most common moves.

A backyard wrestler who found out the hard way was John Nunziato from Chicago. When his opponent pulled the "tombstone pile-driver" on him, Nunziato's head hit the concrete and broke his neck. His "it's just fun" fight landed him in the emergency room, where surgeons had to replace one of his vertebrae with part of his hip bone. He went through months of rehabilitation before learning to walk again.

Is the potential for physical danger and harm even worse? Dr. Joseph Zanga, a Chicago pediatrician who studies children's reaction to TV violence, says, "Paralysis, loss of speech, loss of memory—even death. I saw that potential there," he warns. With over 400 backyard leagues with their own Web sites and an Internet search for the phrase yielding a whopping 16,000 matches, you do the math.[15]

I Am Woman, Hear Me Roar

To borrow a phrase from Helen Reddy's "I Am Woman" anthem, I doubt women have the WWF or WOW in mind when thinking about the possibilities open to them in the twenty-first century. But unfortunately there are many stepping into the ring these days to "get discovered." Chyna has been the well-known prominent figure in women's wrestling, proudly displaying her gargantuan body in *Playboy* and declaring her physique "beautiful." But Chyna's not alone; in fact, she's spawned a string of wanna-be's. Bobbi Billard is an aspiring model/actress/Internet star, racing toward her big break in television. She's strong-willed, savvy, and already making a six-figure income. In the ring Billard flaunts being a "sexy warrior" and has earned the role of "Summer," bringing the *Baywatch* look to the Women of Wrestling circuit. She high kicks women in the sternum and gets head-butted, hoping she'll be the next big pop-culture phenomenon. WOW consists mainly of women mud wrestling, wet T-shirt contests, and good and evil role-playing, where the women put each other through headlocks, half nelsons, drop kicks, airplane spins, and choke holds. Billard's main reason for doing this sport? She hopes that "someone will notice me."

Jarrett, a male wrestler, throws Ivory, a female character, into a mud-wrestling ring. Miss Kitty, another female character, enters the ring, which is surrounded by shouting spectators, and attacks Ivory. They pull each other's hair, push and punch each other as they each attempt to pull the other's clothes off. During the match, Ivory pulls off Miss Kitty's bikini top. Though she is covered in mud and moves to try to cover herself, her breasts are visible.
                                                        —WWF Smackdown!

What Do Parents Think?

Surprisingly, some parents not only go along with it but actively support it. A father in the audience at one of the Extreme Hardcore matches in Ohio brushed off concerns for his child's safety. "Boys will be boys," he said. "There are going to be some bumps along the way, but I don't think that there will be anything major."

Just try telling that to John Nunziato's mother, Roberta. When her son broke his neck, they didn't know if he'd ever walk again. "Wake up!" she urges. "How can you be so incredibly stupid? Look what happened to my son? Do you want that to happen to your child?"

"The abundance of violent and vulgar programs—led by *WWF Smackdown!*—makes it clear that networks and the advertisers who sponsor such programs continue to refuse to address the negative impact that this kind of programming is having on our nation's children," said L. Brent Bozell, Chairman of the Parents Television Council (PTC).[16]

NOTE: The World Wrestling Federation filed a federal lawsuit against the PTC and its chairman, alleging that the watchdog group uses scare tactics to get advertisers to drop sponsorship of the WWF's popular shows, including UPN's *Smackdown!* The WWF seeks an injunction to stop the "unlawful" behavior. Bozell has threatened to counter sue for libel and says, "The allegations are completely without merit."

THE MORE BAD MOVIES, BAD TV SHOWS, AND BAD MUSIC I hear, the dumber I think it's making America.

—MARILYN MANSON, singer/ghoul-rocker[1]

IT REALLY IS AN ART AS OPPOSED TO A SCIENCE. Our mandate is to sell as many records and as many artists as we can. It's not like we have a macro vision to plunder and pillage the "tween" market.

—BARRY WEISS, Jive record label president[2]

The Media, Music, and MTV

THE MEDIA

t's been said that those who control the media control the culture. And nowhere is this fact more evident than in the United States of America. If you watch the evening news, listen to talk radio, played a CD, read a newspaper, look at a magazine, log on to the Internet, catch a movie, read a billboard, or play a video game, you have been touched by or at least influenced by the media. It is so strong and so pervasive in our society that it is impossible to shield yourself or your children from its manipulative grasp.

So who is it that is designating our country's media pace? Just how often does the media affect us? We watch the television and daily news stories about a gang shooting, a family murder, crimes of passion, or teen violence, and they are eerily beginning to reflect the movies we see, the music we listen to, the TV shows we watch, and even the magazines and books we read. In this chapter I touch on a few media formats that heavily influence our culture, society, and even our human nature. But I barely scratch the surface on how much is truly influencing our lives and families. Parents need to know that these little bits of influence that your children and teenagers meditate on (whether it's TV, the news, radio, MTV, or music) collectively affect the way they behave, what they believe in, and how they conduct themselves.

NEWS

We live in a world where everything is news. It used to be that for something to make the news, it had to be newsworthy, an event, a bizarre occurrence, or an out-of-the-ordinary happening. These days, our entertainment, music, politics, sports, and everyday life are reported on the television news programs twenty-four hours a day, seven days a week, whether or not it's "news worthy." Our media-saturated society craves broadcasts about anything and everything, from pop stars to naming stars. Whatever is interesting, unique, and pop culture is what we have become by watching it all day and all night.

Remember that when you view the world through the presentation of any news format, that media is competing for the best and most influential coverage and is often bringing a one-sided bias or political view. Numerous times in recent years the news media has manipulated certain events or situations based on misinformation and fear, resulting in the public reacting to that fear. That manipulation has thrown a presidential election into overtime, induced riots (the '90s Rodney King beating and subsequent looting and burning of Los Angeles after the trial), mass hysteria (who can forget the Y2K propaganda and the weirdest New Years Eve ever?), and violence (victory celebrations after sporting events, gang shootings) that directly affected our society. These reports and the media's preoccupation with creating hype and fear have been responsible for inspiring numerous copycat crimes of the same nature.

Sleaze Leads

Judging by our contemporary society, we seem to be constantly conditioned for bad news. The media has done an excellent job of keeping us in a daily state of fear with an "if it bleeds, it leads" emphasis on the news. This has created a mind-set of fear that readily accepts anything these major networks and cable news have to say. In turn, fear appears to be the biggest commodity the evening news can use to boost their ratings. But sleaze has become a polished addition that's also proven it can get ratings. Fear and sleaze are two key areas parents need to guard their young impressionable children from when watching the news.

Another topic that gets prime coverage is the random shootings that take place at our schools. Kids as young as eight are pulling guns in schools and committing "copycat Columbine" style killing sprees. I realize these horrible events need to be covered, but sadly it's that very heavy television coverage that's appealing to many kids and blurring the lines of reality and bringing serious repercussions on them and their families. In order to get their "fifteen minutes" of fame on national news, they are willing to do the unthinkable.

The more that local and national news cross the boundaries of human decency and good taste, the closer they come to subliminally giving ideas to impressionable children who then "act out" or "react" to that information.

Minorities and Network News

Minority correspondents and women have had their ups and downs as far as landing secure jobs on the network news. With all of the movie story lines using women as news anchors, being able to find a real one on TV is harder than it used to be. Minorities and women have a small disproportionate presence on national nightly news, while white males continue to dominate the newscasts. Hollywood seems to have a bigger vision for women and minorities as correspondents and anchors in movies than the major networks and cable stations do in real life.

False Truth

In *Psychonomic Bulletin & Review,* a study was reported of one hundred college students who were asked to remember facts from a series of slides showing a crime.[3] After inaccurate information was given along with the truth, researchers discovered that misinformation is more likely to register over time with people and be remembered as the factual thing. As the memory of true information tends to blur, people not only recall the false information, but they judge it as the truth. This changes not only the factual truth but the standard of truth as well. The study will help to explain how "false memories" derived from events seen on television, the news, and in the paper end up becoming recalled as facts of truth.

In a society that is bombarded with a surplus of information, experts are beginning to wonder just how much of what some people recall as factual actually happened. Or might it be attributed to "false memories"? If our country had a moral and ethical standard of truth that was inherently a part of all our lives, these kinds of ridiculous studies wouldn't be necessary. This report only verifies what I've said all along: the media really does have a seductive power over many of our lives, enough to make some lie about it!

Radio

The radio is one of the most powerful forms of media we have today. Although television and the Internet are wonderful visual tools, the radio reaches more people on a local and national level in a more intimate way. The interesting fact about radio is that you *never* know who's listening. I've done radio shows where the range of callers on a topic has varied from people like you and me to celebrities, famous athletes, witches, pedophiles, drug addicts, criminals, and very famous religious leaders. Radio provides a truly great forum for participating in our popular culture. Not only is it a venue for popular music, disc jockeys, radio personalities, and contests, but talk radio has emerged on the scene bigger and more competitive than ever before.

Teenagers turn to the radio as an upbeat escape, a popular force they embrace, and a touchstone to energize their world. Many identify with their peers by carrying around a boom box, the latest Walkman, or hand-held techno-invention. But adults are just as involved in identifying with a favorite music station or one that has talk show hosts or a talk format. Radio brings popular culture into our homes, cars, offices, the beach, park, just about anywhere one can carry a radio.

Our twenty-first-century children have been indoctrinated with radio from birth, and many kindergartners can recite the latest lyrics while carrying the tunes to Eminem, Britney Spears, Christina Aguilera, Backstreet Boys, or any other latest hip wonder. One day I overheard a little girl of about six singing, "Hit me baby one more time, Oh baby, baby . . ." She obviously had no idea what she was singing about. But those lyrics are a powerful tool in the minds of impressionable children and teens. The words they sing over and over and the tunes that they meditate on as they play them all day are what subtly shape, affect, and dominate your child's mind.

Almost 97% of twelve- to nineteen-year-olds listen to the radio in a given week. Of all teens, 60% own a portable radio or boom box, and 58% own a small stereo.[4] The peek radio time for teens to listen to radio takes place between 6 and 10 A.M., when they're getting ready and going to school. A music format is the most popular, so most stations concentrate on "morning drive" teams or hosts, because this format has proven to be popular with all ages. Whether it's in their room, on the Internet, in a car, at work, at a friend's house, or on the beach, they listen to an average of two hours of radio a day during the weekdays and five hours on the weekends.

Talk Radio

There's one thing we love to do more than anything, and that's talk. We will talk about anything—our kids, marital affairs, racial issues, politics (Clinton provided so much fodder we still can't stop talking about the man), and pretty much whatever else pops up in the news. Statistics show that people who spend at least one hour a day listening to talk radio are much more informed than people who don't. Talk radio has become a popular forum for delving into the topics du jour and letting people vent about the issues that concern them. But it has also become a levy for our "pop culture" mentality because it gives the select minority interest groups (racial, conservative, special interest, faith based) a chance to be heard and proclaim what they hold to be true.

Talk radio has been around in Los Angeles for thirty years. What began in counseling offices in the '80s with a "me" decade of exploring "dysfunctional issues," justifying behavior, and self-centered attitudes and actions spilled over into the '90s with everyone wanting to talk about it. The popularity increased in the '90s when it became an extension of what was happening on late-night talk formats (Arsenio, Letterman, *The Tonight Show*) and the daytime smorgasbord (Phil Donahue, Jerry Springer, Oprah, Sally, and others). Yes, America has mastered the art of talking, but along with the addicts who can't wait to get their two cents in, there's a silent majority who just loves to listen.

The way you make it big in this industry is to find your niche. Rush Limbaugh discovered his niche in being a self-proclaimed "gift on loan from God" and defender of patriotic American values. Dr. Laura Schlessinger burst on the scene when there were few other women who were hosting local or national shows. Her in-your-face truth was just what the doctor ordered, and her quick solutions to major problems earned her respect from men and women alike. People wanted to be told to be their "kid's mom," "stop shacking up!" and "go take on the day." Now the talk radio industry is a competitive market with many well-known hosts vying for popularity and national exposure. From the conservative to the liberal, hosts such as Dennis Prager, Michael Medved, Imus, and Larry Elder have opened new pathways for talk shows to expand with unique formats and plenty of intelligent dialogue and views.

My Story

In the early '90s I had been a movie critic for *The Orange County Register* for a couple of years when a morning drive team, *Tim & Al*, on KBRT AM asked me to come on their show and discuss family films. It went so well that the program director, Ann Harrison, gave me the opportunity to do a movie review show called *Holly on Hollywood*. When that show grew in popularity, I enjoyed adding a woman's touch to morning talk with a show called *For Women Only*.

After a few years I moved to KKLA in Los Angeles, where the general manager, Dave Armstrong, saw a niche I could fill and gave me a chance with a four-hour talk show called *Saturday Night With Holly McClure*. I reviewed movies, interviewed celebrities, authors, musical guests, and took local calls. I even took my children up to the station with me and have fond memories of those early years. Eventually I hosted a daily show called *Real Talk*, but eventually I left the LA market for sunny San Diego.

In between writing my column and doing TV movie reviews, I host a daily drive show called *Holly McClure Live* on KPRZ in San Diego (a sister station to KKLA) and have been extremely happy working for one of the best general managers in the business. Talk radio is only as good as the on-air talent, and I am fortunate to work for a man who knows how to put it all together and make it work. Mark Larson is not only one of the funniest men I've ever met, but truly one of the kindest in a business that's not always kind, especially to women.

My motto is "Positive Talk With Passion and Purpose" as I interview guests, discuss the latest topics, and take calls from San Diego listeners. I have kept *Holly on Hollywood* on Saturday nights and enjoy every day that I'm on, because you never know who's listening!

Shock Radio

Since the beginning of radio, there have been DJs who have pushed the envelope for many reasons. Usually when they do, they are fired because public opinion weighs in heavily with concern from local advertisers. There has been one, however, who seems to have beaten the system and remains on the air, spewing his vile, sexually perverted, and twisted sense of humor across the airwaves aimed directly at your teenager's ears. Perhaps no other DJ has tested the patience of parents and the limits of the FCC more than Howard Stern. Stern's blatant pitch to grab your teenager seems to have worked because he's still on the air, but his popularity is waning. When he took his radio show to TV, he caused so much controversy with his X-rated pornography topics that only thirty-six of the original seventy-nine TV stations still carry him.

MUSIC

Music has become an integral part of the soundtrack to our daily lives. Volumes could be written on the different styles of music and the many different ways music has influenced and continues to dramatically affect our culture. While I can't devote that kind of time or space to the subject, suffice it to say not a day goes by where the average person doesn't hear some form of music.

Whenever I hear a song from my past, I smile at the memories it invokes and the feelings it stirs. Music has moved me to repent in church, cry for joy at a wedding, sing in my car, dance with my kids, motivate me at a sporting event, weep over a relationship, and inspire a romantic moment. Who can honestly say they haven't been moved by music? Married couples usually have a song from the era when they met that they call "their song." Teenage girls have a medley of favorites that move them emotionally, and the guys have their favorites blaring from their car, truck, or boom box.

We know that music has a strong influence on our culture and a certain power and ability to define reality and life. It can easily influence and shape adolescents and teens (especially their behaviors), but this influence is not new. For many years musical artists have influenced teenagers with their clothing (Cher with her bell-bottoms, Marky Mark and his "sagging" pants), hairstyles (Elvis, the Beatles), language ("street slang," rap, and hip-hop), and behavior (many white kids act and even talk "black" these days). Kids are quick to lock into a group or pop icon who caters to their adolescent image and needs (witness the phenomenon of Madonna passing her torch to Britney.) It is from their own taste in music that teenagers are able to help define their image.

The music industry entered the millennium with a wide range of artists and so many diverse styles that it's hard to say where our eclectic and fickle tastes lie. From Britney Spears, Ricky Martin, and Destiny's Child to 'NSync, Backstreet Boys, Eminem, Faith Hill, Jennifer Lopez, and don't forget Bob Dylan and the Beatles.

My job is to raise my kids and explain to them the difference between entertainment and reality, and other parents need to do the same thing.
—LL Cool J, rapper [5]

New Ways to Hear Music

Sadly the days of Dick Clark and Casey Kasem introducing teens to their favorite tunes are over. From the age of toddlers on up, kids are exposed to more music through Nickelodeon, Disney, and other cable channels that play music videos than any other generation. Hollywood has also learned how important music is to promoting their movie industry. Oftentimes a movie is defined and remembered just as much for the musical soundtrack it's promoting as it is for the movie itself. Multi-artist releases such as *Down To Earth, Valentine,* and *O Brother* are soundtracks from movies compiled with different artists to hopefully sell that movie. Teenagers are constantly singing the praises of a current movie's soundtrack, and that word of mouth alone can help promote a movie more than any advertising could do.

Television shows have also caught on to how important music soundtracks are in selling their shows. *Malcolm in the Middle, WWF All-Stars, Dawson's Creek, Ally McBeal, Buffy the Vampire Slayer, Angel,* and many more use artists to move the story line and sell records all at the same time. MTV was one of the original cultivators of using music videos to promote an artist, and that visual stimulation combined with the artist singing their song has revolutionized the recording industry.

And don't leave the Internet out! It has also become a new source of revenue for the music industry with the advantage of promoting artists and their soundtracks in the convenience of a listener's home. Unfortunately, the Internet has also created a huge headache for the music industry with a company called Napster (created by a teenager) that found a way to spread the music around without paying for it. Mega legal bills later, Napster was legally forced to shut down and stop its operation from sending out current artists' music, leaving millions of fans who enriched their music library disappointed.

Rock is a niche market now needing to be reinvigorated by cool bands. But many feel that the public is starting to get tired of the wanna-be's—both rock and otherwise. Creativity is on the comeback, and poetry in music is likewise a commodity many see a resurgence of in the music scene today.

Oh, Baby, Baby!

If you're a baby boomer who rocked to groups in the '60s and '70s, then started to feel disconnected through the '80s and lost touch with what group was hot or not in the '90s, move over. Gen-Y kids are in the house and in control of what's happening in the music scene. Gen-Yers are spending the money, and that makes them one of the first generations that record companies and marketers have and are bombarding with specific marketing. Fan base for groups like 'NSync, Backstreet Boys, Britney Spears, and others are now starting at about five years old. It's become very clear that entertainment companies are catering to our kids.

Boomers relied on radio and eight-track tapes to keep them happy. Gen-Xers had their Walkmans and MTV. And Gen-Yers? They have it all—radio, MTV, CDs, the Internet, TV, cable, and whatever technology exists today and/or is created within an eighteen-month period. The Gen-Y generation are the purchasing power in music today. The Gen-Y kids have more money and outspend previous generations on more music products than ever before, which is why the Gen-Y kids will change the face of music in the not-so-distant years to come. There's a movement to hook kids at a much earlier age who are passionate about music. A generation ago kids would not have had their first concert experience until about the age of eleven or twelve, but now they're going at age five and six. We've developed a whole generation of young music consumers who are just too important to ignore, as stated in *Seventeen* magazine (whose audience starts at about age eleven).

But take heart, what started out with the Spice Girls in 1997 has continued with groups like 'NSync (who hold the record for opening week album sales of 2.31 million),[6] Backstreet Boys, and artists such as Britney Spears, Christina Aguilera, Ricky Martin, and Destiny's Child. These are groups and artists that parents and kids can enjoy together. Bubblegum or teen-pop (mostly composed of sex appeal, good times, and having fun) have overtaken the industry and sell more than real musical talent these days.

But those times may soon be changing once these teens hit an older age. The genres may soon be blurring, and kids will start to embrace more diverse artists and actually hearken back to music with a message and a real beat. While younger kids enjoy the glamour, choreography, rhythmic driven beats and hip-hop, the older teens are into bands that play their own instruments as do Papa Roach, The Deftones, Incubus, and others.

How will these artists fare in the future? Michael Jackson is a good example of an artist who started out as a kid, and as he grew into manhood, his music grew with him. Britney seems to be spreading her teen wings and leaping into womanhood with her edgy lyrics, skimpy clothing, songs that are changing with her image, and sponsors such as Pepsi that are transitioning her from teen star to pop star.

The Voices Behind the Power

Just as writers and directors in the movie industry have had to do (Kevin Williamson for *Scream*, Oliver Stone for *Natural Born Killers*), musical artists have likewise had to defend themselves over just how much their music has influenced the actions of teens. There is a cause-and-effect relationship between media violence, including MTV's violent videos, and real-life violence. Numerous stories about teens committing suicide or murdering other teens have brought certain artists such as Marilyn Manson, Ozzy Osbourne, and others into focus and to task because of their music's influence. What may surprise you is what some of these artists are like when they're not on stage. Who they are on stage and the music they prefer may just be an act, albeit a vulgar and convincing one, to make money just the same.

Poster Child for Evil

Marilyn Manson is an oxymoron. He revels in contradictions, likes to stir things up, likes to watch *The O'Reilly Factor* on the Fox News Channel, and although he doesn't always agree with the conservative host, he admires him. He also likes to watch tawdry daytime talk shows and see "how backward humans have gone on the evolutionary chart." What offends Manson the most? Bad grammar. Surprised? There's more. Manson doesn't like excessive swearing or rap music, doesn't smoke, and is close to his parents. "They're very proud that I'm doing something that I enjoy. My mom was always a big Elvis fan, so it works out. I'm kind of her version of Elvis."[7] Manson obviously delights in his creepiness and knows he's an unorthodox version.

But what this part ghoul/part O'Reilly does on stage is what has caused problems. Manson has spent a lot of time thinking up ways to offend people, and it's evident in his concerts. He has urinated on groupies, spit on strangers, behaved like an animal, collects prosthetic limbs, and has even stolen bones out of a New Orleans graveyard and smoked them in his pipe.

A favorite whipping boy for parents and politicians, Manson and his confrontational music became easy targets after the massacre in April 1999 at the Colorado high school, where two teen boys killed twelve classmates and a teacher before turning their guns on themselves. In May 1999 Manson wrote an essay for *Rolling Stone* magazine, responding to the bad reputation his music had gotten. "The name Marilyn Manson," he wrote, "has never celebrated the sad fact that America puts killers on the cover of *Time* magazine, giving them as much notoriety as our favorite movie stars." He added, "I'm a controversial artist, one who dares to have an opinion and bothers to create music and videos that challenge people's ideas in a world that is watered-down and hollow. There's a real fine line between entertainers and mass exposure through the media where people know they can get their picture on the cover of *Time* or *Newsweek* by doing something outrageous, either as an artist or by hurting someone. They will always put the killer on the cover before they put the victim, because it's more dramatic for them to help sell fear."

Disputing the notion that violent art leads to violent acts, Manson says, "You can't blame people's behavior on books, music, film, and video games, which are important outlets for emotions. Growing up, I always escaped to music if things got too hard to deal with. When you take away the things people identify with, you create these little time bombs that eventually explode. People feel smothered when they aren't heard."[8] That same year he received a 1999 Grammy nomination.

Who and why does he do all of those repulsive things? Because teenage boys and adult males seem to really love it. "Until you turn eighteen, you don't really have any rights, so in a sense you don't really have a soul. You're not really a person, and I think that's how a lot of teenagers feel in America." Obviously, that's how Manson felt.[9]

His Poster Twin

Eminem has been labeled "the most compelling figure in pop music" by *Newsweek* (5/29/00).[10] He has stretched the mainstream's patience to the limits, and his controversial lyrics, while earning him three Grammys in 2001, also earned him a protested spotlight with Elton John. His rage-filled lyrics lash out against his single mother (whom he describes as "real, stereotypical trailer park, white trash"), his wife (who divorced him in the spring of 2001), gays, pop-rock, and anything else he can sing about. And who is Slim Shady (from his album with the same name)? Slim Shady is his "evil side, the sarcastic, foul mouthed side" (www.ubl.com) that gives him a chance to "take what was wrong with my life and turn it back on others" (*Newsweek*, 5/29/00).[11] He concludes by saying, "Slim Shady is a name for my temper and/or anger. Eminem is just the rapper, Marshall Mathers is who I am at the end of the day."

So what's so bad about this white guy with an urge to rap? His lyrics are appalling, shocking, offensive, and disturbing. I won't print the words to his songs in this book, but if you would like to see where you could get them, I have references at the end of this chapter.[12] One of his songs was written to his daughter, describing how he would kill her mother. Another song describes his account of going to a rave party, getting high on mushrooms with a girl, but then she dies and he's sorry. There are others, but you get the idea. Eminem is a lonely man who never knew his father and is lashing out at the world he felt mistreated him.

I can't begin to name all the controversial groups and artists in the music scene today, but there are several that deserve mention because of their sexual or violent messages. Your children take in more than just the tune or medley. Only you can be a discerning parent and detect that at a young age. Please refer to my Parental Guidance section for more information on how you can be equipped with information on different artists and their influence on your kids and teens.

Music Porn

That's right! Snoop Dogg has struck up a deal to market his rap music with X-rated pornography packaged to say "Doggy Style." The deal is with Larry Flynt and *Hustler Magazine* and will only be sold to teenagers over eighteen. However, it will be marketed on MTV and other prime stations that advertise to kids and teens *well under* that age, so guess who's going to see borderline pornography flashed across your TV screens compliments of Snoop Dogg!

MTV

I remember in the late '70s when disco dominated the music scene. Once John Travolta appeared in *Saturday Night Fever* and struck that famous pose in a white suit, the Bee Gees, Barry White, K.C. and the Sunshine Band, Michael Jackson, and numerous black artists were mostly what people were listening to. Disco ruled our culture, and with that trend, sales in the pop music industry fell. Other music styles, studio musicians, artists, and record companies were desperate for someone or something to save them, and that saving grace came in the form of MTV.

When my daughter was born in August 1981, I remember seeing television reports on a phenomenon that was revolutionizing and energizing the music industry. MTV was a new channel that showed music videos 24/7, and I remember thinking, *What a great idea and way to sell music!* And it was. The only problem was the controversy the videos were causing. Once I ordered cable, I saw what the excitement was all about.

I Want My MTV

On August 1, 1981, MTV began its programming just after midnight with a music video that would forever change the way we "listen" to music and become an in-your-face power that would directly influence our kids and teenagers. From that moment on, the youth of America would "watch" their music, and adults would marvel at the appeal and strange power the new "visual" music would have over their children. Our popular culture has never been the same.

In that first year, MTV reached only 1.5 million homes with limited cable. But with an active campaign (remember "I want my MTV!") and a target audience of twelve- to twenty-four-year-olds, within a year they were well on their way! Today, MTV reaches over 300 million households worldwide, with the largest percentage of the audience between the ages of twelve and seventeen.[13] With possibly over seventy million of those kids attracted to its fast-paced style of programming and advertising, MTV is one of the more powerful and influential forces in the media world today. In fact, the brains behind the network knew that the key to MTV's success would be appealing to the culture of kids who grew up watching TV, listening to music, doing their homework, and talking on the phone at the same time.

These are multistimuli kids who emotionally connect with the MTV format and have adapted to the barrage of images thrown at them in rapid-fire succession. Advertisers have picked up on the MTV style of marketing and lavish products with a loud soundtrack, youthful actors, and lots of camera angles, helping MTV to yield over $100 million in yearly profits and creating an accepted worldwide culture. This culture is made up of a youthful generation that seems to delight in getting away with what the previous generation didn't, and it's evident in every aspect of their marketing and programming. Pushing the envelope of moral decency with defiant, shocking, in-your-face programming is what MTV is all about.

The Influence

MTV revolutionized the music industry in the '80s and '90s with its materialism and capability to sell and design musical artists with visual appeal. That appeal has ended up being one of the most destructive and lethal influences to our youth culture that's on television today. The MTV brand has influenced or touched just about every record company, studio, agent, and industry tycoon in the business. Scoring a slot on MTV is a guarantee of name recognition and eventual sales success. Because this notoriety comes quickly, many artists are developing and marketing a "look" instead of true talent with choreography, clothing, exotic locations, elaborate sets, sexual steam, and women—lots of women. These formulas seem to sell and work well with MTV, whether a group has any talent or not.

Soundtracks became a popular way to sell and promote movies, which eventually led to marketing movies in a whole new way in the '90s. In many cases those soundtracks carried the movie that was made around it (*Fame, Flashdance, Footloose, Salsa, Cool As Ice,* and

Dance With Me). It worked so well that MTV is now releasing its own movies.

In January 2001, *Save the Last Dance*, a hip-hop meets *Dirty Dancing* movie, boogied to the tune of $60 million before its international release. Using the soundtrack has become the way many studios are trying to sell their horrible movies, especially to the teen crowd. Parents should be aware that the soundtrack may be the reason your teenager has an urge to see a bad movie.

MTV has also put a new face on popular music with its televised concerts to raise public awareness, money, and make a difference on social issues. *Live Aid* in 1985 and shows like *Unplugged* in 1989, featuring legendary artists such as Eric Clapton, LL Cool J, and many more, were huge events. And in 1995, MTV had its first Video Music Awards, which are now known for their outlandish outfits, crazy artists, and bizarre, rude, and offensive behavior.

Selling Sex & Violence

What is the youth culture mostly watching on MTV? Music videos are the main attraction with their overtly perverted sexual themes, vulgar messages that objectify women, rage against authority figures, degradation and demeaning of minorities, and the constant perpetuation of promiscuity. Singers and rappers (Dr. Dre, Big Boi, Sisqo, D'Angelo, and many more) seductively woo and seduce women (usually almost nude and gyrating around the singers) with sexual, chauvinist lyrics. Those suggestive lyrics deliver soft pornography that's visually stimulating and many times borders on X-rated.

The backlash against the male influence that used to dominate the market has come in the form of female singers and rappers (such as Lil' Kim, Britney Spears, Toni Braxton, Christina Aguilera, and Madonna) who, with their own style of lyrics, make it clear they are sexually in control. In fact, these post-Madonna women are clearly at the top of the market because of their sex appeal and appeal to sex. Many times the artists deliver their own personal and political messages. Tori Amos sang her message against sexual abuse, and Madonna's entire blond ambition tour had a message promoting sex.

Most of the videos that get airplay on MTV feature or include illicit or implied sex, objectification, dominance, implicit aggression between male and female, and at least one occurrence of violence in

60% of them.[14] The lyrics, videos, celebrity focus, and constant messages of sexual freedom are a strong lure for teenagers who have their hormones kicking in, and the violent messages have unfortunately influenced many youth.

Rap music has become a cry for the urban message, mixing anger with hopelessness and pain in lyrics that promote violence. The angry attitude, clothing, and even rappers' language have influenced a generation of kids who mimic their style.

Yes, sex and violence sell. But should it be sold to children? To latchkey kids who listen and watch while they do their homework? To preteens who watch in their bedrooms and emotionally connect with the sensual appeal? To older teens with spendable income who are fed seductive advertising mixed with music around the clock? Perhaps no other influence in our society has changed our youth worldwide as dramatically and as much as MTV.

He watches VH1 all day and gratifies himself. Whitney Houston, Madonna, Jennifer Lopez. —Snoops, ABC

More MTV

MTV has moved far from its music video roots. Its hedonistic programming and sexual themes have expanded to irreverent shows, specials, regular programs, and features that take pride in edgy, unusual programming. From the grotesque (a man winning a contest for the biggest stool sample) to the weird (nude contestants run around the Las Vegas strip, others had to eat the whipped cream covering off their mates) to the idiotic (spring break nude fests).

Then there are the "regular" shows. What began with a music show, *Unplugged* in October 1989, has morphed into shows that delight in delving into the sexually twisted, humanly perverted, and really strange. Kids love this type of programming and let their parents think MTV is just about music. If parents would watch even a couple of these shows, they would be shocked and a lot more protective.

The most popular show on MTV today is *TRL*, Carson Daly's music schmooze fest, featuring artists and entertainers who come together in a small room that overlooks his fans on the street in downtown New York City. This show is what *all* the kids and teens watch these days. It's so popular it's even getting mentioned in movies.

The Andy Dick Show features Andy parading as different characters with disgusting, twisted topics (usually about body parts) and perverted situations (usually involving bodily functions) that push decency to the edge.

Real World is a ridiculous show that gained popularity because it was the first taste of "reality TV." Unfortunately, you take a group of twenty-somethings and stick them in a furnished home with luxury and goofy challenges, and all you get is unreal situations with unrealistic people. MTV's *Undressed* is devoted entirely to showing couples in their twenties having sex in a soap opera style plot and setting. The sex can take place between a girl and boy, boy with boy, girl with girl, and usually does so blatantly. Specials like *Spring Break* are very popular and feature an abundance of events like the wet T-shirt and edible underwear contests, and couples wearing nothing but edible clothes have their date eat the clothing off of them.

Beyond the sexual shows is one that seemed harmless but proved dangerous. The highly rated show called *Jackass* featured an array of pranks and silly stunts that thirteen-year-old Jason Lind watched. After the show, he decided to imitate one of the pranks with his friends and was severely burned when his feet and legs were lit on fire. The teens said Jason volunteered to reenact the stunt, which took place in one boy's backyard.

Interestingly, a recent MTV poll found that 92% of its *own* audience wanted less sex and violence on television.[15] Nevertheless, even though its own audience clearly says it wants less, MTV continues to shove sex upon its young audience with more than a thousand references to sex every hour.

Other cable music shows such as VH1 and BET (Black Entertainment Television) have made a dent in the music market. They both tend to follow the same music format as MTV but without all the extra shows, and their programming isn't as offensive or insulting. VH1 sticks to decent music videos that aren't as offensive, vulgar, dark, or sexually and morally perverse as what MTV airs. BET airs videos that, because of the style of their performers (rap, hip-hop, pop), have more offensive language, angry lyrics, and sexually suggestive material than VH1.

PARENTAL GUIDANCE
News

Parents must be protective over letting younger children watch the news, *particularly* the evening news. The negative, fearful, deadly, crime-filled, steady stream of words that are spoken in bullet phrases at an elementary level can be picked up easily by your younger children. If you are not careful about what they're hearing, or at least explaining it thoroughly to them, they can carry those fearful, ugly thoughts with them and dwell on them.

Consider what took place during the Clinton scandal. For two years the evening news channels repeatedly introduced oral sex to a generation of young kids long before it was appropriate. Angry parents had to explain to their young children what oral sex meant and why our president was in trouble over his "sexual" indiscretions. Many of the kids who heard Clinton deny he had sex and didn't feel oral sex was sex are now experimenting with oral sex in junior high and justifying it via the example of the president. No one can say that children don't mimic, think about, or "act out" what they hear on the news.

The same righteous indignation that parents had then should be present in your home today as you protect your kids and monitor what they should see, hear, and learn from the news. Here are some points to guide you:

+ Remember that not all the news you hear is the truth. The media often distorts its version or portrayal of stories because they don't always come from a spiritually sound perspective. Much of what they deliver is truth packaged from a world's point of view. So it's important for you and your kids to talk about the controversial topics—abortion, cloning, mercy killing, evolution, etc.—and explain or correct the truth.

+ Be careful about which heroes and role models your kids pick up from the tabloid news. With so much attention given to celebrities, sports athletes, and TV personalities, kids idolize them as heroes.

+ Most junior high and high school students choose actors (from whatever the hottest movie is), musicians

(God help us that Madonna and her predecessor Britney Spears have been named as heroes for young girls), and comedians and athletes (remember when Dennis Rodman was actually someone kids admired?). These "stars" or "heroes" are using their celebrity platform to speak for them, instead of making it clear what they truly believe in and why. Teen heroes get a lot of notoriety and attention because of MTV and VH1.

✦ Even the news media sets a standard of beauty that kids and teens want to achieve. By elevating what society thinks is perfection and who the "beautiful people" are, our kids have a superficial, idolizing mentality toward sex, equating that with beauty. Unfortunately, plastic surgery is the drug of choice for many teens today because the standards are so high among their peers. They are taught to believe they can achieve popularity by being more sexual.

✦ Listening to too much news can cause a heavy depression to set in with some kids. It becomes a kind of morbid fascination with all of the evil and bad that's in the world. This mind-set of depression can actually take root in an impressionable adolescent who's wrestling with hormones, peer pressure, and drama in their life to begin with. That fatalistic view can cause a lot of problems if not checked and balanced with a parent's love and perspective. Be sensitive to your preteen's fascination with the negative things in life, especially from television news.

Radio

A key element to enjoying the stations you listen to is the programming. If you're upset with a host, a type of format, content, songs that are played, etc., let the general manager know. This is the person you want to contact and voice your complaint to. Letting a general manager know what's right or wrong with his station through phone calls or a letter is vital in getting changes made. Likewise, be sure to let a station know if you are happy with what they are doing, particularly if there's a DJ or host you appreciate.

Shock Jocks

Howard Stern, the "shock jock" who drags morals, values of life, and standards to an all-time low, has outraged one group of adults who want to do something about it. Beverly LaHaye's CWA group (Concerned Women for America) has worked closely with Bill Johnson, president of the ADA (American Decency Association), to mobilize their members against Stern through letters. They sent 53,522 petitions directed toward the show's sponsors, Snapple Beverages and the Warner-Lambert Company. Both companies stopped advertising. Of the 9,592 companies that once advertised on the show, 8,470 have stopped supporting him, and the number of TV stations has dropped as well. Letter writing clearly makes a difference.[16]

If you don't like what you're hearing on a station, call the general manager and ask for the advertisers' names that sponsor that show. You can also file complaints to the Federal Communications Commission (FCC) at complaints-enf@fcc.gov or to the Mass Media Bureau, FCC, room 2-c334, 445 12th street, Washington, DC 20554.

Music

The influence of the music industry is strong, and unless your child or teenager is prepared, it will be hard to resist its seduction. Listening to music repeatedly can shape and mold the values, ethic, behaviors, and attitudes your kids or teens will have toward you as a parent and the world they face. Here's what I recommend:

1. Teach your kids that the words they sing mean something. Sing a favorite song with them that they've heard repeatedly. After you sing the song together, ask him to explain what the song means.

2. When your child is in the ten- to twelve-year-old range (or of a maturity to understand what you are doing), ask what his or her favorite songs on the radio are and why. Talk about the lyrics that people hear every day in songs and teach your child to start analyzing the words and what they mean. Listen for a song on the radio with questionable lyrics and ask your child to tell you what the song is about. This is a good way to start teaching your child music discernment and what's acceptable or not, what's offensive

to your faith, your values, your belief system, and the integrity of your home.

3. If you have a young teenager, do the same thing with that teen. I have done this several times with my teenage son, and it's a great time to analyze the lyrics, artists, and style of music that interest your teen.

4. When your child's friends are in your car and you have the radio on, listen to see what songs are popular and how many of the kids sing along to the lyrics. Ask who likes the song and why.

5. My son has to ask first before buying or bringing a CD home. In the case of an artist whom I am not familiar with, I've asked to "borrow" the CD and listen to it or read the lyrics on the insert. When I have found lyrics that are questionable or not right, we have a discussion on why they want a CD with that message on it. Most of the time my son has made his own decision to return or not purchase the CD if we are at the store.

6. In the case of a friend copying or bringing over music and leaving it, the same rule applies.

7. Empower your kids to be able to make tough decisions on their own. Teach them to discern for themselves what music they should and shouldn't listen to and what to bring and not bring into the home.

MTV

I honestly can't think of one good reason to allow your child or teen to get in the habit of watching MTV. The programming is so offensive, vulgar, and morally degrading, the easiest way to avoid the problems is by simply not getting in the habit of having it on. Likewise, make sure your older teen isn't watching MTV in front of your younger children.

VH1 is my favorite for listening to music. If your teen feels a need to watch music videos, tune into VH1.

Center for Parent/Youth Understanding

One of the best references I can give any parent who wants to stay on top of the music and media your child is being exposed to is an organization run by Walt Mueller. He publishes a monthly newsletter that features articles about musical groups, artists, issues, piercing, tattooing, drinking, smoking, and anything else your teenager is currently facing. This is a wonderful resource that you'll be glad you checked out.

> Center for Parent/Youth Understanding
> P.O. Box 414
> Elizabethtown, PA 17022-0414
> Phone: (717) 361-8429
> Fax: (717) 361-8964
> 1 800 807-CPYU
> www.cpyu.org

Generation-Y Web Site

Another informative site that gives you the latest reviews on musical artists, their lives, and news stories about how people are being influenced and affected by their music and the industry is from Kathy Keeley, the music editor of www.katrillion.com.

I THINK WHEN WE LOOK AT THE POWER OF THE MEDIA and look at what it's capable of, it's more important than ever for parents first of all to inform themselves, to understand what they're up against here. And second, to scrutinize every single element of media that reaches into the home, and that would include cable TV, the Internet, video games, even publications, and get involved to the point where they are able to counter this media agenda. Of course, as always, they have to counter with a clear set of moral principles, and there is no better set of moral principles than those which come from the Bible.

—JEFF GOODELL[1]

TO SOME DEGREE, THE INDUS-TRY STILL THINKS in terms of movie or TV shows, when we're actually looking at a whole new beast in online entertainment.

—FRED SEIBERT, MTV Online[2]

THE NET HAS BEEN TOUTED FOR THE PRIVACY and the anonymity it offers users. But with the advent and popularity of hidden cams, you'll see a greater surrender of privacy. Mr. and Mrs. Average Joe can hook up a Web cam and put their most intimate moments on the Web. Those kind of sites are getting more popular, and we're also finding that users will sit and watch a girl sleep in her apartment with greater fervor than they would an actual adult feature. I think people are going to create their own adult industry just by outfitting their home with a dozen cameras.

—SCOTT SCHALIN, COO of iGallery[3]

The Internet and Video Games

I t is amazing to think that at the very end of the twentieth century, man would create a cyber highway to globally unite mankind as we entered the twenty-first century. With each passing day, more and more Americans are choosing to travel on that Internet highway in the convenience of their home, office, car, airplane, while dining in a restaurant, sitting by a pool, or watching their kids' baseball game. In just one decade the Internet has gone from obscurity to notoriety, and the twenty-first century has just begun.

THE INTERNET

It's no surprise that cyberspace is being referred to as the new designer drug, capable of providing compelling hallucinations and addiction to millions of unsuspecting travelers.

Established in 1968 by the Defense Department as a communication network in case of nuclear war, the Internet has not only grown since those early days, but its purpose has changed drastically. In 1983 computers could only be found in about 7% of American households, and a computer was definitely not an item most people could afford. In 1992 there were only a handful of businesses creating Web sites. But by the end of the twentieth century, 60% of households with kids had computers, and the high cost of technology was finally at a place most people could afford.[4]

It's predicted that by 2005 over a billion users will be connected to the Internet.[5] America now has a generation of Gen-I (Internet) Net-savvy kids who've grown up with computers. When you look at where that information trail began about twenty years ago and the wide-open road it has become, clearly mankind has embraced the technology, user-friendly convenience, business potential, and plethora of entertainment venues offered by the Internet. In fact, it's the biggest technology since the invention of the television.

My Introduction to the WWW

In the early '90s I worked on an entertainment business deal with a man who had been in the Hollywood community for years. John (not his real name) was delving into something I had never heard about. He explained that a new form of technology called the World Wide Web was mushrooming at a rapid pace and was destined to be the next "big" thing in our modern-day world.

Being the visionary that he was, John had created the first Catholic Web site that catered to the Catholic community but was not run by the Catholic Church. Even in its infancy stage, the site was causing a huge controversy with the Vatican because not only did they not know what the Internet was, but online Catholics were being exposed to an outside world of information, opinions, and teaching that many had never experienced before.

John was receiving e-mails from priests in the remotest parts of the world, thanking him for giving them a lifeline not only to civilization (some were in tiny villages) but also to fellow friends in the Catholic Church. Some of the priests were writing to one another about their mistreatment by the Church and were uncovering financial atrocities, dirty little secrets, and other information that had benefited Rome. The intrusion into the sacred and cocooned Catholic world via the Internet led to death threats and character assassinations on John's life from high-level people within the Church, but he didn't back down. Eventually, Rome started to see that this "thing" was bigger than the Church's control. Technological advancement was inevitable, and so the Church embraced his idea. John made a lot of money and a lot of enemies from that deal.

The moral of the story is that anything is possible, especially on the new frontier of the Internet and Web TV. If you have a dream and think it could work, you keep pursuing it to make it happen. Don't listen to people who don't have your same vision. That's what's exciting about this new frontier. Anything's possible!

THE INFLUENCE

I see articles claiming that the Internet isn't taking audiences away from TV. That's because there's not anything on the Internet right now that could take it away. But that's precisely what our goal is. I just started Eruptor.com and I am on the equivalent of Channel 3. Channel 4 is Disney, Channel 5 is Warner, and 6 is Fox. We're all on equal footing and the best content wins. The gloves are off.

             —Brad Foxhoven, President of Eruptor Entertainment[6]

That's Internetainment!

Hollywood's reaction to the Internet has been much the same as that of the Catholic Church—slow to accepting technology that will change the future as they know it. Hollywood has had to acquiesce to the inevitable. At first, a number of adventurous Hollywood players (Steven Spielberg and Ron Howard's www.pop.com) ventured into the unknown abyss of the Internet to be a presence. But by the end of 1998, Hollywood had just about given up, and many of those well-funded entertainment entities pulled out.

Now, just a few years later, with 56k modems standard, broadband capabilities, and other technological advancements, the Internet can truly function as an audiovisual entertainment medium. So it looks as though Hollywood gets another chance at online entertainment, and everyone gets the chance to define what those two words mean.

In terms of entertainment, most people think of movies and TV shows. But parents, teens, and kids get ready! Entertainment on the Internet is actually taking shape in a variety of formats, presentations, and unique subject matters. Those who choose to delve into that medium are going to be faced with creating innovative subject matter as well as new ways to generate distribution deals and systems to produce the material.

On the Internet, the development time, risks, and costs for projects are far less than in TV or movieland. The public ridicule isn't as opinionated or vested as what studios presently go through, and the best part is that the field is wide open and the playing field is level. There's also the fact that the creative world has a chance to usher in unknowns—writers, directors, and animators who dream of grabbing a stake in the entertainment industry. These people might never get their work seen in close-knit Hollywood circles, but on the Internet there's a world of possibilities.

One of those new avenues has been chartered by Ben Affleck and Matt Damon. The successful duo who wrote and starred in *Good Will Hunting* exercised their good will and faith in the Internet by holding a "Greenlight" contest, accepting scripts from hungry writers. The winner of their contest will see his or her script produced by the dynamic duo and hopefully have an instant hit.

The Hollywood Reporter did an interview with Brad Foxhoven of Top Cow Comics about the challenges he faced when he tried to develop Top Cow characters for film and TV. Brad explained how he turned to the Internet for his creative outlet and developed www.eruptor.com. "Eruptor's audience is kids that are being raised on the Internet. They're bored with the passive experience of TV, and they're hungry for something new. If the networks realize this stuff is a threat, they won't acknowledge it. But I know my competition isn't other original content sites—it's MTV, ESPN, and CBS. We're competing not for online time, but for viewing time. When someone goes to the Net or watches TV, the only question is who can entertain them the best."[7]

What the Internet does for everyone who goes on it, whether it's advertising, entertaining, or displaying your wares, is make you equal. Programming will eventually be integrating commercials into the content, new and creative ways to entertain will emerge, and the audience will be the ones who benefit. Hollywood is shape-shifting into a new market where the studio lots will be keyboards, the crews will be few in numbers, egos will be replaced by enthusiasm, and the premieres will be attended by potential millions. It's hard to tell who the big and little players will be, and that's what makes the future of Intertnetainment so exciting.

HOLLYWOOD JOINS THE TWENTY-FIRST CENTURY

Receiving huge criticism for being slow to embrace the Internet, studios have all agreed to start putting movies on the Net within six months. MPAA president Jack Valenti expressed concern from Hollywood about Napster-style free sharing of material on the Net and says Congress should continue supporting copyright protections. A few films such as the *X-Men, Planet of the Apes,* and *Star Wars* benefited from their fans' Web buzz and actually did well because of the hype. But false rumors, on-location guests who leak false information, and bad reviews by test-screening audiences can really hurt if spread on the Internet first.

Postings on most Web sites are anonymous, so studios have actually manipulated some of the sites that have attacked their movies by entering postings that praise their current releases, giving a false impression that test audiences loved it. They manipulate the very audience that has attacked and trashed them in the past.

Switching Channels and Technology

+ By 2004 there will be 55 million households with electronic program guides and 12 million households with the ability to surf the Internet on their TV sets. (Forrester Research)

+ By 2009 personal video recorders will be in 82% of all households. (Forrester Research)

+ Half of U.S. adults or 94 million Americans aren't online, which leaves lots of room for growth.

+ 71% of those polled agreed that the Internet would help them find information more easily.

+ More and more new talent will be discovered, not through agents but by visiting Web sites on the Internet. (Brad Siegel, president of Turner Networks Television)

+ Digital technology will permit video on demand, letting viewers watch any movie they want at any time, and eliminating the need for video store rentals. (Bruce Leak, president of Web TV Networks)

✦ The main reason for turning off the Net is fear and lack of interest. More than half of those not online believe the Internet is a dangerous thing. (Pew Internet & American Life Project poll)[8]

Screen Time

Kids are spending 4.4 hours in front of some kind of electronic screen every day, with TV dominating about 3.3 hours a day.[9] Whether it's on the computer, playing video games, watching the VCR, or vegging in front of the television, kids are being passively entertained but aggressively influenced. And that influence is not coming from a morally sound, values-based, protective society. That aggressive influence is coming from a world ready to seduce your child, rob their innocence, and destroy their obedience to you, the parent. That seductive entertainment mentality from the world of the Internet, TV, and video games is a Pandora's box waiting for your child to open. Where are the parents during those 4.4 hours? Can you say you are *truly* raising your kids, or is the entertainment world doing it for you?

A Net That Traps Your Kids

One afternoon I inadvertently interrupted my seventh-grade son and his friends who were online with a young girl who was trying her best to impress my son with lines such as "You're a hottie," "I like your body," and silly questions asking how he felt about her. After he signed off and the boys left, we had a long talk. While the incident itself was fairly harmless, my main concern was about how comfortable Nathan and his friends felt about going online with this girl and dialoguing like that in the first place.

The Internet provides an easy and nonthreatening way for teens to quickly make friends. Teens will tell you that it's easier to ask intimate questions and advice from online friends who can't see you, don't know how you look, can't judge you, and have no idea how shy or scared you might be. These days the talk is open and personal, girls are brazen, and neither sex seems to worry about how the other person will react. Friendships can be deepened at faster rates than face-to-face. Relationships and puppy love that used to coyly take place on the playground or at lunch now turn into a mad crush or love with a few brave words.

How risky is it to take an online relationship to the next step of physical contact? The papers are full of stories of girls and boys who thought it was an exciting way to meet someone who "really" cared for them, only to find an older man preying upon them. Police constantly warn how risky those rendezvous are and how big the exploitation business is becoming. People can pose as anyone and lie about what they say. You have no way of knowing if they are who they say they are.

Later, Nathan and I browsed through some of the sites he had been visiting. I asked him who his online pals were, and he showed me some of the dirty jokes and cartoon pictures that friends had sent him. Then we talked about what was acceptable, what wasn't, and why. After talking, I put limits on his site, what he could and couldn't download from the Internet, and what behavior was expected from him when he was on my computer. Nathan understood my requests were for his own good, and he seemed to appreciate it. I have never had a problem with Nate since, and because he is older now, some of them have changed.

A New Breed of Communication

The Internet has revolutionized the way kids meet, talk to each other, gather information, and flirt. It's become a trendy way to be daring, take chances, take on a new personality and create your own persona, especially when parents aren't around. Newsgroups are one of the most dangerous areas to go into because of the prevalence of explicit material and blatant sexual topics, and, of course, teenagers are especially attracted to these areas.

If you are a parent with adolescents or young teens, I urge you to set aside a half hour, sit with them, and ask to see some of the sites they visit. It might be an eye-opening experience. The respect of privacy among family members is certainly an important area to discuss with your kids. But the abuse of privacy and taking advantage of a situation because it's "easy" to get away with is equally important to discuss. I'll be the first to admit I've made more than a few mistakes with my three teenagers. But I would rather make a mistake that I can chalk up to caring too much or being overprotective than not caring at all. And if you asked your kids to be truthful with you about how they feel, they would too!

The best tactic for a parent and child is a balanced use of the Internet and a healthy respect for how to use it. Although the perverts and pornographers are out there, you shouldn't have to scare your child into not using the Internet. Instead of fear tactics and horror stories, educate, equip, and engage your child or teen to be discerning about the sites they visit. Along with educating them on the risks, show them you are using a parental "guide" approach rather than a parental "watchdog" role.

The best part of the whole Web culture is that no one knows the answers . . . the whole game can change tomorrow.
                                        —Warren Zide, www.inzide.com

Kid Stuff

Ever wonder how computer use affects your child's development? It's a common question parents are asking because the technology hasn't been around long enough to have any scientific evidence or proven track records. Does sitting in front of a computer screen for hours on end harm your kids? Will their imaginations be damaged because of too much screen time?

One of the early pioneers of childhood TV media, Sesame Workshop (creator of *Sesame Street*) launched the Web site www.sesamestreet.com, infusing some of the latest sound, animation, and interactive technologies into its time-honored brand of pre-schooling. Each Muppet has a link to its own home page, which young users visit by clicking on the "Muppet piano," a musical grouping with each character's head across the bottom of the screen. Elmo giggles when tickled; Oscar jumps out of his garbage can; Big Bird has an e-mail account, and all with lots of kid-friendly animation. One of the most innovative touches on the site merges parental content with kid content. A child and parent can play a game about eating while the parent takes in tips about fussy eaters as they roll through a traffic light in a corner of the screen. It's a proven tactic the thirty-two-year-old TV show has used over the years to entice parents to watch and interact with their youngsters.

Sesame Street numbers indicate that young users play on the site for twelve to sixteen minutes, which its developers consider safe for preschoolers. Stephen Gass cites the company's survey of parents and children, done with the National School Boards Foundation, indicating that computer-using youngsters spend the same amount of time in physical play, but less time watching TV, as children who don't use computers. "Thirty years ago the naysayers were there saying, TV is a wasteland. There's nothing good on for children. Then there was

Sesame Street," says Stephen Gass, group president at Online Sesame Workshop. "We're hearing similar kinds of arguments now . . . but we have this responsibility to deliver wherever kids are, whatever the medium happens to be."[10]

News on the Net

The spectacular growth of the Internet in recent years has reshaped our culture in a number of ways. On the bright side, seekers of truth can learn about important news stories without the filter and spin of the left-leaning mainstream media. On the Internet, there's a world of sites to view. Some of the best sources where you can get information quickly are Worldnet Daily, Conservative News Service, and www.newsmax.com.

Witchcraft on the Net

Witchcraft is the largest religion on the Internet today, and occultists refer to it as the "portal of transcendence." The neopagan explosion (which can be largely attributed to the Internet) is becoming popular with older kids, teens, and adults from all walks of life and all over the world. Recent TV shows (*Buffy the Vampire Slayer, Charmed, Sabrina the Teenage Witch,* and *Angel*) have catapulted its popularity and turned witchcraft into a glamorous, hip, manipulative religion that gives the illusion of power and control. White magic is increasing in popularity with spells, incantations, charms, and ritual magic sought after on the Web. Pagans from all over the world can now communicate and even perform ritual magic online through an ever-expanding number of highly networked occult-oriented chat rooms.

Funerals Online

A Japanese company, NTT, has launched a service that lets mourners visit gravesides at temples via the Net. The first funerals online have been launched to let those who can't get around, those living abroad, and the elderly visit the graveside.

Virtual Visitation

A New Jersey appeals court ruled that a Web designer could move to California with her nine-year-old daughter and build a video enabled Web site to help her ex-husband keep in touch with the girl. This case is the first of its kind and allows the non-custodial parent the ability to have more frequent contact with the child without physically being there.[11]

Virtual Adoption

The first case of adoption over the Internet was infamous because it involved twin girls who were adopted twice. Tina Johnson, the adoption broker, took $6,000 in fees from a California couple and, two months later, took $12,000 from a couple in Britain. It is illegal to buy and sell babies or children over the Internet, but I predict there will be more situations like this that no one can monitor.[12]

The Singles Scene

Chat rooms have become one of the most popular and easiest ways to meet other singles in today's world. I have known people who said they met and even married someone they met online, but the dangers of doing that far outweigh the thrill. Although there are many sites out there, being safe is the first priority. One site that is honest and will get you results in a healthy environment conducive to finding the love of your life is www.eharmony.com. It is relatively inexpensive, completely safe and private, and they partner you with healthy people who are ready for a relationship. Dr. Neil Clark Warren is a noted psychologist and author whose site is one of the firsts of its kind to help you get connected on the Internet the right way!

Predators

Eric Eisner, who is a porn site creator and the twenty-six-year-old son of Disney CEO Michael Eisner, says, "We see a backlash toward political correctness. The Internet has enabled people to express themselves in a way they hadn't before, which is raw, not sugarcoated, and irreverent." In June 2000 his vulgar men's site had 183,000 users compared to 8.2 million for Shockwave and 1.7 million for Atom Films. Unfortunately, their numbers are growing every month.[13]

It is ironic that Eric's father is the head of a company many parents expose and entrust their children to on a daily basis, whether through TV, radio, video, or the theme park. Disney's PR is promoting itself as wholesome, kid-safe, and kid-friendly. Eisner's son is the CEO of a men's site dedicated to animal sex, people sex, and dirty humor. The greater irony is that Disney has tried to live down accusations of implied sexual innuendoes in their animated children's films for years. Moms, keep your young, impressionable boys and men away from this Web site.

Internet Pornography

There is however a darker side. While cyber enthusiasts promise a cultural renaissance filled with unlimited knowledge, courtesy of the information superhighway, they fail to take into account man's fallen nature. Computers help reinforce man's general tendency toward moral and spiritual corruption, encouraging a desire to seek self-centered, self-satisfying pleasure regardless of the consequences. This can best be illustrated by a recent investigation by Yahoo!, one of the largest search engines on the Internet. They found that eighteen of the twenty most common search words used were "sexual" in nature. That means 90% of those who use the Internet primarily seek out sexually explicit, pornographic material and are literally inviting pornography, pedophiles, and perverts into their homes. The sheer volume and depravity of this electronic age will only increase with its availability to younger and younger consumers. Which is why it's more important than ever to guard your child's innocence, your marriage, the sanctity of your home, and the purity of your marriage from the "death" of pornography.

I read that there were about 70,000 obscene sites on the Web visited by twenty million people a week. One out of three people look at adult content, and a surprising seven million of those visitors are women.[14] In fact, there's a growing trend of women visiting and purchasing pornography on and off the Internet. These women are usually at home, but sometimes it's even taking place in the workplace.

When was the last time you heard about anyone being prosecuted for pornography? The prosecution of pornography fell over 80% during President Clinton's administration.[15] In part, there's a lack of legal clarity, since there are states such as Utah, Texas, and Oklahoma where stores selling pornographic materials can't ship to. And partly because pornography's so prevalent, there's a defeated sense of futility in trying to crack down on it locally. Will the Internet be different? Will we see a day when sex offenders will be caught and prosecuted for preying on young teenagers and children?

Church Porn

A Zogby poll showed that 20% of Christian men admit to surfing Internet porn sites. Christian men who find themselves tempted to log on now have another tool to help them resist temptation.[16] The new computer program is called "Covenant Eyes," and it records all sites visited on a computer and then sends a list of the sites to an Internet server. The program is based on Job 31:1, which says, "I have made a covenant with my eyes. Why then should I look upon a young woman?" At the end of the month, a log of questionable sites is sent to two men the subscriber identifies as "accountability" partners. The accountability issue is very important, especially to men who need the support of other men.

Since the Christian faith believes in forgiveness and restoration, there are several ministries reaching out to help. Emerge Ministries (www.emerge.org), headed by Christian psychologist Richard Dobbins, helps ministers from different denominations find deliverance with intense counseling and God. Dobbins warns that cyberporn can take hold in a matter of hours or days, but rehabilitation from habitual pornography takes six to eighteen months. "The church needs to be more transparent on this issue," he said. "Addiction to pornography and masturbation is increasingly common among Christian males in our society. Once a person is addicted, marriage will not cure this problem. A person addicted to pornography faces a more complex recovery than an adulterer."[17]

Pure Life Ministries (www.purelifeministries.org) provide resource materials, sponsors support groups, and offers a twelve-week program of weekly telephone counseling sessions called Overcomers-at-Home. Their live-in program lasts from six to twelve months and has ministered to more than 500 men. Steve Gallagher, the founder of Pure Life, said, "I learned that overcoming sexual sin was a process of maturing as a Christian. The church tends to deal with sexual issues by ignoring them, denying them, and repressing them. Only 10% of Christian couples talk about their sex life."[18]

Kiddie Porn

If you think your kids don't go to these sites, here are some statistics that will make you think twice about leaving your children alone on the computer. NetValue, an international Internet measurement company, discovered that 27.5% of those under seventeen on the Net visited adult sites in one month. Of the minors who visited the sites, 21% were fourteen and younger. If you think your boys are the only ones interested, think again. Young girls and women are becoming more intrigued and involved on porn Web sites. Girls made up 40% of the visitors. Another alarming find was that once they were there, kids spent 65% more time on porn sites than on game sites.[19]

VIDEO
The VCR & DVD

If you think about it, the VCR has allowed viewing audiences to time-shift for years. In the early years, the idea of being able to record a program and watch it at your convenience later revolutionized television and the workforce. It actually encouraged customized TV viewing for years. About 94 million homes have VCRs, and many have more than one. Only TVs, radios, and telephones are in more homes.

Consumers buy VCRs because they are cheap and allow people to collect a library of tapes to watch. In fact, more than twice as many VCRs (7.4 million) were sold as DVD players (3.5 million) over the 2000 holidays.[20] Even though the DVD is gaining in popularity because of technical improvements, experts are predicting the VCR has many years of popularity left. DVD players began selling in 1997, but the VCR continues to outsell the DVD because of the "record" luxury. People still like to record television programs and movies to watch later, and the DVD doesn't do that.

The main reason for a VCR in most homes, though, is for movies! Human nature likes the communal experience of watching entertainment together, and renting a video has provided that. Putting a video on has comforted a toddler, nursed a sick child, romanced a couple, provided a cheap date, been a friend to the lonely, told the truth, taught the lost, entertained a slumber party, and made family fun nights . . . fun! The VCR has influenced an untold number of lives.

Personal Recording

Devices like Replay and Tivo are making customized TV viewing easier and easier, but the personal video recorders are changing it even more. The design and technology of these machines make the VCR look primitive. With the personal videos you can click on a program and record a show with a specific actor. Request a specific type of program like *20/20* or *60 Minutes*, and it will show you everything coming up in that format. The VCR is limited to using videocassettes, which take up space. The personal recorder records digitally on a hard drive similar to computers. That capability allows the consumer to record anywhere from ten to thirty hours of shows. If you come in while it's recording, you can start the program while the recorder continues to record the rest of the show. With these kinds of recorders, a person can surf through and zap commercials along the way, which will eventually change the way advertisers support television.

WebTV

The first boast WebTV can make is that it brought the Internet to TV. But WebTV is quickly catching on in American homes because of the interactive capabilities and easy time-shifting. For the 800,000 households that currently subscribe to WebTV, viewers are involved in many aspects of programming such as playing along during broadcasts of *Jeopardy* or rendering a verdict when watching *Judge Judy*.[21] In Europe, TV viewers have what they call Canal+, with over five million homes joining in the fun to make it one of Europe's biggest pay-TV operators. Viewers can call the shots while watching a sporting activity because the boxes let viewers have instant replay, select something to be seen in slow motion, or choose from several different camera angles to find the one that interests them. This kind of television viewing is spreading in popularity and is quickly changing the overall entertainment experience. Interactive TV has all sorts of future possibilities, the most important being the way the viewer receives content. In future years the opportunity to allow the viewer to decide how and what kind of programming they will get is the direction WebTV is heading.

Interactive Television

The natural evolution of a convergence of the interactive television industry will be multifunction entertainment devices such as a combination DVD/Internet/game machine or a digital video recorder that has a built-in cable converter and cable modem for Internet access. In 1999 Motorola Semiconductor Products introduced a reference design for implementing a multimedia platform dubbed the Streamaster. The technology is designed to enable the convergence of audio, visual, and interactive tasks under one roof. This device supports everything from DVD-Video to games, cable, satellite transmissions, and broadband Internet access. This is the wave of the future in home entertainment.

VIDEO GAMES

In computer games, players are given the power to go beyond the natural ethical and spiritual boundaries and are frequently encouraged to seek revenge, kill, and destroy. The effect can be intoxicating and dangerous. Video games are now required by law to include a disclaimer warning players that they "may induce previously undetected epileptic symptoms even in persons who have no history of prior seizures" and that "loss of awareness, disorientation, or involuntary convulsions" can result.

From our fascination with Pong machines to the Pac Man days, Game Boy, Nintendo, PlayStation, and many others over the past quarter of a century have joined the ranks of addictive video games. A generation of video addicts have turned into adults, raising another generation of video game-addicts, and now the $10-billion-a-year industry occupies 40% of American households with video game systems. It is estimated that kids spend an average of ninety minutes a day playing them.[22]

But somewhere in all the competitive fun, action, intensity, simulated realism, expert levels, and reality scenarios, a new breed of killers was born. A generation of kids who believed video games were just for fun are now seeing the fruits of all that "game" training as they are randomly being stalked on school campuses by fellow classmates. Classmates who may have reviewed their training on how to use their gun by practicing on video games. Obviously there are a multitude of reasons beyond video games why kids and teenagers take guns to school and randomly kill classmates. But violent video games have definitely been attributed as one of the major causes.

The FTC and Video Games

A media watchdog group, including several senators from Washington, have recently attacked the video game industry who, they say, still markets inappropriate games to kids. The industry began using voluntary ratings in 1994 and has a review board to enforce guidelines on advertising. Although the games are rated, the retailers are still selling the adult-oriented games to children under seventeen. The task force is intent on getting legislation passed that would allow the FTC to take action against the video game industry.

Violence Breeds Violence

As mentioned before, video games are now required by law to include a disclaimer warning players about serious health concerns. Obviously the effects of playing these games a lot can be not only intoxicating but also dangerous.

But aside from possible health issues, we need to look at the philosophy of playing these games. In certain computer games, players are forced to cross the lines and given the power to go beyond the natural ethical and spiritual boundaries in life. They are frequently encouraged to seek revenge, kill, and destroy. Therefore the argument has been made that violent video games can lead to aggression in adolescents and teenagers. Recent studies support that idea and further state that violent video games not only can increase aggression but also can lead to delinquency. Those two combinations are lethal to an adolescent or teen already feeling anger about his or her world. This volatile combination can encourage a stupid mistake when addressing a situation or person who's upsetting them.

Recent studies tell us that:

+ Violent video games with realistic action, strategy, shootings, blood, and combat are not just "entertainment." The violence that a child or teen reenacts in turn makes him think and act more aggressively. Males in particular may even see the world as hostile after playing these games.

+ Violent video games promote not only thinking violently but also practicing the violent skills to get good in the game. By practicing the violent acts over and over that information may lie dormant until a child or teen may recall it for real-life situations.

+ There is a relationship between playing violent games and delinquent behavior. The more the violent video games are played, the more delinquent behavior occurs.

+ There is a relationship between "screen time" and poor grades. The more time that was spent playing games led to lowered academic achievement.[23]

A New Video Generation

By the mid-'90s more than two-thirds of American homes had

one or more VCRs. The access to video home entertainment and the abundance of games and choices have now set a physical standard among America's males. A recent survey of 13,000 teens showed most prefer video games to healthy physical exercise. "Blacks, Hispanics, and Asians are less active than whites," says University of North Carolina researcher Penny Gordon-Larsen. A third of adolescents say they're moderately to vigorously active five or more times a week. Black youths play video games for about thirty hours a week, while whites average nineteen, and Asians and Hispanics fall in between. The couch-potato lifestyle has made youth obesity "a major public health problem" says Gordon-Larsen.[24]

Reverse Psychology

You aim the gun, pull the trigger, and boom—a man rises and walks away. You have just played "Bang, bang (you're not dead?)," a multimedia exhibit on the Internet. Instead of killing things and reducing them to "gibs" (a pile of body parts, in gaming terminology), you shoot gibs, a limp flower or a lifeless bird, and resurrect them. Kathleen Ruiz, digital artist and assistant professor at Rensselaer Polytechnic Institute, doesn't expect players to become addicted to the game. But she hopes it makes them think about a topic consuming the nation and Congress: the link between video game and actual violence. Ruiz keeps an open mind: Violent games "could be cathartic for some, for others they can be desensitizing."[25] But she adds, "It's a waste of technology to focus on the violent games when we can use the technology to express more of the human condition, not jut killing."

Game Creator

Video game creator Keiji Inafune, the designer of *Mega Man,* which first appeared on the original Nintendo in 1988, has designed *Onimusha: Warlords.* Inafune's most recent project takes him in a more mature direction with cutting-edge graphics and bloody action, and combines the works of Japanese film legend Akira Kurosawa. In the game, players control a samurai as he battles a supernatural army, and unlike his Mega Man, *Onimusha* is clearly designed for a mature audience with graphic scenes of attacks and characters bleeding profusely. In other words, it's gory and for adults only. Inafune says, "When I create family games I concentrate on making a game that is suitable and fun for kids of the targeted age. When I create adult-only games, my target is to make a game enjoyable for adults." I believe the question should be raised: why is this kind of bloody game "enjoyable" for adults to begin with?[26]

No Guidelines for Games

Japan does not have a ratings system for games, so there are no guidelines to warn or tell parents. The country has seen a rise in teen violence over the past few years, sparking the same kind of media examination that is taking place in the U.S. In the past, teen violence was never a problem in Japan, a culture known for its lack of violent crime. But violence has become a big issue with the youth in Japan, and the country has to take a hard look at how their violent games and entertainment media may be affecting their country. Among several violent incidents of crime in 2000 was the case of a fourteen-year-old boy who cut off and mutilated the head of an eleven-year-old.

Although the number of crimes by juveniles has dropped in Japan, violent crimes have increased. As in the U.S., all facets of their culture are under examination by politicians and psychologists alike. Some point to aimlessness among youths, others look to the education system, but many target video games. Japan's leading politicians think the younger generation "lacks the basic ethical sense of the importance of life and of the difference between good and bad."

Several years ago the Japanese video game industry created a trade organization called the Computer Entertainment Software Association (CESA) that is similar in concept to the U.S. Interactive Digital Software Association. CESA provides leadership in the industry, represents it to the government, and has both permanent staff and appointed executives from within the game industry who serve one-year terms. *Onimusha* and other games published in Japan must be approved by CESA, but the interesting fact is that CESA has no written code and no guidelines for warning labels on games.

So should we in America question some of the games our kids get from a country that doesn't have a standard of guidelines or warnings? Absolutely![27]

New Way to Watch Video

Console video games will also be staking out a niche as an overall home entertainment machine. The next generation console from

Nintendo will support DVD and the Internet. Sony PlayStation 2 can access the Internet and play DVDs and CDs. Even La-Z-Boy and Microsoft are selling a home video designer console called The Explorer that retails for $1,049 and has everything: plug for laptop, jacks for internet connections, and a fold out-tray table.[28]

Virtual Reality

Kids can go to game rooms and not only play the traditional electronic games but also partake in the latest form of interactive technology that creates an illusion of being in an artificial world. The user puts on headgear with a special viewing screen and a glove that's computerized. As the person enters the world of choice, the events that take place, the people he meets, and the interaction he encounters all look and feel real.

More advanced equipment will use a suit that will recreate sensations the whole body can experience, both pleasurable and painful, which could be used as an excellent educational or training tool. But realistically, the biggest concern about virtual reality for younger kids and teens is its misuse for sex. By climbing into a body suit and entering that world, kids and teenagers could feasibly have virtual reality sex with anyone, anywhere, anytime.

Movie plots have been using virtual reality or hologram characters in story lines for some time now. But it was in *The 6th Day* that for the first time a very sexy and seductive virtual reality female was used as a girlfriend to one of the characters. That fantasy grabbed the attention of most kids and teens.

PARENTAL GUIDANCE
Who's the Gatekeeper?

YOU ARE! You as a parent are the only one who stands between your child and the World Wide Web, videos, video games, or any other form of media influence. Can you possibly be there at all times monitoring what your child does? Of course not! There is no way you can deny the powerful influence and potential the media has to manipulate and/or affect your child's life. But there are ways to teach your child how to resist that manipulation and educate them about how the entertainment industry and media want to take their money and addict them to entertainment.

Tools and Rules

With a few tools that are now available for concerned and protective parents today, you can set guidelines, standards, and rules for your child or teen on the entertainment you will allow in your home. Respect for how the different forms will be used in your home and what consequences will be incurred if they aren't should be established. Your kids are under your parental authority and need to know what's acceptable in your eyes . . . *your* eyes.

Remember: *More is caught than taught with your kids.* Your child or teenager will be watching what your Internet and video viewing habits are, what sites you go to, what movies you spend time viewing. Truthfully, they look to see if your behavior, lifestyle, and actions line up with your own words of advice.

Ultimately, the values and ethics, the do's and don'ts, that you set for your home will send a message to your kids that they are loved. The right values in your home empower your kids with intelligence, security, and discernment. And that kind of "discernment" is what your kids will rely on when making wise Internet, video game, and entertainment decisions when you aren't around. That gift of discernment is your Gate Keeper!

Net Safety

I was thrilled to discover AOL had parental controls that let me monitor some activities. They've also produced a *Safe Surfin'* video with the National School Boards Association. Microsoft is a partner of GetNetWise and has produced a CD-ROM called *Stay Safe Online.* The company is offering a service called *Microsoft Kids Passport* to give parents the power to say yes or no on whether kids may disclose personal data at a certain site. Parents create the passport account, and the kids can't go shopping, etc., until Mom and Dad say so.

The results of a study presented by the National School Boards Foundation, the Children's Television Workshop, and Microsoft indicated that most parents consider the 'Net a "safe" place. The Children's Online Privacy Protection Act is backed by the Federal Trade Commission and requires commercial Web sites and online services to inform parents and obtain "verifiable consent" before collecting or using personal information for kids under thirteen.

If you're looking for a book with practical advice about online protection, pick up Aftab's *The Parent's Guide to Protecting Your*

Children in Cyberspace (McGraw-Hill). GetNetWise.org is a resource created by corporations and nonprofit organizations that include a safety guide and a place where you can report trouble to the authorities. It also has lists of appropriate kids' sites from The America Library Association, Children's Partnerships, and several others.

Here's a list of a few programs that will help you protect your child on the Net:

www.growingupdigital.com
www.getnetwise.org
www.cyberangels.org
www.cyberpatrol.com
www.junkbusters.com
www.netnanny.com
www.safekids.com
www.safeteens.com

Interesting Sites

The Internet has increased the competition from the media to get news, views, rumors, gossip, but mostly entertainment to you first. With innumerable Web sites out there on the Net, I have come up with a few that can make your life fun, a little easier, and a lot more informed. I'll let you be the judge. Enjoy!

Net Navigator

Are you hung up on where to go to look for information on the WWW superhighway? Do you wish you could go to one place and be able to let them browse for you to find all the things you need? Go to www.etour.com and find over 132 categories to click through remote control style that makes it fast, fun, and easy to use!

Other popular search engines are Lycos, Yahoo!, Webcrawler, AltaVista, and Excite. Some of the major online services such as AOL, CompuServe, and Prodigy provide the Internet, e-mail, chat rooms, games, shopping, reference help, and more.

Movie Reviews

The following are a few entertainment and family Web sites with information and opinions that will help you and your family enjoy surfing the Web.

Family Friendly Entertainment Choices

www.hollymcclure.com—the BEST

www.screenit.com

www.kidsinmind.com

www.hollywoodreporter.com

www.imdb.com

www.comingsoon.net/2001.htm

www.variety.com

www.terriblemovies.com

>   The site explores the worst of the worst so you can
>   avoid renting one.

www.dove.org

www.crosswalk.com

www.christianity.com

www.gospel.com

www.oneplace.com

www.jewishworldreview.com

Fun Ones

www.videogameheaven.com

>   Run by video game lovers and industry people. A
>   good source for learning about and choosing video
>   games.

www.radiodiaries.org/teenagediaries.html

>   Teenage diaries, hear firsthand about life from a
>   group of teens from all around the country.

www.voxxy.com

>   A site for girls where Jennifer Aniston hosts a monthly
>   live chat session with celebrity guests.

www.sonicnet.com

>   Learn about today's popular music, featuring a lis-
>   tening room.

www.parentsoup.com

>   An extensive parenting site for every parent's needs.

www.parentstv.org

>   For up-to-date, comprehensive ratings and information
>   on all network television shows. A must for parents!

www.cpyu.org

>   Center for Parent/Youth Understanding. A *great*
>   resource for any parent who has a teen and needs
>   answers for every aspect of their teen's life.

www.family.org

Focus on the Family, family oriented programs, books and videos.

www.christianity.com/drlindahelps

A site that can give you sound advice from an expert in her field.

Friendships

Why I think meeting and carrying on an online friendship is risky business:

✦ I know it sounds obvious, but people can present themselves falsely on the Internet, and kids seem to be oblivious as to how this could affect or harm them and your family!

✦ Teenagers aren't at a fully matured stage of reasoning, so good judgment and good decision making is still in a formative process during adolescence. There's no way you can "trust" your teen to "just know" if a person online is "safe" or not.

✦ "Safe" can mean mentally as well as physically, and if the person is pathological, they may be extremely needy or dependent.

✦ You can't always screen the online person correctly. People who want to exploit and hurt teens are good at false identities and manipulation.

Personal information opens the teen, child, or family to cyber predators. Warn your kids about giving out your phone number, or predators can look it up in reverse directories and locate your home.

A Parent's Job

All of the above sites can help in educating your child about the dangers of the Internet, but there's no protection like a parent's protection. I've listed a few commonsense tips for you to consider. I've discovered it never hurts to be too practical.

1. First of all, talk with your kids about their use of the Internet on the *appropriate age level* they can comprehend. There's obviously a balance in what you will want to establish with your kids, preteens, and teenagers. Be honest with them and encourage them

to keep an open dialogue about what their experiences are on the computer. Be careful not to be too judgmental or negative.

2. If your kids are younger, place the computer in the family room, a busy area, or your bedroom. Keep it somewhere you can monitor easily.

3. If you're not sure of your younger child's computer skills or what they know on the Internet, have them look something up for you, cross-reference it, and save it in a separate file. Screen the sites your younger children go to.

4. Find out where the "history" is contained in your computer and then check it about once a week/month to see what your kids or teens are viewing.

5. Find out what programs offer clean Internet sites (there are lots of them).

6. Go to school and meet the teacher who teaches the Internet to your children or teens, then look at some of their curricula and ask the teacher to e-mail you with progress reports about your child's abilities, as well as ask about current sites teens and kids are exploring. You can learn a wealth of information from this teacher.

7. Talk with your child about giving out personal information (name, phone number, where you work, schools, what they would like to buy on the Net, etc.). I had to talk with my son about this because he was signing up for Napster, drum information, skateboard stuff, and giving out our personal information. I educated him on what people could do with that information and how pedophiles can track kids down with even a few details. He thanked me. In fact, he said, "Mom, I never even thought about that." He had no idea. Kids usually don't, so be honest with them about having a healthy "fear" and "respect" for that portal into your home.

8. Warn kids about the intentions of people and how they are not always what they seem to be online. If someone makes them feel unsafe or "funny," obviously they should log off immediately and tell you, a teacher, or another adult who is present. If your child understands common sense and will oblige, that's great. But what if your child doesn't tell you? What about the child or teen who acts as though he's hiding something because of embarrassment or is concerned that you'll get mad? Here's what you do!

   Sit down with your child or teenager and say, "Let's log onto a site and see how easy or hard it is to meet someone online. Let's see if they try to ask me personal questions." Then let your child watch as you both play a game of exploration. Go to a couple of places (try letting your child or teen tell you where to go, because chances are they've already tried it) and explore a chat room, skip around to a few places, and then let your child answer a few questions in a chat room. The confidence you place in your child, the ease at which you let them learn to venture out on their own, and your forgiving heart when bad answers or mistakes are made will make that learning experience a positive one. It will also let your child see that adults can be vulnerable too and have to be smart at all times. Hopefully an ease and trust will form with your child, and they will see how easy it is to be conned or tricked on the Internet.

9. Software filtering programs such as Cyber Patrol, CYBERsitter, and Net Nanny can block objectionable material, but they can't block it all. Some are educators or information specialists such as KidsClick!, which was created by librarians from the Ramapo Catskill Library System in Middletown, New York. A good place to find a number of search engines for kids in one place is Ivy's Search Engine Resources for Kids at www.ivyjoy.com/rayne/kidssearch.html.

Videos

Young children are introduced to language, sex, and violence in strong doses through movies, but mostly it comes through the home with the TV, Internet, video games, and videos. When parents rent an R-rated film for themselves, their children or teenagers sometimes pick it up and watch it the next day. The consequences of this easy access to explicit violence and sexual material demands that parents take an active role in stepping in to monitor what is watched and *hiding* the R-rated or PG-13 movies that are inappropriate for kids.

+ Go into video stores with your kids and, as inconspicuously as possible, walk the aisles close to your child or teen and observe what movies he or she is immediately attracted to. Okay, let's call it what it is . . . spy on them . . . but this will help you see what their tastes really are when they don't think you're looking. Don't try it with a sixteen-year-old . . . they're on to you!

+ Ask your child or teen, "If you could rent any movie in this video store, and I had to let you see it, which movie would it be and why?" Be prepared for the worst answer and take one of two approaches: (1) Ask them why they want to see this movie. Tell them why you (the parent) would or probably wouldn't want them to see it, then talk about those answers. Trust me, you will get lots of giggles, but perhaps some interesting thoughts and viewpoints will emerge. Or (2) Take the video home and watch it with your child or teen. It makes a profound impact on your child when you make an effort to sit down and *try* to see *their* viewpoint. Barring that the movie is pornographic or demonic, discuss the story, characters, plot, morals, hero, etc., with your child afterward and find out what your child thought was right and wrong with the movie. Ask them what they thought was inappropriate, immoral, or unacceptable behavior.

+ This is a good way to show your child or teen what you believe *is* appropriate for them. Tell them why you like or don't like their selection, how you feel it's a good movie, or how it might harm your child to see it. Ask him or her if this kind of movie could hamper their spiritual life. Have them then analyze why they still want to expose themselves to that kind of entertainment. Let them see *how willing you are* to take a look at their choice of entertainment and hear their opinions.

✦ If your older kids come home with an unacceptable movie, sit down and watch the movie with them, or you watch it later but *still* discuss the good and bad aspects of it with them. It's important you get *their* opinion about their likes and dislikes.

Video Games

Many parents are simply unaware of the entire negative effects violent media have on their children. By dropping the kids off at the video store to rent the games they want, then allowing them to run home and shut themselves off from family to play a game for hours, isolating themselves away from your discerning eye, you could be encouraging an eventual mini time bomb.

Before you think I'm some vast right-wing conspiracy nut! Happy and healthy kids with sound morals and a hopeful outlook on life can pick up a violent video game, play it, and not be affected by it. I'm not saying it won't linger in their memory, but I likewise don't believe video games kill people. People kill people. In other words, realistically it would take a lot more than one game to snap a child's or a teen's stability, and we all know that. But it's not the healthy, happy, hopeful kids that concern me.

It's the angry kids who already have issues with their parents, teachers, friends, peers at school, or the world, for that matter! Angry kids who are loners and spend lots of time in their rooms playing violent games over and over, meditating on the violence as a means to "get back" at someone. Role-playing how the power trip of killing would feel, fantasizing about the fifteen minutes of fame and notoriety . . . those are the kids I'm worried about! Those are the hurt, rejected, and wounded kids who need to be looked in on, talked to, and loved. Those are the kids who can be stopped.

As a movie critic I observe kids as they run out of theaters after seeing an action adventure or a martial arts movie with a lot of fights and high energy. They run around jumping, kicking, fighting, and copying what they saw on screen. That same adrenaline reaction is stirred up when they play a video game.

A Note to Single Parents

As a single mother who has raised three teenagers (two boys and a girl) on my own, I can assure you that just because you're single (and most likely working) doesn't mean your kids have to run wild in the streets, get picked up by local authorities, or go on a killing spree. In a day and age when teens are turning to violence as a means to make a statement before ending their life, it pays to be detailed about what influences your kids are spending time with. Are they withdrawn and consumed with playing video games while listening to music? Do they choose aggressive, violent games for most of their playing pleasure? It pays to be too careful these days, instead of discovering you didn't care enough!

Here's my advice about handling video games:

✦   Take a look at the games your child or teen has in his or her room or game room. Ask them to show you how to play and play a round with them. Ask what the objective of the game is, who the hero is, and why they like this game. Discuss why you do or don't approve of the game, and as you play, point out the elements you think are good or bad for your child. Making a decision about future purchases and rentals is all part of teaching your child or teen how to be discerning and how to make wise entertainment choices.

✦   Encourage alternative games that are creative but not violent, ones that require skill rather than violent responses. For example, opt for a skateboard video that has good music and special effects (*Tony Hawk's Pro Skater 2,* PlayStation, Activision) or a game that motivates and challenges your child or teen with some aggressive contact and action (*Madden NFL 2001,* PlayStation, Electronic Arts). The aggressive action in a skating or football video will give them that contact-sport rush without all of the bloody violence. My young teenage son loves these two, and I've personally seen and played them with him . . . he *loves* when I come in and sit on his bed and say, "Can I play?" Just fifteen minutes makes his day, and you get to be the popular parent!

✦   Find games that demonstrate healthy behavior and positive moral values with characters that can be a hero role model. If your child doesn't have a video game like that, go to the store and help him select or buy an appropriate one, discussing why you won't agree to some of the other ones.

✦   Go to an arcade/game room with your child and designate $5 or $10 to play any games your child or teen wants to play. Go with them to each game and watch their reaction to the game, what they choose to play, how well they can play it, etc. Then have an ice cream or treat afterward and talk about the games your child selected to play. Let them tell you why they liked certain ones better than others and observe their physical behavior (if they are wired, bouncing off walls, jumpy, etc.) as they leave the building.

Obviously, doing any of the above means you have to be involved in your child's life and take time to monitor and supervise his or her media habits. Time is usually a parent's worst enemy, and though it may not seem as if there's enough left to follow through with the suggestions I've made, the sacrifice is well worth it. By spending a little time with them, you show how much you care about what your child sees and does in his or her life. By taking the time to teach, listen, and give them your perspective, you are *training* your child to be a discerning young adult and *equipping* them with the tools they need to *discern for themselves what's right and wrong.*

If you give your child the time it takes to watch a movie or play a game with him or her, then you have invested yourself wisely. That gift of time translates into love, and that love translates into memories that will be remembered for a lifetime.

CULTURE—A compilation of ideas, customs, skills, arts, beliefs, traits, values, religion, social organization, ideals, economics, knowledge, attitudes and opinions, representing a people or group of people in a shared community or society. Collectively, it socially transmits a way of life meant to govern and guide generation to generation.

THERE'S A SCHOOL OF THOUGHT SUGGESTING ANDY WARHOL'S fifteen minutes of fame is now an overestimate, that given the public's constant hunger for new stimuli and the media's desire to oblige, fame is ever more fragile and evanescent.

CHAPTER

Our Popular Culture

oday's popular culture is reflected by and constantly being changed by the deluge of movies, television, music, video games, Internet, advertising, books, and media on our lives. This bombardment of mass entertainment and media is reshaping the social and cultural landscape of American life. It influences what we like and dislike, what we eat, how we dress, shop, exercise, and work, what hobbies and interests we have, and what music we listen to.

We see how powerfully it changes our children, sways our politics, shapes our trends, tempts our religious beliefs, instructs our education, and robs our values. It occurs every day because the entertainment industry is such an integral part of our daily communication, reaching and speaking to all classes, races, cultures, and countries.

It's important to remember that when motion pictures were attracting almost every middle- and lower-class family to go and see them on a weekly basis in the late '20s, the most important social influence in America was the family. After the family came the church, the local neighborhood or community, the school, and last came the media. If you were to put an order on these today, where would you place the family's influence?

We live in a much different world and American culture now. Families have been torn or touched by divorce, the family unit has been culturally dismantled and redefined, many families don't go to church or even have a faith, and the cost of living and/or divorce have forced women into the workplace and left children alone to fend for themselves at home. Schools have become the gatekeepers of our children and are teaching classes on sex, tolerance, and social behaviors.

I know parents are concerned about the effects that pop culture has on our youth. If you think this is a current trend, think again. The entertainment industry started focusing on the youth market soon after WWII. As a result, our culture went through major changes that transformed the America before WWII into a much different nation in the '50s. Hollywood forever changed the moral climate of America and introduced a new temptation to the American teenager—movies!

RESTLESS YOUTH

After WWII America experienced a huge growth spurt. Young middle-class couples were buying homes, having babies, and buying cars. A respect for freedom and patriotism was "in," and war heroes were honored both in film and in our society. A shift in mood and attitude took place in music, and rock and roll became the popular art form with the youth. The major studios were producing big blockbusters aimed at the general audience, so smaller, independent studios decided to capitalize on the youth market and turned their attention to the postwar baby boomer set with movies that would appeal to teenagers.

It started in 1955 when a very cool guy named James Dean epitomized the "restless youth" in his hit movie *Rebel Without a Cause* and Elvis became king in *Love Me Tender* (1956). In the early '60s, a new independent film company was formed, American International Pictures (AIP), which focused on the youth audience and produced low-budget movies that showcased rock groups and others that were aimed at the college crowd. Baby boomers were the first generation weaned on television and raised on movies, and the youth market became the principal audience studios targeted. Their search for freedom from a restrictive middle-class culture was explored through filmmaking.

During the early '60s, the bigger studios stuck to family-friendly musicals and "safe" controversial films such as *Cat on a Hot Tin Roof* and *Guess Who's Coming to Dinner*. But the independent studios made movies with controversial themes aimed at the youth: *The Graduate*,

Bonnie and Clyde, 2001: A Space Odyssey, Valley of the Dolls, Easy Rider, Alice's Restaurant, and *The Wild Bunch.* These movies ended up making a lot of money and brandished social messages that promoted drug use, sex, graphic violence, and rebellion against the establishment. Paradoxically, the social angst and rebellion America saw on the big screen was being mirrored in our nation. Drug use, sexual revolution, protests against the establishment, the Vietnam War, and racial upheaval were all taking a serious toll on our culture.

Mainstream Hollywood felt the pressure from the independent filmmakers to banish the Production Code, and with that act, the dismantling of the studio system closed an era of Hollywood that once protected our morality, decency, and values.

It's not our business to promote the culture of the country or to make art films. It's to make money for the studio.

—The head of production at MGM in 1969[1]

A NEW HOLLYWOOD FOR THE UNDER-THIRTY CROWD

The '70s were about change in movies and our culture. Hollywood explored old themes (action-adventure, science fiction, horror, and comedies) in new ways and challenged our religious beliefs, social structure, educational, political, and cultural views. Movies were made for the entertainment savvy, under-thirty crowd. Message films such as *The Deer Hunter, The Godfather, Chinatown,* and *The China Syndrome* were successful. But it was the romance sappy *Love Story* and special-effects, soundtrack-driven, hip-directed movies such as *Grease, Close Encounter of the Third Kind, Jaws, Star Wars, Sting, Superman, American Graffiti, Rocky, Alien,* and *Saturday Night Fever* that made box-office history and revived a sinking film industry.

The Exorcist debuted as the granddaddy of all scary movies, followed by *Carrie* and *Poltergeist.* These movies brought back the horror film aimed at the teen crowd, but this time around special effects and brutal bloody deaths. And really scary bad guys made movies such as *Halloween, Prom Night, Friday the 13th,* and *Nightmare on Elm Street* incredibly popular, accounting for nearly 60% of the domestic releases in 1981 with twenty-five of the fifty top-grossing films that year![2]

TEEN THEMES

The '80s were ushered in by MTV as well as by Steven Spielberg and George Lucas, who brought their marvelous special effects in sci-fi style and gave young audiences movies with an old-fashioned balance of morals, values, and chivalry. *E.T. the Extraterrestrial,* the *Indiana Jones* blockbusters, along with *Blade Runner, Alien,* and *Terminator* dominated the box office.

The teen themes changed with smarter writing, cool stars, more dating dilemmas, peer pressure, and the communication gap with parents. That was seen in *Sixteen Candles, The Breakfast Club, Pretty in Pink, Ferris Bueller's Day Off, Say Anything, Flashdance, Footloose,* and *Dirty Dancing.*

But Hollywood continued its slide into loose morality, sexual themes and situations, drinking, partying, drug use, and gross behavior. *National Lampoon's Animal House, Porky's, Fast Times at Ridgemont High,* and *Risky Business* were very popular and very immoral.

MEDIA STEREOTYPES

For years Hollywood has promoted ethnic stereotypes with characters that embody them in memorable ways. Movies such as *The Godfather* was and still is a powerful influence on the way we think Italians are linked to the Mafia. *The Quiet Man* and, more recently, *Far and Away* were stories built around the Irish traits of drinking and fighting. *Fiddler on the Roof* embodied Jewish customs, their culture, and humorous quirks that reflected their tradition. Movies reflect stereotypes—life, human emotions, characteristics of people—and that perception depends on the writer and director who put the thoughts and ideas together.

A new Zogby International poll says that some of the stereotypes teenagers are being bombarded with from the entertainment media today are negative of certain ethnic, racial, and religious groups. Italian-Americans are perceived as crime bosses or restaurant workers; Arab-Americans as terrorists or convenience store clerks; African-Americans as athletes or gang members; Hispanic-Americans as gang members or factory workers; Irish-Americans as drunkards, police officers, or factory workers; and Jewish Americans as doctors, lawyers, or teachers.

The purpose of the survey was to find out whether teenagers, in general, and Italian-American teens, in particular, recognize stereotyping on TV or in the movies. And if they do, how much it affects them. The nationwide poll of 1,264 teenagers, aged 13-18, was conducted in the summer of 2000 at the request of the National Italian American Foundation. Apparently other interest groups are also upset. A suit against HBO was filed in April of 2001 against the hit show *The Sopranos,* charging discrimination against Italians and asking for an apology for, among other issues, stereotyping that implies "all Italians are connected with the Mafia."

THE FAMILY

Hollywood has targeted teenagers for years, and through the '90s the tone was increasingly liberal. Television can still be a family's friend, but it can also easily be a parent's worst enemy. The borderline porn that some stations carry, the vulgar dialogue, and the graphic violence and indifference to life are slowly tearing down our moral fiber and seeping into our values, society, and culture. How is your family influenced directly or indirectly by the media of today? Let's take a look at a few areas.

Morals Matter

In August 1999 a survey was conducted by Peter D. Hart Research Associates for the Shell Oil Company and printed in the *USA Today* "Snapshots" section.[3] The results of the survey indicated that the moral decline ranked as follows:

✦ Families not teaching children good values (88%).
✦ Rise in drug abuse (83%).
✦ Society too tolerant of bad behavior (80%).
✦ Adult language/sexually explicit TV (73%).
✦ Pornography on the Internet (62%).
✦ Reduced influence of religion (62%).

When you look at this list, one observation is abundantly clear: There is no substitute for good, active, healthy parenting, with family living focused on loving relationships and spiritual leadership in the home. Make sure you model moral character for your children so that they can trust your insight and counseling. Know what moral dilemmas your children and teens are facing by getting into nonjudgmental discussions about these issues. Teach your kids character traits that will empower them with godly wisdom. Talk to them about your trials and tribulations as a teenager (my kids love to hear my stories) and admit where you went wrong. Sometimes confession of the soul opens a floodgate of honesty, and that human vulnerability is what your child or teenager needs to see and can relate to.

Count on the fact that the entertainment media and today's culture will try to undo your moral training. That's why it is important to get kids involved with groups that will reinforce similar moral standards to your own—youth groups, church groups, sports, scouting, music programs, etc. Moral values are more "caught than taught."

Have a Little Faith

Faith is a part of our nation's heritage, but today's faith is changing to accommodate the pop culture. Forty-five percent say they are guided by "their own views." Eight-six percent of Americans believe in God or a universal higher spirit (8%), 54% call themselves religious, and 68% of those belong to a church or synagogue. One in four Americans proclaim a different faith as adults than their childhood faith. Many feel there is a lot of hypocrisy in organized religion and prefer to have their "deep" moral beliefs while not disengaging from the church completely. I found it interesting that 86% believe there will be a day when God judges whether you go to heaven or hell, and 50% say even being a good person isn't "good enough" to get you to heaven unless you believe in God.[4]

Trust Issues

Have you felt that Americans don't trust one another much? An Ohio State University study in the *American Journal of Sociology* indicated that from 1975 to the late '90s trust in our fellow man declined about 10% according to findings. Despite the deplorable Clinton era, trust in government and religious organizations didn't dip overall. But it did go down with trusting our fellow man! People have a problem with people today. Most people feel that people would try to take advantage of them if they got a chance.[5]

The Divorce War

In the last thirty years we have nurtured a "culture of divorce" that has almost killed the strength of the family unit. When the stigma of divorce started to disappear from our society, a comfort zone set in that unraveled the sacredness of the family. Gay and lesbian couples stepped up their demands to unite, female celebrities are now having babies out of wedlock and touting it as "the new family" of the millennium, and people are choosing to live together over getting married because they can't see the point in marrying just to divorce later. The deception of each of those areas is monumental, and so is their influence on our entire culture, and particularly our youth, our future families of tomorrow.

Sadly, nearly half of all marriages end in divorce and 60% of second marriages follow the same pattern. In the 1990s, 40% of all married adults had already been divorced. Since 1970 at least a million children a year have seen their parents divorce, and half were under the age of six when the breakup occurred. Children from divorce are three times more likely to be referred for psychological help at school, one in four start to use drugs and alcohol before their fourteenth birthday, and by the time they were seventeen over half were drinking or on drugs. Children of divorce are sexually active earlier, have more children out of wedlock, less marriage, more divorce, and one in five females will have sex before age fourteen. Twenty-five percent of all children will spend part of their childhood in a stepfamily, and in young adult children of divorce, 66% feel closer to the stepdads, while only 47% feel close to stepmoms. Only about a third of adult children think of their stepmothers as parents, while about half regard their stepdads as parents. And we wonder why the family is "changing"?[6]

Grandparents Raising Kids

Research shows that grandparents are increasingly providing a large part of the caregiving for their grandchildren. In fact, about 7% provide extensive caregiving to their grandkids. That works out to 30 hours of childcare in an average week or at least 90 nights a year, according to the April 2001 issue of *The Gerontologist*. Approximately 20% of grandparents care for preschool-age children of working parents. Thank God for these grandparents! They are bonding closer to their grandchildren and sparing them from being raised by day-care workers or nurseries.[7]

Kids and Teenagers

In the beginning of the twenty-first century, our children and teenagers are going through amazing changes in a world that's far more hostile toward young people than ever before. Our kids are facing more stress, social pressures, family problems, media influence, entertainment seduction, and fears (especially school violence) than ever before. Take a look at the following topics and ask your child or teen if they can relate to any of these issues. Ask your child about their peer groups at school, and which one he or she belongs to. Ask them who's popular and who's not? Talk about your experience in high school, who the popular kids were, and who you hung around with. Maybe ask your child what areas he or she feels inadequate, embarrassed, confident, or positive about. Dialoguing in a natural way about any of these topics can create a positive "parent connection" with you and your child.

Growing Up Too Soon

In a survey of 375 mothers with children twelve years old and younger, *Sesame Street Parents* magazine found that moms are trying to slow down the clock and prevent children from rushing into new behaviors. Parents say they hear more requests from increasingly younger children to practice "grown-up" activities, such as to listen to older pop music and wear trendy clothing or makeup. In a day and age when girls are now showing signs of puberty at ages eight and nine, the idea of slowing down their "grown-up" activities seems like a good idea. Mothers are divided over how ready their children are for these changes. They formed two groups: 57% were identified as "sooner moms," who allow their kids to be exposed to the media culture; the remaining 43% were tagged as "later moms" because they limit their children's exposure. One question brought almost universal agreement: 93% say it's harder to be a mom in today's world.[8]

Kiddie Stress

Stress in children has increased 45% over the past thirty years, and pediatricians are seeing a record number of kids for physically related stress illnesses. Changing social structures, such as the breakdown of families, are leaving kids more vulnerable to stress and anxiety. As a result, our children are facing stress-related illnesses, childhood emotional disorders, etc.

What do children worry about? Researchers studied the normal worries of schoolchildren between the ages of 7 and 12, asking them about 14 areas of worry. When a child identified a specific area of worry, the researchers asked more detailed questions. The average number of worries per child was 7.64 and covered a wide range of topics, but most worried about health, school, and personal harm. The most *frequent* worries were about family, classmates, and friends. The most *intense* worries were about war, money, disasters, personal issues (e.g., grades), social relations, and death and social issues such as homelessness and the environment. When kids were asked what they would like to change the most in their lives, the frequent answer was "*to have parents who are less stressed and tired.*" [9]

Obviously, parents' stressed lives are affecting their kids. As parents we need to seriously think of ways to decrease the stress in our homes. Kids need an opportunity to practice relaxation that doesn't include our adding more stress to theirs. If you find yourselves running from event to event, it's time to slow down and rethink your priorities.

We should also regulate the amount of news our kids are watching on TV. I'm sure some of these kids are reacting to their parents' stress and imitating some of the same mannerisms they've observed or lived with. But topics of concern about war (an interesting "worry" from children who have only lived in peacetime), disasters, homelessness, and the environment are constantly being heard on the nightly news or television programs. It would have been interesting for the researchers to have logged how many hours these kids sat in front of a television listening to these reports. They might have discovered the *real* source of why these kids are so stressed.

Teen Stress

A September 2000 survey sponsored by *Teen* magazine and Sears found that out of 400 teenage girls, ages 12 to 17, 74% said their teen years are more stressful than those of their parents. Of those surveyed, 68% say their fellow teens are also stressed, and 58% said the biggest stress-inducer comes from being overscheduled.[10]

Female Teen Role Models

In that survey, girls were also asked who their positive female teen role models were, based on image, behavior, and/or style. Julia Roberts is the pretty woman most teen girls picked; Drew Barrymore and Christina Aguilera were next. What about Britney Spears? She was the pick for setting a "bad example."

Peer Pressure

What group does your teen fit into? Dozens of factors contribute to our youth culture, but a significant one is fitting in with a group of peers. Being popular usually involves different traits for boys and girls. The number one requirement for boys is athletic ability. For girls, it is first looks and then clothes and socio-economic status.

Would you describe your son or daughter as a prep, cheerleader, goth, punk, raver, or headbanger? Are they in the gay clique, racial clique, smart clique, bohemian clique, or freak clique? Apparently, even the "outsiders" have a loser clique. If this is confusing to you, imagine what your teen is going through.

Since bullying and teasing have become big issues with kids these days, getting into a group and feeling a part of one is a very big deal to them. Patricia Adler, co-author of *Peer Power: Preadolescent Culture and Identity*, says, "Finding a niche is the most important thing in a young-ster's life, it defines who you are. It sets the tone of your everyday experience. Without a group, your life could be hell."[11]

Although parents are extremely important in an adolescent's life, social scientists are now suggesting that "family disconnect" drives kids earlier to their second family of peers and pop culture. That's where teens find the acceptance they crave and claim that they don't have at home. The sad part is that there are no adults and no rules in that second family, and that's where smoking, drinking, drugs, and sex begin to take their devastating toll on their lives.

Teen 'Tudes

Josephson Institute of Ethics, a California-based institute that teaches character-building skills to teens, did a random survey among 15,000 teens at schools nationwide. Their results showed that 75% of boys and 60% of girls said they had hit someone in anger in the past year. Is it "OK" to threaten or hit a person who angers them? Forty-three percent of high school boys, 19% of high school girls, and 37% of middle-school boys said yes. Sounds as though these kids need a little attitude check. Talk to your teen and ask how he or she would react if someone did that to them?[12]

Teen Intervention

Parenting in our culture of perceived stress isn't easy. For years parents have been reading books and following trends from tough love to no spanking, raising self-esteem, instilling family values, drugging hyper-dyslexic kids and using other medications. Kids as young as nine are having sex and using drugs, and more kids (especially girls) are expressing violent, angry behavior.

What are some of the symptoms for problem teens?

✦ Unusual disciplinary problems.
✦ Dysfunction in schools.
✦ Deliberate defiance with parents.
✦ Frustrated most of the time, often angry.

It's no wonder many parents are confused and wanting answers. That's where teen-intervention programs such as Wilderness Quest in Monticello, Utah, come in handy. Starting with a handful of programs in the '70s, there are hundreds of programs available today. Parents pay about $14,000 for a six-to-nine week program for counselors to help guide troubled teens off of the course of self-destruction.

"Most come to the program with a history of using prescription drugs and seeing counselors since they were knee-high," says Larry Wells, director of Wilderness Quest. They arrive with an "entitlement expectation" that someone else is responsible for them. "Teenagers paint a picture of a very unfriendly teen world full of drugs, sex, and violence, unlike any generation before them. They're fearful of school, and the harassment and scapegoating of the weaker kids. There just seem to be a lot more pressure in their world and there's not much fun."[13]

And what's the worst mistake a parent can make when dealing with an out-of-control teen? Giving up too soon and trying to cajole with rewards.

School Shootings

Violence in the schools has become the number one concern on most teenagers' (and even children's) minds these days. Since the Columbine shooting on April 20, 1999, in Littleton, Colorado, nine other school shootings have taken place as of April 2001.

In March 2001, right *after* the San Diego shooting at Santee, California, a Gallup poll asked 1,015 parents about the likelihood of a school shooting happening in their community. Of those polled, 37% said it was very likely, 34% said somewhat likely, and 20% said somewhat unlikely. The fact is it could happen anywhere, anytime, by male or female, and that's the real world we live in. Like it or not, it's time to be honest with ourselves and our children.[14]

Every violent act reminds us to look for the warning signs of potentially violent kids. There are some identifiable risk factors, but it doesn't always guarantee a teenager will act out violently. Truthfully, there simply are no guarantees. But a 2000 study on school violence conducted by the Secret Service analyzed thirty-seven shootings in twenty-six states since 1974 and advises the following:

- ✦ Encourage your child to tell authorities about over-heard threats, even if it sounds like a joke. Take threats seriously.
- ✦ Promote trust between students and the adults who supervise them so that students won't fear telling someone in authority.
- ✦ In more than two-thirds of shooting cases, the shoot-ers felt persecuted, bullied, threatened, attacked, or injured by others.
- ✦ In almost all cases, the attackers acted after careful planning. More than half listed revenge as motive.
- ✦ Most of the time suspects told someone about their plan, expressing concern, anger, or fear.
- ✦ In nearly two-thirds of cases, attackers got their guns from their own home or relatives.
- ✦ Finally, there is no accurate or useful profile of a school shooter. Rather, behaviors and communica-tions have to be the deciding factors if a student is appearing to plan an attack.[15]

My Son's Experience

My son's school had an eighth grade boy threaten to bring a gun and "shoot the popular kids." Nathan came home and excitedly told me about it. I joked with Nathan that he didn't have to worry because he "wasn't popular," and he laughed. Then he told me that earlier in the day he sat in front of the troubled boy and had asked him if he was on his list. The boy said no, patted his shoulder, and told him, "No, man, I like you." I thought Nathan was joking, but he wasn't.

The whole incident hit me very hard. Although the boy didn't have a gun and it turned out that he was just a problem kid wanting attention, my son didn't know that. Kids have a hard time realizing a fellow student could (or would) commit such a horrible act. Nathan and I talked about what he should do in the future if something like that ever happens again.

Parents, as surreal as it feels, you need to talk with your child about what to do if another kid brings a gun to school or if violence breaks out. Although it may feel like an overreaction, we live in a time when that discussion just might save your child's life.

Suicide and Depression

Suicide is now the third leading cause of death among people between the ages of thirteen and twenty-four. According to a recent survey of high school students, 60% of teens often think about killing themselves, and 9% say they have made an attempt at least once. In the past three decades, teen suicide has risen 300%.

Signs of teen depression are sleeping more than usual, not sleeping well, and feeling tired, appetite changes, restlessness, isolation from friends and family, concentration problems, losing interest in activities, hopeless and guilt feelings, sudden mood changes, changes in grades and health, and a feeling that life isn't worth living.

Dr. Linda Mintle (author of *Kids Killing Kids,* Creation House) says, "Sometimes, as parents, we feel overwhelmed by the dangers our teens face. But there is hope and much you can do to help a depressed and suicidal teen. Suicide is preventable. You are not powerless to help." These are the preventative steps she offers:

- ✦ Talk about their suicidal feelings. Talking about suicide does not cause someone to do it. Ask if they have a plan. If they do, they are more at risk.

- ✦ Don't promise to keep suicidal feelings a secret. Make it clear that people must be told so that help can be given.

- ✦ Communicate that there is a way out of whatever they face. Suicidal teens are convinced that killing themselves is the only answer. They have options that need to be presented.

- ✦ Don't lecture. Teens will talk if you listen. Make yourself available.

- ✦ Reassure them they are not a burden. Assure them you want to hear what they are thinking and feeling and will take it seriously.

◆   Remove any means for self-harm. If there are guns, pills, knives, or ropes available for harm, get rid of them.[16]

Healthy Humor

If you want to live longer, rent a funny video! No joke! (Go to www.hollymcclure.com for my selections!) Watch a funny video with your family and laugh it up! According to Lee Berk, associate director at the Center for Neuro-immunology at the Loma Linda School of Medicine, laughter will give you a healthy, balanced life and can keep you healthy. In *Parenting* magazine, Berk and other researchers concluded that laughter helps in a lot of areas. It produces NK cells that fight infections, including pneumonia and bronchitis. Laughter also suppresses the release of cortisol, a hormone that weakens the immune system. It functions as a natural analgesic that raises the body's pain threshold and acts as a muscle relaxer. Lighter laughter increases circulatory capacity and strengthens organs, helping the body to become more resistant to infection while boosting energy levels. Children can find something to laugh at an average of 400 times a day, so parents need to get a sense of humor. Laughter is, indeed, the best medicine![17]

ENTERTAINMENT TRENDS

Star Moms Without Dads

Several years ago former Vice President Dan Quayle criticized Hollywood for glamorizing single momhood on the show *Murphy Brown*. Although Candice Bergen, who was married at the time and a mother, admitted after the show was off the air that she agreed with Quayle, the damage that the writers set out to do worked.

A decade later in Hollywood there's a growing trend of "celebrity moms" who have decided to opt for "motherhood without fathers" and raise their children either with their lesbian partners, other partners, or alone. Some of these celebrities are Rosie O'Donnell, Jodie Foster, Macy Gray, Linda Ronstadt, Sandra Bernhard, Janine Turner, Madonna (until 2001), Kate Jackson, Camryn Manheim, Melissa Etheridge, and Calista Flockhart. Camryn Manheim and Jodie Foster chose to be single birth moms without revealing the father, but the rest have adopted. When asked if it was hard to raise kids without a father,

O'Donnell said, "Everything in life is easier if you're famous."[18] I guess everything is, except for buying a father.

Family Films

When I started to review movies for parents back in 1987, there were only a handful of movies that catered to the family. I grew up on Disney when the name was synonymous with family entertainment (*Mary Poppins, The Parent Trap,* etc.). But through the '70s, Disney seemed to have lost its magic, particularly with animated films that lacked the "special effects" and "exciting plots" of movies such as *Superman, Star Wars,* or *Close Encounters of the Third Kind.* In short, animated Disney was boring. So smaller film companies took over with *Benji, The Life and Times of Grizzly Adams,* and *Pete's Dragon.*

In the '80s there were a few movies from bigger studios such as *The Muppets Take Manhattan, An American Tail, Benji the Hunted, The Land Before Time,* and *Who Framed Roger Rabbit.* But the real breakthrough was the hit *The Little Mermaid* (1989).

Disney utilized a new color computer technology on *The Little Mermaid* that allowed more colors on the palette to create a brighter, more colorful movie to accompany its great soundtrack and lovable characters. That technology literally revolutionized and revitalized the animation industry and rebirthed the Disney legacy. A string of hits followed, each one improving on the previous success with techniques, skills, story lines, and characters: *Aladdin* (1992), *The Lion King* (1994), *Pocahontas* (1995), *Toy Story* (1995), and *The Hunchback of Notre Dame* (1996).

When *Pocahontas* debuted in 1995, many parents were upset about the seductive shape of Disney's heroine along with the strong new age philosophy and historical inaccuracies sprinkled throughout. Disney did it again with *The Hunchback of Notre Dame* (1996), making sexy Esmeralda the desire of the evil minister who sings seductive songs of desire for her. This time when parents complained, Disney got the message and toned down the sexy female leads for younger children in *Hercules* (1997), *A Bug's Life* (1998), *Mulan* (1998), and *Tarzan* (1999).

Credit also has to be given to WB, DreamWorks, Paramount, Sony, Universal, and Fox for their efforts in the '90s to create a wonderful family market that challenged Disney and one another. Those movies included *The Little Princess, The Iron Giant, Lassie, The Princess Bride,*

The Black Stallion, Free Willy, Babe, The Indian in the Cupboard, The Prince of Egypt, Antz, Andre, and others.

THE SUPERNATURAL AND OCCULT

Any time the dark side of the supernatural world is presented as harmless or even imaginary, there is the danger that children will become curious and find too late that witchcraft is neither harmless nor imaginary. In a culture with an obvious trend toward witchcraft and New Age ideology, parents need to consider the effects that these ideas may have on young and impressionable minds.

—Linda Beam, *Focus on the Family*[19]

Harry Potter

J. K. Rowling's "Pottermania" magically floated to our book stores in September 1998 with *Harry Potter and the Sorcerer's Stone,* and it turned the publishing world upside down. It was soon followed by *Harry Potter and the Chamber of Secrets* (June 1999), *Harry Potter and the Prisoner of Azkaban* (September 1999), and *Harry Potter and the Goblet of Fire* (July 2000). By April 2001 there were 1 million audio versions, 40 million books in print, translations in over 40 languages, and Rowling's publisher has cleared well over $200 million, making Rowling the highest paid woman in Britain.[20]

Rowling's books have generated a hotbed of opinions not only among concerned parents but among the Christian community as well. The books are clever, funny, well written, well researched, and deliver an exciting story you don't want to put down. Although Harry represents good, he uses lies and deception and magic to triumph over evil, so the roles of good and bad are blurred. He's a witch who tries to do good, which is not a "standard tale of good versus evil."

By following the orphaned Harry through adventures with his best friend Ron and other magical characters, the reader gets a glimpse of good and evil, hatred, forgiveness, loyalty, compassion, friendship, and self-sacrifice. Harry's world has its own vocabulary, an evil wizard who killed Harry's parents and is after Harry, Quidditch (a world cup flying soccer-like game played on broomsticks), and Hogwarts (a boarding school for magical boys and girls).

Some say that Rowling has delivered what most Christians enjoyed in the C. S. Lewis books, a fantasy story where the good guy wins. Christian author Chuck Colson describes Rowling's magic as "purely mechanical, as opposed to occult," explaining that, "Harry and his friends cast spells, read crystal balls, and turn themselves into animals—but they don't make contact with a supernatural world."21 *Christianity Today* takes a similar stand, toning down concerns by calling the Harry Potter books "literary witchcraft."22

But others are concerned about the books' dark side. If *Harry Potter* is as harmless as these two representatives of the Christian faith say it is, then why are so many witches praising Rowling's books? Why do you have practicing Wiccan (witch) Phyllis Curott say, "Sure, you are seeing witches in *Harry Potter* do things they don't do in real life. But it is positive. They are friendly. They are good. The book might change the way people feel about us." Or check out the High Priest Egan of the First Church of Satan in Salem, Massachusetts. He said, "Harry is an absolute godsend to our cause. An organization like ours thrives on new blood—no pun intended—and we've had more applicants than we can handle lately. And, of course, practically all of them are virgins, which is gravy."23

Perhaps we should take this approach. If Rowling's books are truly ideologically on an equal level with *The Chronicles of Narnia* (C. S. Lewis) or *The Lord of the Rings* (J.R.R. Tolkien), then why aren't more witches praising those Christian authors with the same passion and praise as Rowling? It's because they relate to her book through the witchcraft. So if witches connect with these books and praise them for their accuracy with the occult, doesn't it stand to reason that children could become swept up and enamored with the occult in the same way?

I've spoken with several people who have studied the occult and witchcraft. Rowling claims that she is "bemused that anyone who has read the books could think that I am a proponent of the occult in any serious way,"24 but she clearly knows *way* too much about her subject to not have studied it. Rowling intertwines numerous references to ancient and modern occultism, sometimes hiding them in characters' names. So while she may not believe in the witchcraft she wrote about, she's definitely channeling occult knowledge from somewhere.

My concern for younger children who read these books is the adult level violence, gore, cruelty, and language along with the scary characters. My concern for the older ones is their getting "hooked" on the stories and desensitized to witchcraft and the occult practices. Some children will handle this issue without a problem, but others won't. The same is true of kids who watch a violent movie or play a violent video game.

Author Richard Abanes has written an excellent book that I recommend, *Harry Potter and the Bible* (Horizon Books). It is an intelligent exposé on the book series that covers all of the areas of concern extensively with common sense and objectivity. No one wants to be a Bible-thumping spoilsport, but whether Harry Potter is unhealthy for certain children must be addressed.

If you have read all of the books, ask yourself this: How much darker can the series get? I contend they will get a lot worse. And after the *Harry Potter* movie is released by Warner Brothers, I am certain that our children will crave almost anything and everything to do with witchcraft. Kids are already flocking to Wiccan Web sites for spells and potions. The movie will give children a visual image of what they've been reading, and as soon as that "fantasy world of witchcraft" comes to life, it is going to seduce kids of all ages to emulate what they saw on screen, "acting out" the "darker side."

Warner Brothers is going to make a fortune on this movie and so will the toy companies. Hasbro and Mattel are coming out with Harry Potter action figures, trading cards, role-playing games similar to Dungeons & Dragons, high-tech toys, and a line of clothing. Video games, computer games, book bags, and candies based on the wild-tasting "Every Flavor Beans" eaten by Harry and his companions will make the cash registers ring.

With the swelling momentum for Harry Potter, parents need to know where they stand on this matter. If you have a child who insists on reading *Harry Potter* books, why don't you at least take turns reading it to each other. Then discuss what you read and find out what (if anything) scared or bothered your child.

They're Just Mad About Harry

Many schools are reading Harry Potter books in their classrooms, which has upset many parents and prompted them to organize protest groups. There are twenty-five school districts in seventeen states where parents have challenged the reading of *Harry Potter*, defining their cause as less about the issue of "good book versus bad book" and more about "appropriateness and undermining parental authority." Their contention is simply: If Harry Potter's brand of witchcraft gets attention, so should Christianity and Judaism and Islam. It's not fair to allow a teacher to read a book that some regard as promoting the religion of witchcraft and deny other religions their rights.[25]

Nite Stine for Kids?

R. L. Stine of *Goosebumps* fame has a new series of spooky stories for kids called *The Nightmare Room*. He was inspired by the old *Twilight Zone* TV show, but he says *The Nightmare Room* is more straightforward. In the books a normal kid takes one step, opens one door, and suddenly has stepped into a nightmare. Stine made the Guinness World Records 2000 Millennium Edition for the best-selling children's book series.

Pokémon

As a family film reviewer, I'm always keeping my eye open for entertainment trends that could harm or inspire adverse behavior in children or teens. When I first heard about the Pokémon movie, I shrugged it off as another attempt by Hollywood to capitalize on a popular kids' game. When I took a closer look at the trading cards and did some research on Web sites, I was shocked at how dark this "children's game" really is, and how deceptive the occult and fantasy themes are.

The video game debuted in Japan in 1995 but didn't become popular in the States until last fall. Since then the phenomenon has spread and become a $5 billion-plus craze that's sweeping the country and enticing our children with everything from trading cards, a Nintendo video game, a Saturday morning cartoon show, and a full-length movie, *Pokémon: The First Movie*.

Pokémon (POH-kay-mahn) is short for "Pocket Monster," the name given to little monsters that roam in the wild. It's the creation of a Japanese man named Satoshi Tajiri, who created a universe inhabited by monsters and the children who can train them. Each monster has a characteristic special power, and most can evolve into a meaner, more powerful monster. What powers do these cards possess?

Exeggcute can hypnotize; Pinsir can paralyze; Gloom poisons and sends a foul odor; Abras teleport their way out of trouble; Kadabra sends waves of mental energy that cause headaches; Staryu, Mr. Mime, and Alakazam have psychic abilities; Haunter puts opponents to sleep while draining their energy; Psyduck mesmerizes with a piercing stare and then unleashes a barrage of pent-up mental energy.

The point of Pokémon is to collect all 151 monsters and become a Pokémon master, which means parents have to buy as many packages as they can afford and pay premium for rare cards that retain no value. Aside from becoming an obsession with kids, the game seems to separate the winners from the losers. In Japan there's a Pokemon song that goes, "Can you name all the Pokemon?" and then lists the 150 names. Apparently, kids who can't memorize all the names are socially shunned.

So how is this game affecting our kids? Parents are reporting behavioral (aggression, bickering, hyperactive) changes in their children. Schools have banned the cards from classrooms because kids are so obsessed with trading they can't study or concentrate, and many kids are actually getting into fistfights.

I was a bit mystified as to why more parents weren't openly complaining until I read a quote by Jenny Bendell, public relations manager of Wizards of the Coast, which makes the Pokémon trading card game and markets Dungeons & Dragon: "The running joke is the older you get, the harder it is to understand. But the kids seem to get it." Norm Grossfield, executive producer of the Pokémon TV show, sounded a similar theme: "One of the reasons [for Pokémon's success] is that it's a magical world created for kids which is so complex that really only kids can understand it. It's their own secret, private thing they can all become experts on."26 This exclusive child-product relationship adds a type of adult-free independence to the experience. The idea of child autonomy is even built into the premise of the TV show with the main character leaving home at ten years old on his quest to become a Pokémon trainer. Once again, parents are taken for passive fools and excluded.

Digimon

Twentieth Century Fox released *Digimon: The Movie* in hopes of making the kind of money the Pokémon films did. *Pokémon: The First*

Movie grossed an impressive $85.7 million, and the second film, *Pokémon: The Movie 2000*, has taken in more than $42 million. Pokémon (pocket monsters) and Digimon (digital monsters) both have trading cards, cartoon series, and lots of merchandise. Monster see, monster do. But the fact that they are similar isn't surprising. The Japanese don't seem to mind copying if it is a good idea, i.e., if it makes money. Digimon, in which kids are unexpectedly transported by "digivices" to a colorful and enigmatic world full of small monsters, supposedly has more action and is more intense than Pokémon. But both seem to have run their course in America.[27]

I THINK THEY'RE DETERMINING EVERYTHING—from what we watch, to fashion, to music, to what films are getting made, to what product is being produced. If you can tap into that group, I think you're gold, because they are influencing kids younger than they are, and closely watching and emulating what's gong on with the group that's older than they are.

—T. L. STANLEY, Editor of "What's Hot Now"[1]

A CHILD'S LIFE IS LIKE A PIECE OF PAPER on which every person leaves a mark.

—CHINESE PROVERB

Marketing
Our Culture

Children see 20,000 TV commercials a year. More kids know the Budweiser frogs, Joe Camel, Britney Spears, the Simpsons, and The Rock than know the name of the vice president of the United States.

ADVERTISING

Many advertising agencies continue to push the boundaries of good taste in the never-ending pursuit to get their product noticed. In the past, advertisers were careful not to offend their target audience for fear of a financial backlash. Today they seem to relish the idea of creating controversy served in provocative ways. Magazines are using gender neutral ads or nudity, and provocative underwear catalogs look like issues of *Playboy* without the articles. Billboards on major freeways have become soft porn for commuters, and hard porn for children in car seats who snicker at the nudity. How do these advertising ploys on television, the Internet, newspapers, magazines, and even billboards affect us?

Let's take a look at the many ways this medium influences our lives.

Kid-fluence

The buying power of children is so strong that it's now called "kid-fluence." This "kid-fluence," as James McNeal of McNeal & Kids Consulting calls it, is expected to grow 5% to 20% over the next ten years and will undoubtedly influence where families' entertainment decisions will be made. They will ultimately demand more from the entertainment industry. But that's not all. Of the twenty-two million five- to eighteen-year-olds that went shopping on the Web in the year 2000, 67% did research and made almost $300 million in purchases on the Internet.[2]

Teen-Influence

According to a recent survey conducted for Marshalls by Opinion Research Corporation, 63% of teens felt that friends and peers are the most important factor influencing their fashion choices. That far out-weighs magazines (10%), television (7%), music stars and videos (5%), movies (3%), family members (3%), models (1%), and other factors (5%). A mere 3% of responding teens felt there was no influence of their fashion choices.[3]

Parents' Influence

Many affluent parents, who have given their children a comfort-able lifestyle, are worried that the emphasis on money and material possessions outweighs or is out of balance with their perspective on life and reality. The U.S. Trust Department reported that in their research:

- ✦ 61% of kids today place too much emphasis on material possessions.
- ✦ 57% are naïve about money and how hard it is to earn.
- ✦ 54% spend beyond their means.
- ✦ 47% let initiative be undermined by material advantages.[4]

Kid Fixated

America is returning to a society focused on our children. Parents are moving away from the "latchkey-kid syndrome" of the '90s and finding 11% more time to spend with their kids.[5] Parents are giving our millennial kids love, material things, and more of themselves. But with seventy-nine million of them, our pop culture is doing the same. I'm referring to our television shows, movies, advertisers, marketing companies, magazines, and media that are *obsessed* with marketing to our kids and teenagers. Our "kid-minded" and "tween-fixated" pop culture has offered them a steady diet of narcissism and idol worship.

Cross Promoting Products

Next time you're in a store, look in the software section and see if you recognize characters from your child's favorite books, movies, toys, and TV characters on the software. Look familiar? Cross promoting products is booming in this country, and the key market is children. Multimedia leveraging is transforming everything from *Barbie* to the *Rugrats* to *Sesame Street* and turning cartoons into books, books into TV shows, TV shows into movies, and that's not counting the merchandise. "Edutainment" software for your preschool to sixth grader has matured, and now we're seeing *all the brands your kids are familiar with* ready to plug into your computer. Brand recognition is tricky and can get very expensive, so ask yourself this question, "Will the game engage my child or will it just eat up space on my PC?"

TV Ads

For those who say the media doesn't have the power to influence or seduce our culture for the brief time that an image is on television, then how do you explain the staggering prices that advertisers pay to be a part of the Super Bowl commercial lineup every year. Of all the events that highlight commercials, it has become more popular than the game itself. In the 2001 Super Bowl XXXV, fifty-five advertisers paid as much as $2.3 million for each thirty-second spot to air before a U.S. audience of 144 million.[6] The TV network determines the prices each year, and for those millions of dollars, advertisers are hoping you watched their ad just *once* to make their investment worth it. Product placement, TV commercials, Super Bowl ads, and even Internet ads are costly for a sixty-second reason—the power of suggestion to influence consumers to spend their dollars.

Regarding product placement, advertisers in the not-to-distant future will have to reinvent the way they relate to programming. Instead of being scheduled to air between programs, we will see them increasingly embedded in the program itself. Experts in the industry say that in ten years, half the people watching TV won't see the ads. TiVo was designed to let the viewers fast-forward through commercials, and although it's new, it's gaining in popularity.

Magazines

Magazines have taken on a more seductive look than ever before. Provocative covers, some with nudity and most with seductive sexual themes, have made *Cosmopolitan, Glamour,* and others the target of Morality in Media (MIM), which launched a campaign against magazines with explicit headlines. MIM sent letters to more than 350 national and regional chains urging them to pull the magazines or shield their covers.

MIM is not alone in this battle. A national survey revealed that 73% of people believed provocative magazine headlines are inappropriate.[7] And fashion is only one front in which your child will be culturally challenged. Look at most of the magazines at the grocery check-out counter, and you quickly see the overt sexual messages to which kids are exposed. Your job as a parent is to be the cultural guardian of your family. This means you have to guard your child's mind and heart starting at an early age.

If the original Barbie were a real live woman, she'd stand 7'2" tall and have 40-22-36 measurements. The average woman in North America is 5'4" tall, a size 12, and 37-29-40.

SEXUAL IMAGE

Girls pay attention to the images they see on television, in magazines marketed to tweeners, and even in Barbie doll shapes. At a time when teenagers struggle to understand their sexual development and are undecided about sexual choices, they are encouraged to try to live up to these sexual fantasies in the media. It's as though there's a "national cult of thinness," says clinical psychologist Mary Pipher, author of *Reviving Ophelia.* "In all the years I've been a therapist, I've yet to meet one girl who likes her body. Girls as skinny as chopsticks complain that their thighs are flabby or their stomachs puff out. They have been culturally conditioned to hate their bodies."[8]

Cosmopolitan Girl, "a cool new magazine for teens," tells girls how to give "an absolutely heavenly New Year's Eve kiss."[9] The kissing guidelines are graphic and erotic. An advertisement for a Maidenform bra reads, "Inner beauty only goes so far." These magazines are provocative and ignoble, offering graphic guidelines for French kissing and other inappropriate behaviors to tweeners. They expose tweens to sexual messages prior to their emotional readiness to handle them.

In an oversexed culture, it's important to teach young girls the balance between trying to be nice-looking and obsessing on beauty.

Being obsessed with appearance often causes girls to develop eating disorders. As a parent, you must counter these harmful cultural messages. As you teach your daughter respect for her body, incorporate how she dresses as an outward expression of that respect. This doesn't mean she can't be fashion conscious. It means they have to stay within certain guidelines. Be clear on what those guidelines are.

Kid Plastic Surgery

Teens are now one of the fastest-growing plastic surgery markets. *Cosmetic Surgery Magazine* was launched in the fall of 1999 and provided ninety-eight pages of ways to improve your looks. What's the message to budding pubescent girls? Since outward appearance is everything, consider plastic surgery and learn how to arouse a guy.

Nine-year-old girls are dieting, and teens are wanting (and getting) breast augmentation. Why? They want to look like Jennifer Lopez, Christina Aguilera, or the many models and thin celebrities they see in the media. It should not surprise us in that the dominant message of the new millennium is that looks count for more than your inner person.

Parents, take a look at the *Teen People* or *Cosmopolitan Girl* magazines marketed to young girls. Read the articles and discuss the appropriateness of the sexual content with your daughter or niece or granddaughter. Sit with her and ask if this is helping her develop self-control and an acceptable view of her body. Help her understand the culture's obsession with beauty. Then discuss your acceptance of her just the way she is, and God's acceptance of her, emphasizing how important her heart and character are.

Anorexia and Bulimia

Since WWII, the media (television, movies, magazines, etc.) have increasingly held up thinner body images as the ideal for women. Study after study repeatedly has determined that young girls are constantly targeted more than boys about looks, romance, and image in magazines, and it's taken its toll on them.

Anorexia and bulimia signal a troubled body and soul. Eating disorders such as anorexia nervosa and bulimia are common among college students, says registered dietitian and author Ann Selkowitz Litt. Anorexia nervosa is a psychological disorder in which a person purposely loses weight as a result of dieting, but the dieting gets out of control. The dieting is a symptom of emotional issues, says Litt, who works with people who have the disorder. Bulimia is characterized by binging, eating a large amount of food in a short period, then purging to get rid of the food by vomiting, laxative abuse, and/or diuretic abuse. The numbers for these cases have skyrocketed in recent years. The media's driving force is to focus on one image—to be successful, popular, and beautiful you have to be thin.

Tattoos and Body Piercing

Tattooing and body piercing is the popular trend with today's teens and twenty-something's. What was once considered a socially lower-class thing to do is now the rage with celebrities, sports figures, and especially our youth sporting "tribal bands" and artistic creations.

But for some, tattooing or piercing is not edgy enough. Now that a large segment of our society is doing it, those who are "on the edge" and want to be "different" are getting "implant" body modification. This is a new art form that implants beads under the skin on your wrist. It's known as three-dimensional body modification, but it doesn't stop with beads. As the practice becomes more popular and widespread, men are having shapes put under the skin on their genitals—and others are placing barbells, spheres, and rings under their wrists and . . . are you ready for this? Even horns placed on foreheads. Yes, they look satanic. In fact, the practice stretches the skin so that the horn passes through it. One end sits under the skin and the other on top!

SMOKING
Cigarette Advertising on TV?

Sure there is! Although cigarette advertising on TV has been illegal for almost thirty years, you wouldn't know it by watching it! Increasingly, there's blatant promoting going on in shows such as *Sex and the City*, where actress Sarah Jessica Parker lights up more than she beds down. You'll see smoking on *Frasier* and *West Wing*, and even Tyne Daly on *Judging Amy* is lighting up. Cable is just as bad or worse with smoking in movies.

We're seeing more actors smoking on the big screen than ever before. In fact, we watched people drag on those cancer sticks in 78% of the movies in the last ten years. Dartmouth Medical Researchers found that of the 250 movies studied, 217 featured tobacco use and 180 featured an identifiable brand. In other words, the cigarette industry has blatantly continued advertising even though there's been a ban on tobacco.[10] John Travolta (a popular star with the under-eighteen crowd) smokes in most of his movies and even had the nerve to portray an angel who was addicted to the nasty habit in *Michael,* yet he doesn't smoke in real life. What a drag!

How can advertising cigarettes be off limits but promoting them with character endorsements is not? Children aren't the only ones who are influenced subliminally by it. Adults are influenced just as much or more because many have already tried the habit and quit.

Product placement is where companies pay to have their product used, endorsed, or even just sitting in front of the camera? Perhaps Washington should check into the promotion of smoking on TV and see if it is a coincidence or a new way to advertise.

What About Kids?

With the daily bombardment of television programs and movies that show characters smoking, is it any wonder that kids emulate what they see instead of what they're taught? More than a fourth of the 8,388 schoolchildren who were in a fourteen-year study program designed to prevent schoolchildren from smoking are now regular smokers, says a report in the *Journal of the National Cancer Institute*. The experiment began in September of 1984 and was based on social influences and teaching the children skills to ignore social pressures to smoke. By the twelfth grade, 24.4% of the girls and 26.3% of the boys smoked—a rate identical to that of students who weren't in the study. An even higher rate of smoking took place two years after high school.[11]

Are Teens Influenced?

Hollywood relentlessly shows teens and adults smoking in movies and on television shows. Although it's illegal in many states for any-one under eighteen to own, possess, or smoke tobacco products, we know that's where it begins for most smokers. According to a 1998 survey by the Centers for Disease Control and Prevention, men are more likely to smoke than women (26.4% of men, 22% of women), and adults who did not finish high school smoke more than those with a college education. It's estimated that 90% of smokers pick up the habit in high school, which contributes to the death of 40,000 people a year.[12]

However, teenagers are more likely to quit because they are concerned that their secondhand smoke is hurting others more than they fear for their own health, says a survey in the journal *Pediatrics.*

Anti-Smoking Web Sites

If you have a teen that you suspect wants to try smoking or already has, here are a few Web sites that could possibly change his or her mind:

✦ www.thetruth.com was created by teens for teens. It's an incredible site backed by a foundation that is financed by the 1998 master settlement between the states and the tobacco industry. It shows in sickening detail just what tobacco can do to you: lost teeth, cancers of the nose, throat, mouth, tongue, cataracts, and hair loss.

✦ www.tobaccofree.org was a project of Patrick Reynolds (the grandson of R. J. Reynolds), who turned his back on his family business in 1986 after losing his father and oldest brother to tobacco-related deaths. On this site teens can read a speech Patrick wrote and check out before-and-after photos of Sean Marsee, a track star whose chewing-tobacco habit made him lose part of his jaw, nose, neck, and tongue before he died at age nineteen. It may sound disgusting, but sometimes seeing the truth makes more of an impact than hearing it.

Put This in Your Pipe and Smoke It!

"Roughly 18 million American *adults* think it's OK for parents to let their children smoke," says Arthur Cosby about a national survey from the *Social Science Research Center* at Mississippi State University. "Every tenth patient coming in thinks it's OK for their kids to smoke. That 10% is important, and it's a large number that surprised me." The report, *Smoking in America: 35 Years After the Surgeon General's Report*, was created to study how Americans view smoking after years of anti-campaigns and no advertising.

So how did we do? About 70% of American households are smoke-free, but the survey found that 31 million households allowed smoking in the house or car. Children are exposed to smoke in 21.6 million homes. Apparently Americans are ambivalent, confused, or all of the above about smoking. Why? Because like anything else, we are used to seeing people smoke, and we've been told to be "tolerant" of others' rights. So we let people do what they want to in our presence, even though we feel it's wrong for ourselves. The good news is that there are 40 million fewer smokers who don't because of the public health campaigns.[13]

Cell This!

A study done in England by the *British Medical Journal* with a number of fifteen-year-olds who smoked found that smoking dropped from 30% to 23% between 1996 and 1999. It also discovered that cell phone ownership rose from 23% in January of 1999 to 70% in August 2000. The author's theory is that because teens love to socialize with one another, bond with their peers, and mimic adults, they get the same gratification from cell phone conversations that they get when they smoke socially with each other. With the cost of cigarettes skyrocketing, talking on the phone with one another may not only be more pleasurable but more affordable.[14]

DRINKING

Older teens who drink are seven times more likely to have sex at a younger age and more likely to have several partners than teens who don't use alcohol or drugs. The Center on Addiction and Substance Abuse (CASA) at Columbia University found that out of 34,000 teenagers, 63% of those who used alcohol also have had sex, compared with 26% of teens who don't drink.[15]

Apparently there's also tremendous peer pressure on girls to drink. The behavior and influence of their five closest friends was the single biggest reason girls start to drink, but research also found that when parents were regularly involved and communicating with teens, they were less likely to drink or smoke.

Substance abuse is on the rise and is a major problem with teenagers today. Drugs and alcohol often become coping mechanisms for teens who are having problems in life. With that dependency comes addiction, and with addiction comes depression from not being able to function without alcohol or drugs.

I've had wonderful experiences with drugs, I mean really wonderful. In teaching personal epiphanies about life. About a different perspective.
                                                                —Keanu Reeves[16]

This drug dealer, who's in my book, said to me, "If God invented anything better than dope, he kept it to himself." When I heard that I thought, "Yeah, that's pretty good." But then, it occurred to me—there is one thing that's more powerful than dope, and that's movies.

—Richard Price[17]

DRUGS

A survey of nearly 600 teens in drug treatment in New York, Texas, Florida, and California indicated that 20% have shared drugs other than alcohol with their parents, and that about 5% of the teens actually were introduced to drugs—usually marijuana—by their moms or dads.[18] Classmates or neighborhood friends remain the most likely sources, but some baby boomers who went through the drug culture are enablers for their children who experiment with drugs. Some parents believe that sharing an occasional joint with their teenager can ease family tensions and make a parent seem more like a buddy in whom their teen can confide. Other parents regard marijuana use as a relatively harmless rite of passage for young adults.

Almost 60% of the baby boomers born in the USA from 1946 through 1964 say they have smoked pot at some point in their lives. But since their days of rebellion, the drug landscape has changed.[19] A smaller percentage of youths are using drugs regularly. But marijuana and other drugs are more potent than ever, and first-time users are more likely to be in middle school than in college. Many parents say they believe that most people will try illegal drugs at some point. Some parents, counselors say, naively figure that they're "protecting" their kids by allowing or even encouraging some drug use in the home.

THE DUMBING DOWN
OF AMERICA

The three buds from Budweiser's "Whassup" commercials provided one of the funnier commercials that debuted as a Super Bowl prize and charmed a nation of fans who liked hearing these three use their famous phrase. It's funny to laugh at until we see national statistics that prove we aren't getting smarter; we're getting dumber. In fact, the mentality and attitude that permeates MTV and other youth-oriented programs is indifferent to education. So WHASSUP with that?

Illiteracy

- ✦ 1 in 5 high school graduates cannot read his or her diploma.
- ✦ 85% of unwed mothers are illiterate.
- ✦ 70% of Americans arrested are illiterate.
- ✦ 21 million Americans cannot read.
- ✦ Illiteracy costs the USA about $225 billion a year in lost productivity.[20]

In case you'd like to help your kids read better, or maybe at all, here are some interesting sites to check out children's interactive media:

- ✦ www.childrenssoftware.com
    a magazine that provides reviews.
- ✦ www.kidsdomain.com
    a children's site with reviews written by parents.
- ✦ www.superkids.com
    reviews by teams of educators, parents, and kids.
- ✦ www.mediafamily.org
    offers ratings on content from the National Institute on Media and the Family.

YOU KNOW THAT EVERYTHING we're exposed to influences us. . . . Those violent films influence us, and the TV programs we see influence us. The weaker your family is, the more they influence you. . . . The problems with families in our cities are catastrophic. But when you put violent programs before people who haven't had a lot of love in their lives, who are angry anyway, it's like pouring gasoline on the fire.

—TED TURNER[1]

HOLLYWOOD IS A PLACE WHERE THEY'LL PAY YOU $10,000 FOR A KISS and fifty cents for your soul.

—MARILYN MONROE

CHAPTER **TWELVE**

Raising Your Kids to Be Media Savvy

IT BEGINS WITH YOU!

O K, parents! Having read about the many ways the world of entertainment and the media seduce and affect our culture, did you recognize areas that influence you or your family? If you did, you probably want to make some changes and look for ways you as a parent can empower your child or teenager.

Hollywood cannot be blamed for your children watching a late night adult show on TV, or buying an Eminem CD, or going into a theater to watch an R-rated movie. Despite the fact that there are documented cases of movies and television shows that have influenced people of all ages to commit crimes, dangerous stunts, or unhealthy acts, the key word here is "influence." Bottom line, it all boils down to each one of us making choices that allow those influences to affect our lives.

Parents, like it or not, the burden of preparing your impressionable and imitative children and likewise educating your family about those seductive choices of Hollywood and our culture starts with you! Parenting is a full-time job not to be taken lightly. If you don't lay a foundation of morals, upright values, honest ethics, integrity, self-discipline, self-respect, responsibility, accountability, and trustworthiness in your children's lives, the world will step in and substitute its own system!

It starts with teaching a basic fundamental value system of knowing how to discern right and wrong, good and evil, along with bringing a balanced moral accountability. These give children the tools to embrace a values system that respects human dignity and life while being accountable for the way they live. Teaching your children how to discern between the fantasy world of entertainment and the reality they live in will give them the fundamentals to become media savvy in their seductive youth culture.

For instance, you not only owe it to yourself and your children to talk to them about anger issues and carrying out that anger in violent acts, but each parent owes it to society. No matter what entertainment medium a child or teenager is exposed to, the fact that he or she would carry out that anger with an atrocious, violent act is an obvious sign of deeper issues and larger problems at home. As we have seen in so many cases, the parents were either uninvolved in that child's life or too busy to notice the problems that were developing.

You need to realize there is a price "hands-on" parents pay for taking a stand to protect your kids. You have to forfeit a self-centered lifestyle and perhaps lose a popularity contest with their children. But the reward is a solid parent/child relationship and a family with a strong foundation. This will never happen for parents who close their eyes and hope their kids turn out for the best when they leave their kids to be raised by the television, peers, their teachers, and, ultimately, our culture.

Most Christian parents not only don't manage the flow of media into their homes or into the lives of their kids, they actually consume statistically the same amount and very much the same kind of product as people who make no claims to being Christians at all.
—Larry Poland, CEO of Mastermedia Inc.[2]

Biblical morality is being assaulted relentlessly in our culture every day. In Proverbs 4:23 the Lord instructs us: "Watch over your heart with all diligence, for from it flow the springs of life." Our eyes and ears are gateways into our heart, and our will is the gatekeeper. What we choose to let through those gates will affect the quality of life in our "well." If we allow philosophical sludge and immoral debris into the well of our heart, then we will pollute our own water supply. In our physical bodies, a weak immune system cannot resist disease; likewise, a polluted soul cannot resist sin.

For years the church as a whole has treated Hollywood as a taboo. Hollywood is a temptation clearly enjoyed by most, but an enigma to confront. The need for contemporary Christians to educate themselves and their children on becoming more media and entertainment savvy has never been more important than it is today. Jesus Christ didn't dodge seductive or negative cultural influences that continually surrounded and attacked His disciples and their ministry. He didn't run from Satan and His temptations. Instead, Jesus taught His disciples how to handle each situation using parables (an early form of a screenplay) and God's powerful words to confront and combat the problems in their culture.

Some parents remove the television sets from their homes because they are so disgusted with the immoral and offensive programs. They likewise regulate any movies that aren't PG or G rated. While I applaud monitoring television programming and movie picks for your family, I think there's a danger in completely sheltering your kids from the culture they have to confront and live in. Unless those children are being prepared to understand *why* and *what* you are protecting them from, they will become curious and seek answers on their own.

My sister Amy and her husband, Casey, received Masters degrees in communications at Regent University, and both know the power of movies and television. They have monitored what my nephew Ben and nieces Madeline and Audrey are allowed to watch on video, television, or at the movies. I even have to ask her permission on certain movies before I send videos to the kids! My sister's reasoning makes sense. She doesn't ban all television or movies from their home. Rather, she selects what TV shows the kids can watch and what movies can stay in the home to be seen over and over again. She says, "If they are going to meditate on these movies by watching them several times, eventually memorizing some of the lines, then I want to make sure the message they are getting is one I want my children to take into their hearts, minds, and spirits." She's trying to teach her children to guard their hearts by making good entertainment decisions.

When children see or hear something just once, it is catalogued in their memory. But when children watch something repeatedly, such as their favorite videos, it becomes embedded in their heart. Have you heard the expression "memorizing" or "learning by heart"? When we take information to heart, it becomes a part of us. The VCR is a very effective tool for meditation and memorizing, both positively and negatively. If the show contains positive lessons, the repetitious viewing will build upon and reinforce the moral truth parents are trying to impart. If the shows' themes are negative, every viewing will act as a battering ram to tear down what parents have tried to build.

While it is important to protect and guard your children, if you completely isolate them from Hollywood's negative influences inside the home, you deprive them the chance to be emotionally and mentally prepared to handle it outside the home. Are you teaching your kids that all television viewing and movies are bad, or are you balancing your media message with practical, sensible advice? Are you discerning on what comes into your home, but likewise balancing that with information to help your child face influences outside your home? This is what separates a discerning, caring parent who is teaching their kids to be media savvy from a parent who hides behind "religious reasons" as their excuse to shirk parental responsibilities.

The media tells us what to think and, to a great extent, how to think.
—Marlin Maddoux, *Free Speech or Propaganda*

EMPOWER YOUR KIDS TO SAY NO!

Isn't it ironic that one of the easiest first words we humans learn to say ends up being one of the hardest words to say when we grow up? Teaching your child or teenager to say "no" to their peers (and to themselves) when confronted with negative or harmful entertainment choices (movies and clubs) or behaviors (smoking, drinking, drugs) is one of the most empowering tools you can give your child or teenager in life. It's that simple. That "no" answer could end up being a life-or-death, peer-pressure decision. Does your child or teenager feel confident enough about who they are and what they believe in to feel empowered enough to use it?

When my daughter Sarah was seventeen, a group of her friends wanted to go see the movie *Southpark*. Sarah told them she didn't want to see it, but they convinced her it would be funny. She watched for fifteen minutes, utterly disgusted by the language and crude story. Then she politely excused herself and told them she would meet them afterward outside. Within five minutes the rest of the group followed Sarah. They all got their money back and left. One of the boys said to her, "That was really cool that you left. I didn't want to stay either." My daughter learned an invaluable lesson about the importance of not compromising her values and the power the word "no" can have among peers.

America has a real strong Puritan Ethic. I don't like it. Pushing the edge of broadcast standards is something I've always done. Broadcast standards simply are whatever they'll finally let you do. That becomes the new standard.
    —Steven Bochco in an interview with *TV Guide*

HOW YOU AND YOUR FAMILY CAN FIGHT BACK!

There are three areas that parents need to learn special skills on how to raise their families to recognize Hollywood's seductive power and fight back. The three areas are "hands-on" parenting, raising kids to be media savvy, and raising kids to be culturally savvy. Ultimately, your goal is to send your mature teenager into the world to live as a moral and responsible adult in a world full of choices. How your young adult discerns those choices will be determined by the fundamentals you have helped build into their lives.

I. "Hands-On" Parenting

What do I mean by "hands-on"? I'm talking about parents who set limits on what movies their kids can see, what kind of television shows they can watch, when and where their kids can go out at night, what CDs they can or can't listen to in the home, and what friends they should or shouldn't socialize with. These are parents who raise children who are less likely to be heavily influenced by drugs, drinking, sex, and the seductive influences from the youth culture that preys on them.

Teens Want Parental Influence

Raising three teenagers as a single mom meant I had to not only be the fun-loving, nurturing mom but the "hands-on" disciplinarian as well. I had to be a 24-hour a day, 7 days a week parent! And you know what? That investment of time and parenting paid off! I have three very loving teenagers whom I've raised to be "media savvy" and see life practically with a discerning eye. They are fully aware of the real world that wages a constant battle on their sensibilities, and although they make mistakes like everyone else their age, they've learned by their mistakes. They have also allowed me to make my mistakes (and there have been many), which has been a good lesson for me as well. I have three happy, level-headed, goal-oriented teenagers with a balanced "media savvy" perspective on life and a godly faith that keeps them centered. They can differentiate between good and evil, right and wrong, and choose to hang with friends who believe the same way.

In a recent survey of high school students, 44% of the teens believe there is a "moral and social breakdown" in society today. They agree that communication with their parents is a positive thing. Some 59% cite their mother or father as the person with the greatest influence in their lives, and 67% say they will raise their children the same way as themselves.[3]

Parents who are "hands-off" and fail to set rules or monitor their child or teenager's behavior put those children at risk. As much as teenagers may complain about the rules their parents set for them, they see that parenting as a sign of care and love, which instills a sense of security in their lives. Kids and teenagers have an inherent need to feel their parents care enough to want to protect them.

8 Ways to Be a "Hands-On" Parent

1. *Communicate with your kids by making them feel "safe."* Most parents (58%) and almost three-quarters of the kids (73%) spend less than one hour a day talking to each other. Amazingly, nearly half the kids (46%) and a quarter (27%) of the parents say they talk less than one-half an hour each day. Only *one in five kids* (20%) say it's easy to talk to their parents about things that really matter, and more than 26% said it was "somewhat difficult" or "very difficult" to do. Creating a "safe" environment for your kids to talk to you in is *extremely important.*[4]

Parents, the only way your kids are going to know where you stand on important issues in *their* lives is to communicate with them. You can help your preteens and older teenagers feel comfortable by relating your own experiences with dating, smoking, sex, drugs, and drinking situations when you were young and how you handled those situations, good and bad. Talk to them about how you feel about these important issues *now* and what you expect them to do in these areas. The same technique (age appropriate, of course) can be used with your younger children, because they too are being tempted by many of these issues. Don't just have the discussion once and mentally "check it off your list." Keep your discussions ongoing. And don't try to be a buddy or pal with your kids. Be the parent they need you to be. Don't interrupt and be willing to listen to the "little" stuff, the trivial issues of early adolescent or teen life.

2. *Set limits and impose a curfew.* Every leading child psychologist will tell you that kids appreciate boundaries. Take time to set limits and boundaries on what influences your child's life (movies, TV, music, the Internet, video games, peers, and so on). Use discernment for different ages, giving privileges to the older siblings so that younger ones will want to earn that same freedom. Keep curfews on older teens as well as keeping a respect for the rest of the family in perspective.

3. *Know where your kids are after school and on weekends.* If possible, have an adult (if not you, then a grandparent, friend, trustworthy neighbor, relative) present when your child or teenager comes home from school. Some parents think childhood is the most important time to be a stay-at-home-mom, but the teen years are just as important and critical. Cell phones, pagers, relatives, and/or friends for kids to "check-in" will allow you to keep tabs on your child's whereabouts after school and during weekends. Make sure you are getting truthful answers of whom your kids are with, where they are going, and what they are going to do.

4. *Make the dinner hour a designated time to be with your children.* Whether you eat in, out, or drive-thru, make that a time to get in touch with your child's life and find out what went on in their day. Make few exceptions to this time together so that your family will begin to count on this time as quality "family time." Be sure to turn the TV off during dinner. It robs you of precious time you could spend with your children.

5. *Teach your kids that lying is wrong.* Lying has become a cultural problem in our society for adults and children alike. Lying ultimately destroys a person's *accountability*. Expecting the truth from your kids will make them take *accountability* for their *decisions* and *actions*. This is one of the greatest lessons you as a parent can teach your teenager today. Accountability will instill in your child or teenager the ability

to make responsible media decisions for themselves when a parent isn't around. But remember, as a parent, it's important to make sure your role is one of integrity, truth, and wisdom, so that your child will grow to respect you and your word. Be the "adult" example in your child's life and take a stand on teaching your child how important telling the truth really is and how important a person's word should be.

6. *Help transition your child from obedience to responsibility.* Every parent knows that eventually his child will be exposed to entertainment choices that contradict the moral truths that child was taught. Our goal should be to help our children transition from *obedience* to us to *responsibility* for themselves. Their reason for saying "no" should grow from "My parents wouldn't want me to see this" to "I choose not to see this because I know I won't benefit from it."

7. *Monitor media consumption in and out of the home.* Start with monitoring TV time and shows for all ages in your home. Ask what movie your child or younger teenager (under sixteen) is going to go see and be a part of that decision. Look over the information sites I've listed and ask questions about movies afterward to confirm if they saw the movie they said they did.

8. *Be a fun parent!* Make your home a friendly and fun place to be! A home your kid's friends will want to "hang out" at. And learn how to be creative and make the most of the time you spend with your children. One day I took Nathan to the top of a lookout point in Laguna Beach, California, to ride his Go-ped on the back mountain trails. As we were unloading his gear, three motorcycle riders pulled up to enjoy the view. The men and women exchanged comments with Nathan about his Go-ped, and as we were walking away one of the men yelled out, "You're really lucky you have a fun mom, kid. I wish my mom would have been like yours." Nathan yelled back a "thanks," then looked at me with a big grin and said, "I'm glad you're a fun mom." Kids appreciate the kid in you. Be fun!

People sometimes say that the way things happen in the movies is unreal, but actually it's the way things happen to you in life that's unreal. The movies make emotions look so strong and real, whereas when things really do happen to you, it's like watching television—you don't feel anything.
—Andy Warhol[5]

II. Raising Your Kids to Be "Media Savvy"

You must teach your kids to be "media savvy" and understand the seductive power of Hollywood. What does being "media savvy" mean? Children and teenagers should be taught how the entertainment industry tries to influence them to spend their money on movies, television, music, video games, magazines, and so on. After they have spent their money in one of these areas, the next influence comes through the messages, materialistic value, addiction, or obedience they choose to give that influence. Give your child or teenager helpful suggestions on how to not only recognize the influence but also how to realize if it will positively or negatively influence or affect their life.

8 Ways to Raise Media Savvy Kids

1. *Take your mature preteen (11–12) to a PG-13 movie you don't want them to see and watch it together.* Have your child review the movie for you and tell you why he or she liked it. Discuss the moral, ethical, and cultural influences the characters and story deal with (implied sexual situations, manner of dress, tattoos, whatever issues you feel you need to talk about) and talk about the reasons you as a parent don't approve of this movie and why you think it's harmful to see movies like this on a continual basis.

2. *Watch what your kids watch on TV.* Almost half of the children ages 8-17 have no parental restrictions on how much TV they watch or what programs or channels they watch.[6] Fifty-eight percent of American kids have a TV in their bedroom and 32% of them are ages 2-7.[7] Clearly there are unsupervised kids who may be watching programs they shouldn't. Walk in and sit down to watch a television show that's already in progress, preferably in the evening. Watch it with your older child and discuss casually some of the same points as mentioned above, remembering your child's age level. Ask who your child's favorite characters are and why. Regulate viewing habits with your child and teach them self-discipline about spending too much time in front of the tube. Teach your family when it's time to turn off the TV.

3. *Teach your pre-schooler to discern cartoons, and discuss it in language your child will understand.* Ask your child who the good guys and bad guys are, who their favorite character is and why? Start to do that with your child on a regular basis, letting them tell you about different

shows they watch. You may be surprised how much your young child retains. Do this with magazines, TV shows, and other entertainment aimed at this age. By your example of what is accepted and not accepted in your home, your children will learn to discern what's good or bad on TV.

4. *Put restrictions on what CDs your kids can buy and what music and lyrics are acceptable in your home.* Ten- to fourteen-year-olds now account for 9% of all CD sales in America,[8] so it's not just the older teenagers who are buying music. I recommend you do what I have done: go with your kids to the music store, read the lyrics on the covers of CDs they would like you to buy for them, and listen to a few songs before they purchase the CDs. It was eye-opening what messages were subtly hidden in many songs. If it's not something you approve of, ask them why they want it. You should also check the tapes or CDs their friends make and give to them.

5. *Keep the computer in a family area or your bedroom.* Make sure you have all the passwords and have clearly stated restrictions for its use where age appropriate. Periodically monitor what sites your children and younger teens are visiting. Check your computer to see what sites have been visited recently (see my Internet section).

6. *Pick up a teen magazine and sit down with your younger teenage daughter or son to look through it.* Ask your teen what clothing styles, articles, and ads he or she likes. Find out where your son or daughter stand on some of the sexual articles. Ask your daughter what fashions she finds offensive (if any) and what she would like to have in her wardrobe. If it's something you won't let her wear, discuss why. Ask your son what's seductive to him. Keep an eye on the magazines lying around your house, especially ones such as *Victoria's Secret* or *Teen People.* Remember, many of their ads are borderline soft porn.

7. *Consider the ages of your children and their maturity level.* Is your child mature or immature for his or her age? Take into account his viewing skills. Does he understand right from wrong and what or who is good or evil. Can he repeat a story after he has watched or listened to it? Does he have nightmares, sometimes wet the bed, and come into your bed late at night? Each child in your family is unique. Many parents blanket their family with the same lack of censorship because it's

easier to "let everybody watch it" than arrange for a young child to be out of the room. Be sensitive to the little things that disturb or bother your child when they see it (a scary space monster, a bloody body) and take into account their maturity level.

8. *Look for various forms of entertainment reviews from organizations you can trust and keep current on trends.* Visit different Web sites and stay current on what your kids and teens are watching, listening, and learning from, and *teach your kids and teens how to use these references when they are looking for entertainment choices.* Train your kids to learn to discern for themselves and empower them to make the right media choices.

It's a war. It's a cultural war, it's a moral war. It is a battle that's being fought out in many venues, from education to the media, entertainment, academia, and so on. So if people don't see that there is indeed a cultural war going on, they're not looking at the facts.

—Marlin Maddox, syndicated talk show host and author

III. Raising Your Kids to be Culturally Savvy

Young people today are growing up in a youth culture that expects them to look, act, and talk as though they are adults. Clothing advertisers, magazines, and television networks all cater to the "tweener" market with fashions that have an adult sexiness to them. Ads are designed to lure the younger market with sexy images, adult themes, name brand placing, and a focus on body parts (lips, legs, belly) for subtle objectification. *Teen People* and other teen magazines are mostly about sex. In fact, for as much sex as our society dishes out in one day through all the mediums, it's interesting how many young teenagers aren't prepared or educated to deal with sexual issues.

Girls are starting puberty earlier now (at eight and nine years old), yet many parents don't feel comfortable talking about sexual issues or body development with their child. Kids are discussing "blowjobs" (the term they use) in sixth grade, and in junior high STDs (sexually transmitted diseases) are being reported in record numbers from kids who are still claming they are still virgins.[9] When teens don't get answers from a parent, they turn to the media for answers to their questions about life, love, and sex.

A divorced father was upset when his eleven-year-old daughter was allowed by her mother to wear eye makeup and dress in older teen styles. He was truly heartbroken about it and told me, "I think it's sad that she was only allowed to be a little girl for a few short years. Now, because I've told her she can't wear makeup at my house, she's not coming over to visit me, and her mother is encouraging all of this!" Unfortunately, the girl's mother reflects a large segment of parents who are helping their children be robbed of their youth by a culture that caters to premature adulthood. The seductively dressed Britney Spears (this generation's Madonna) is a poster girl for how our society encourages kids to act older and be sexier than their age.

We have a nation of millennial kids swept up in a youth-oriented, seductive, self-important, "entertain-me" culture whose moral relativism is based on feelings and expediency rather than right or wrong. Standards of right and wrong have been replaced by personal preference and choice, and instead of being "media savvy," kids are "media addicts." So how can we further help and protect our children? By being the gatekeeper and teaching our kids what's socially or culturally appropriate and inappropriate. *These are teens, remember? Not adults.* They think they know things when they don't.

8 Ways to Raise Culturally Savvy Kids

1. *Understand today's culture.* Values and perspectives on life can change quickly, and you need to be hands-on with your kids. Research shows that kids still think parents are their main source of information. Take time to listen.[10] As uncomfortable as it might be, you need to admit if you have a hard time communicating with your child. Realize that your values, morals, and spiritual way of looking at life may differ from your teenager. The two of you won't always see eye to eye on entertainment choices, but talk about these differences.

2. *Know what moral dilemmas your child faces with his or her peers.* Talk over issues such as lying, drugs, and cheating. Teach your child integrity and character at a young age by making values-based decisions and reinforcing them over and over. This will help them face these moral dilemmas and act responsibly when you're not there.

3. *Teach your child social skills.* Help your child learn how to read the social responses of others. And help kids know the difference between anger, frustration, and anxiety, and learn how to control all

three emotions. Guide your child on becoming socially competent in a group and learning to take the social initiative.

4. *Role-play situations your child faces.* Go through what happens in a clique, with peers and friends. Ask questions such as "Why did this person say that?" "What else could you have done?" Then help by developing humorous responses your child or teen can use to keep things light and get them out of the situation. With TV shows and sitcoms rattling off sarcastic one-liners these days, we have a generation that respects a snappy retort. But teach the difference between put-down sarcasm and humorous retorts.

5. *Help your child learn to develop a sense of humor and tolerate teasing.* It's important children learn to have a sense of humor and be fun to be around. There's a big difference between teasing and humiliation. Kids who are hypersensitive to teasing are disliked by their peers and made bigger targets.

6. *Stay out of your child's disagreements.* Unless your child is in danger, he needs to learn to work issues out with his peers.

7. *Help develop genuine self-esteem.* You cannot instantly make this happen, but you can provide opportunities for your children that build self-esteem based on genuine accomplishments. Find the good and positive things to compliment your child on. Try not to be too critical, as these are very important years for developing self-esteem. I think this is harder for dads than it is for moms. Dads, your approval is *so important* in building self-esteem and self-worth in your son or daughter, and hearing loving words from you can change that self-esteem. Moms, your words are equally as important in developing positive self-images in your children.

8. *Moral absolutes must be taught to counter what the culture says.* Remember that outside entertainment influences are always more powerful when your home life or personal situation is at risk. In an environment of divorce, a stepfamily, parents fighting, alcoholism, sexual or physical abuse, and working parents, these create situations where children and teens are always more susceptible to outside influences. We can fight the cultural message of the world by teaching our children the counter-culture messages from the Bible. These messages lay a foundation that will last eternally and are the most powerful and effective tools a parent can use.

WHO'S FIGHTING THE CULTURAL WAR

From a frustrated parent's perspective, it seems that Washington's politicians are the only ones powerful enough to stand in the gap between Hollywood and the people who care. But there are many other organizations and people working hard to not only stop some of the destructive things that the entertainment industry and media are collectively doing, but to help change that powerful influence as well.

There are some religious organizations that have declared war on Hollywood and the media, demonizing the powerful mediums by exposing valid truths. Unfortunately, most of it ends up being name calling that does not effectively change anything.

I admire a different approach taken by people who are daily speaking and acting on changes to better our society and culture from a biblical perspective. Some of these are Michael Medved, a syndicated talk show host and the author of *Hollywood vs. America*, Dr. James Dobson with Focus on the Family, Beverly LaHaye with Concerned Women for America, and Dr. Laura. These men and women have targeted many cultural and spiritual battles our families constantly face and have admirably led campaigns that remind Hollywood of the "silent majority" that opposes their negative influences.

There are even organizations that give "Christian awards" to Hollywood, trying to not only honor the studios for their family-friendly films and contributions but convert them to the Christian mind-set in producing and making their films. Although the intentions are good, year after year these awards have not swayed or influenced Hollywood to "become Christian" or "change their evil ways." The studios gladly show up and accept their awards because it is good business, and they make their films to be recognized and generate money. Often industry people are "turned off" by these awards, and I've heard comments that they view them as "religious brainwash."

Clearly, Hollywood resists the notion of ever becoming "Christian." So it's a bit ridiculous to believe they will adopt Christian standards and principles in all of their films. After all, this is an art community full of "artists" who feel they have the right to their freedom of expression. Truthfully, the real "religion" of Hollywood is money. That's what they believe in and are influenced and governed by. It's all about money and the deals that make it.

To effectively make changes in the entertainment industry will require intelligent strategy, willing participants, effective ideas, powerful influences, and new approaches to the studios. There are those who are already doing this by tackling the problem from within and working with Hollywood.

I applaud the philosophy and mission statement behind Biola University in Southern California. They've created a media task force comprised of people in the entertainment industry led by Rick Bee and Tom Nash. The board of members consists of varied occupations in the business such as producers (Ralph Winter, Ken Wales), directors (Michael Warren, Phil Cooke), cinematographers (Ralph Linhardt), agent/authors (Victorya Rogers), film critics (myself), and many others in various professions, who all have a common purpose and goal. The purpose is to help recruit, mentor, and inspire serious college students who want to get their degree in the entertainment or communications field and work in the industry.

Hollywood is never going to knowingly turn their studios over to Christians and agree to only make "wholesome Christian entertainment." But if Christians are trained *to do the jobs in the industry*, eventually (it's already happening) the industry will change from *within*. Changed by professionals creating better television programming, producing movies with a powerful message, writing better scripts, and so on. Professionals, whose efforts are respected, valued, and lasting.

Will Christians ever completely take over Hollywood? I think that's an impractical approach. But do I think Christians can make a *difference* in Hollywood just as they do in the workplace? You bet!

PARENT TO PARENT

I am ending this book the way I began it, by speaking to you parent to parent. The battle between good and evil has always been waged in some form or fashion in this world. But we don't have to be defeated by it! The power to make positive changes and overcome the dark immoral cultural influences in our families and our world today is possible through the wisdom, hope, and strategy God gives those who are willing to take a stand and be used by Him.

Hollywood's greatest danger is that it seeps into the subconscious of the world and has become a global enigma. It acts powerfully to fill the unspoken needs of today's predominately un-churched youth culture. But all it takes is one person to be that salt and much needed light to bring about positive changes and hope for this millennial generation.

Parents, that's the challenge I leave with you. My hope is that you will be inspired to make some changes in your home, family, and lifestyle. Since Columbine rocked this nation in 1999, I have seen more and more teenagers all over America speaking up for what they believe in and taking a bold stand for how they want to live. Changes can and are being made all around us. I am encouraged that there is a new and different millennial generation who hunger for a return to decency and a moral foundation for their future.

Parents, it's up to you. You can speak into your child's life and make more of an impact than any other influence. You're the one who can empower your child or teenager to handle the influences of the world around them and equip them with tools that can change the course of their fate. You're the one who can change the direction of our youth culture today, by sowing your excellent parenting skills into the future generation of tomorrow.

I disapprove of what you say, but I will defend to the death your right to say it.

—Voltaire 1694-1778

WHAT CAN YOU DO?

Here is a list of a few organizations that are making a difference and will gladly provide helpful resources and information for you, your family, your neighborhood, community, or church. Although the following list of helpful organizations is by no means complete, it's a place to start gathering information, resources, current statistics, and tangible suggestions on how *you* can make a difference in your home and the world you live in. Most importantly, these organizations will connect you with *others* who are as passionately opposed to the destructive influences permeating our society and families as you are, and they will provide a means for *you to be as involved as you want to be!*

Federal Communications Commission (FCC)
   complaints-enf@fcc.gov
Parents Television Council (PTC)
   www.parentstv.org
Center for Parent/Youth Understanding (CPY)
   www.cpyu.org
The Dove Foundation
   www.dove.org
Mastermedia International, Inc.
   www.mastermediaintl.org
Concerned Women for America (CWA)
   www.cwfa.org
American Decency Association
   www.americandecency.org
American Family Association
   www.afa.net
Morality in Media
   www.moralityinmedia.org
Kaiser Family Foundation
   www.kff.org
Media Fellowship International
   www.mediafellowship.org
Focus on the Family
   www.family.org
Dr. Laura Perspective
   www.drlaura.com
For a *Death by Entertainment* video call Jeremiah Films
   1-800-828-2290
Movies Unlimited
   1-800-4-MOVIES or movies@moviesunlimited.com
   For the largest and most complete video/DVD selection

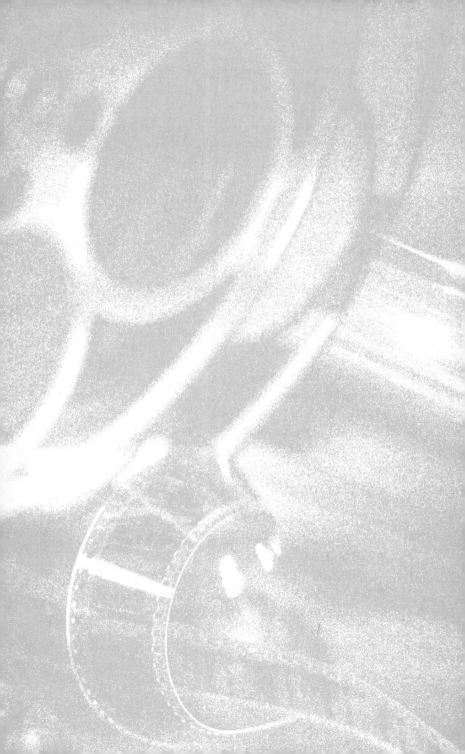

ENDNOTES

Who's Who

1. Ann Oldenburg, "Kid-Fluence," *USA Today*, November 10, 2000.
2. William Strauss and Neil Howe, "Millennials Rising: The Next Great Generation," commentary.

Chapter 1

1. Quentin J. Schultze, *Redeeming Television* (Downers Grove, Ill.: InterVarsity Press, 1992), p. 46.
2. Elisabeth F. Brown and William R. Hendee, "Adolescents and their Music: Insights into the Health of Adolescents," *Journal of the American Medical Association*, September 22, 1989, 1659.
3. Janet Weeks, "Hollywood Is Seeing Teen," *USA Today*, December 22, 1997.
4. "The Top Films of 2000," *Entertainment Weekly*, January 19, 2001.
5. Webster's New World Dictionary–Third Edition (Simon & Schuster, Inc.), p. 453.
6. The Concise Columbia Encyclopedia is licensed from Columbia University (New York: Columbia University Press, 1995).
7. Victor B. Cline, Ph.D., *Pornography Effects: Empirical Evidence* (1988). Dr. Cline is citing a study by Dr. Bryant of 600 American males and females of junior high age and above.
8. *USA Today/CNN/Gallup poll*, June 2-4, 1995.
9. Scott Bowles, "Many adults help their kids see R-rated fare," *USA Today*, September 26, 2000.
10. Karen Peterson, "We're more kid-caring, more entertained, and not as sleepy," *USA Today*, September 11, 2000.
11. Ibid.
12. Ibid.
13. Cesar G. Soriano, "Box office gets boost with year-end flurry," "Lifeline," *USA Today*, January 2, 2001.

Chapter 2

1. Michael Medved, *Hollywood vs. America*, talk show host and movie critic.
2. "Morality and Entertainment: The Origins of the Motion Picture Production Code," *Journal of American History 77*, no. 1, June 1990.
3. Warren I. Susman, *Culture as History: The Transformation of American Society in the Twentieth Century* (New York: Pantheon Books, 1984), p. 154.
4. *Cinema Timeline, Movies Unlimited*, p. 322.

5. Larry Poland, Ph.D. Chairman and CEO of Mastermedia International, Inc., quoted in "Death by Entertainment" video by Jeremiah Films.

6. Cathy Lynn Grossman, "In Search of Faith," *USA Today*, December 23, 1999.

7. Michelle Healy, "Just give us that new-time religion," *USA Today*, January 10, 2001. Quoting Public Agenda Research Agency, November 2000.

8. Cindy Hall, *USA Today*, December 2000.

9. Pat Robertson, *700 Club*.

10. Cinema Timeline, *Movies Unlimited*, p. 80.

11. "1999 US Economic Review: Theatrical Data," Motion Picture Association of America.

Chapter 3

1. Stephen Lynch, "Talkin' about our generations," *Orange County Register*, June 16, 2000.

2. Cesar G. Soriano, "Box office gets boost with year-end flurry," "Lifeline," *USA Today*, January 2, 2001.

3. "Worldwide Movie Ticket Sales Expected to Increase 20% by 2003," *Los Angeles Times*, September 1, 1999.

4. ACNielsen EDI, January 3, 2001.

5. Josh Chetwynd, "Bits of brilliance in Hollywood's bumpy year," *USA Today*, January 3, 2001.

6. "Lifeline," *USA Today*, January 3, 2001.

7. *Entertainment Weekly*, January 19, 2001, p. 50.

8. Elizabeth Wing, "Hollywood's family season," *USA Today*, November 16, 2000.

9. Ibid.

10. Elizabeth Wing, "Hollywood's family season," *USA Today*, November 16, 2000.

11. "Lifeline," *USA Today*, January 26, 2001.

12. Michael Cieply, West Coast editorial director for www.inside.com.

13. Anne R. Carey and Kevin Rechin, "Reading at the movies," *USA Today*, August 1999.

14. Josh Chetwynd and Andy Seiler, "Skip the book; read the movie," *USA Today*, December 15, 2000.

15. Jeff Gordinier, "1999 The Year That Changed Movies," *Entertainment Weekly*, November 26, 1999.

16. Cesar G. Soriano, "Where are they now?" *USA Today*, December 29, 2000–January 1, 2001.

17. Andy Seiler and Tim Friend, "And man created man," *USA Today*, November 21, 2000.

18. Movieline International, *USA Today*, January 25, 2001.

19. Kimberly Shearer Palmer, "Movie reflects interracial issues," *USA Today*, January 22, 2001.
20. Cesar Soriano, "Cornering the teenzine market," *USA Today*, January 16, 2001.
21. Josh Chetwynd, "Talk is expensive for disliked films," *USA Today*, August 30, 2000.
22. Ibid.
23. Keith Alexander, "More movie screens to go dark as companies downsize," *USA Today*, January 7, 2001.

Chapter 4

1. Cinema Timeline, *Movies Unlimited*, p. 484.
2. Adam Sandler, "Hwood: 'R' Kind of Town," *Variety*, September 1994.
3. "The Big Pictures: America's 100 All-Time Favorite Films," *Entertainment Weekly*, 1994.
4. MPAA Web site statement.
5. Josh Chetwynd, "Hollywood films a happy ending," *USA Today*, January 3, 2001.
6. Josh Chetwynd and Andy Seiler, "At the movies, we go less, pay more," *USA Today*, March 7, 2001.
7. Josh Chetwynd, "Escaping 'R' Bondage," *USA Today*, November 22, 1999.
8. Josh Chetwynd, "Bits of Brilliance in Hollywood's Bumpy Year," *USA Today*, January 3, 2001.
9. Andy Seiler, "Entertainment marketing to children blasted," *USA Today*, September 14, 2000.
10. "The Ratings Games at the Cineplex," *New York Times,* February 18, 1996, FTC Report, Alliance for Childhood.
11. Chris Woodyard, "In-flight movies jettison adult scenes," *USA Today*, August 8, 2000.
12. *Entertainment Weekly*, July 1999.
13. Ibid., p. 11.
14. Andy Seiler, "Two studios offer new ad plans," *USA Today*, September 14, 2000.
15. Excerpt from the executive summary of the Federal Trade Commission's report on the marketing of violent entertainment to children.

Chapter 5

1. Michael Medved, Talk Show Host (*Hollywood vs. America*), From the video "Death by Entertainment."
2. "Facts About Media Violence," American Medical Association, p. 1997.
3. Webster's New World Dictionary, Third Edition, p. 916.
4. *Entertainment Weekly*, September 2000.
5. Josh Chetwynd and Andy Seiler, "Movie sex isn't marrying kind," *USA Today*, November 10, 2000.

6. Ibid.

7. Karen S. Peterson, "Younger kids trying it now, often ignorant of disease risks," *USA Today*, November 16, 2000, 1D.

8. Ibid.

9. Ibid.

10. "Teens and oral sex," *Family Planning Perspectives*, published by Alan Guttmacher Institute, December 2000.

11. Kristen Harrison, "Scary Films Stay With You," University of Michigan Study, March 1999.

12. Michelle Healy, "Blame Game," *USA Today*, September 1999.

13. Stephen F. Rhode and Roger L. Kohn, "Report of the Beverly Hills Bar Association Ad Hoc Committee on Violence and the Media," *Beverly Hills Bar Association Journal* (Spring 1996).

14. *Entertainment Weekly*, September 2000.

15. 1999 Crime Victims Survey, Bureau of Justice Statistics.

16. James L. McGaugh, "Preserving the Presence of the Past," *American Psychologist* (February 1983): cited by Cline, *Pornography Effects: Empirical Evidence*, 1988.

Chapter 6

1. Co-creator of *Will & Grace*, in *Entertainment Weekly*, October 6, 2000.

2. "Facts about Media Violence," American Medical Association, 1997, March 24, 1998.

3. "What a Difference a Decade Makes: A Comparison of Prime Time Sex, Language, and Violence in 1989 and '99," Parents Television Council, online at www.parentstv.org.

4. "TV Dinner," *USA Today*, December 4, 2000, Jerry Shriver, "Personal chefs are no longer just for the rich," *USA Today*, February 9, 2001.

5. "What a Difference a Decade Makes: A Comparison of Prime Time Sex, Language, and Violence in 1989 and '99," Parents Television Council, online at www.parentstv.org.

6. NTI Annual Averages, from Television Bureau of Advertising, Time Spent Viewing—Person, TV Basics.

7. Veronis, Suhler & Assoc., Wilkofsky Gruen Assoc., from Television Bureau of Advertising, Consumer Media Usage, TV Basics, www.tvb.org.

8. *USA Today/CNN/Gallup* poll, *USA Weekend*, June 2-4, 1995.

9. "What a Difference a Decade Makes: A Comparison of Prime Time Sex, Language, and Violence in 1989 and '99," Parents Television Council, online at www.parentstv.org.

10. "What a Difference a Decade Makes: A Comparison of Prime Time Sex, Language, and Violence in 1989 and '99," Parents Television Council, online at www.parentstv.org.

11. Ibid.

12. Jim Impoco, "TV's Frisky Family Values," *U.S. News & World Report,* April 15, 1996.

13. "What a Difference a Decade Makes: A Comparison of Prime Time Sex, Language, and Violence in 1989 and '99," Parents Television Council, online at www.parentstv.org.

14. Claudia Puig, "Youths in Poll Say TV Is Harmful Influence," *Los Angeles Times,* February 27, 1995, p. 1.

15. "Television's Effect," National Institute on Media and the Family, July 28, 1999, www.mediaandthefamily.org.

16. "Children and the Media," National Institute on Media and the Family, July 28, 1999, www.mediaandthefamily.org/mediaeffect.html.

17. Edward C. Baig, "Surround your kids with safety," *USA Today,* April 5, 2000.

18. Thomas Robinson, "Limiting TV May Cut Children's Aggression," *Archives of Pediatrics and Adolescent Medicine,* Stanford University Medical School, January 2000.

Chapter 7

1. Becky Yerak, "Small wireless TV firm takes on satellite industry," *USA Today,* November 29, 2000, p. 9b.

2. "What a Difference a Decade Makes: A Comparison of Prime Time Sex, Language, and Violence in 1989 and '99," Parents Television Council, online at www.parentstv.org.

3. Parents Television Council study, "The Family Hour: Worse Than Ever and Headed for New Lows."

4. Ibid.

5. "US Economic review: VCR and Cable Data," Motion Picture Association of America Page, n.d., www.mpaa.org.

6. "Television and Day Care Centers," National Institute on Media and the Family, July 28, 1999.

7. Gary Schneeberger, "Daddy (Not Quite) Dearest," *Citizen,* November 2000, Vol. 14, p. 11.

8. Robert Bianco, "Give it up Spike: WB and UPN sitcoms looking on up," *USA Today,* October 20, 2000.

9. Parents Television Council study, report on WWF, viewable online at www.parentstv.org/smackdown/smackdown.html.

10. Mike Clary, "Defense Pulls Pro Wrestling Into Murder Trial," *Los Angeles Times,* January 25, 2001.

11. Ibid.

12. Ibid.

13. Ursula Owre Masterson, "Backyard wrestling takes America by Storm, but when is enough enough?" Fox News, September 15, 2000.

14. Ibid.

15. Ibid.

16. "What a Difference a Decade Makes: A Comparison of Prime Time Sex, Language, and Violence in 1989 and '99," Parents Television Council, online at www.parentstv.org.

Chapter 8

1. Tucker Carlson, "Marilyn Manson Has a Secret," *Talk* magazine, November 2000, p. 75.

2. Edna Gundersen, "Where will teen tastes land next?," *USA Today*, September 22, 2000.

3. Julie Snider, "Truth bears repeating," *USA Today*, February 15, 2001.

4. Walt Mueller, *Understanding Today's Youth Culture* (Tyndale House Publishing, 1999), p. 169.

5. *Newsweek*, October 9, 2000.

6. Ibid., Gundersen.

7. Ibid., Carlson, p. 76.

8. Ibid., Carlson, p. 76.

9. Ibid., Carlson, p. 77.

10. Walt Mueller, "Eminem—Meet the real Slim Shady," CPYU, YouthCulture@2000, fall 2000, p. 2. Contact cpyu@aol.com or go to www.cpyu.org to request the lyrics or view the article.

11. Ibid., Mueller, p. 3.

12. Ibid., Mueller.

13. Ibid., Mueller, p. 81.

14. Ibid., Mueller, p. 88.

15. *Gallup* poll, *USA Today*, December 14, 2000.

16. Catherina Hurlburt, *Family Voice*, November/December 1999, p. 17.

Chapter 9

1. Jeff Goodell, "The Fevered Rise of America Online," *Rolling Stone*, October 1996.

2. Fred Seibert, MTV Online.

3. Scott Schalin, COO of iGallery.

4. Don Tapscott, *Growing Up Digital: The Rise of the Next Generation* (New York: McGraw-Hill, 1998), p. 22.

5. Chuck Crisafulli, "Webbed Feat," *The Hollywood Reporter*, December 1999, p. 28.

6. Brad Foxhoven, president of Eruptor Entertainment, *The Hollywood Reporter*, December 1999, p. 33.

7. Ibid.

8. Barry Garron, "Changing Channels," *The Hollywood Reporter*, December 1999, p. 61.

9. Barry Garron, "Telling Visions," *The Hollywood Reporter*, December

1999, p. 24.

10. Karen Thomas, "Big Bird flies into online flap," *USA Today,* November 14, 2000.

11. Janet Kornblum, "Ruling encourages virtual visitation," *USA Today,* January 11, 2001.

12. John Bacon, "Arkansas judge nullifies twin girls' adoption," *USA Today,* March 7, 2001.

13. Jefferson Graham, "For men, a bawdy romp online," *USA Today,* August 24, 2000.

14. John W. Kennedy, "Bypassing Pornography," *Computing Today,* January/February 1998, p. 13.

15. James Hirsen, author of *The Coming Collision* (Huntington House, 1999), guest on "Holly McClure Live," on KPRZ.

16. Peter K. Johnson, "Assemblies of God Tackles Problem of Porn Addiction Among Ministers," *Charisma,* January 2001. p. 24.

17. Ibid.

18. Ibid.

19. Janet Kornblum, "What, kids look at porn sites?," *USA Today,* December 19, 2000.

20. Mike Snider, "VCRs aren't stuck on pause," *USA Today,* January 24, 2001.

21. Garron, *Telling Visions,* p. 56.

22. Video Game Violence; *Media Scope,* April 7, 1998, Katie Hafner, "Choosing Technology," *Lancaster Intelligence Journal,* April 14, 1998.

23. Linda Mintle, Ph.D., *Kids Killing Kids* (Creation House, 1999), www.christianity.com/drlindahelps.

24. "Video Generation," University of North Carolina, Penny Gordon-Larsen for *Journal of Pediatrics,* June 2000.

25. Janey Kornblum, "'Bang' offers not too violent alternative," *USA Today,* August 24, 2000.

26. Steven Kent, "Japan struggles with violent games," *USA Today,* November 10, 2000.

27. Ibid.

28. "Sit down, tune in, log on at the e-cliner," *USA Today,* November 10, 2000.

Chapter 10

1. Russel Nye, *The Unembarrassed Muse: The Popular Arts in America* (New York: Dial, 1970), p. 389.

2. Izod, "Hollywood and the Box office, 1985-1986," p. 180.

3. *USA Today,* August 1999.

4. Cathy Lynn Grossman, "In search of faith," *USA Today/CNN/Gallup* poll, December 23-26, 1999.

5. Pamela Paxton, "Trust in individuals Decline," *American Journal of*

Sociology, Ohio State University, November 2000.

6. Walt Mueller, "A compelling look at our culture of divorce," a statistical summary of "The Unexpected Legacy of Divorce," YouthCulture@2000, Winter 2000, p. 8.

7. "Child care falls to grandparents," *The Gerontologist,* April 2000.

8. Sesame Street Parents magazine survey, *Sesame Street* magazine, November 2000.

9. Marco R. Della Cava, "Stress short-circuits tech families lives," *USA Today,* January 29, 2001.

10. Survey sponsored by *Teen* magazine and Sears, *Teen* magazine, September 2001, p. 86.

11. Patricia Adler, "Peer Power: Preadolescent Culture and Identity" (Rutgers University).

12. John Bacon, "Most teens report having been violent," *USA Today,* April 2, 2001, discussing survey conducted by Josephson Institute of Ethics.

13. Karen Thomas, "Parental intervention advised," *USA Today,* March 26, 2001.

14. "Americans fear school shootings," *Gallup* poll, *USA Today,* April 24, 2001.

15. Patrick O'Driscoll, "Unheeded warning signs dismay safety advocates," *USA Today,* March 6, 2001.

16. Linda Mintle, Ph.D., *Kids Killing Kids* (Creation House, 1999), www.christianity.com/drlindahelps.

17. "Television and Day Care Centers," National Institute on Media and the Family, July 28, 1999.

18. Ann Oldenburg and Kelly Carter, "Star moms find life without father," *USA Today,* January 26, 2001.

19. Linda Beam, "Exploring Harry Potter's World," Teachers in Focus, December 1999, available online at www.focusonthefamily.org.

20. Reuters, "From Hogwarts to Easy Street," August 21, 2000, available online at www.abcnews.com
Morgan Murphy, "Magic Coins," *Forbes Magazine,* March 20, 2000.

21. Chuck Colson, "Harry Potter and the Existence of God," Breakpoint Commentary, July 14, 2000, available online at www.christianity.com.

22. "Why We Like Harry Potter," *Christianity Today,* January 10, 2000.

23. Thomas Hargrove, "Many Americans believe in ghosts and witches," Scripps Howard News Service, October 31, 1999.

24. Elizabeth Mehren, "Upward and Onward Toward Book Seven— Her Way," *Los Angeles Times,* October 25, 2000.

25. Malcolm Jones, "Why Harry's Hot," *Newsweek,* July 17, 2000, p. 55.

26. Erica D. Rowell, "It's a Mad, Mad Poké-Monde," Fox News, September 29, 1999.

27. "Studio is hoping Pokémon fans dig Digimon, too," *USA Today,* October 2, 2000.

Chapter 11

1. T. L. Stanley, editor of "What's Hot Now" (www.whnx.com), talking about marketing to the "tweeners" in the *USA Today*.
2. Ann Oldenburg, "Kid-Fluence," *USA Today,* November 10, 2000.
3. Survey conducted for Marshalls retailers by Opinion Research Corporation, results printed in advertisement for Marshalls, Fall 1999, July 26, 1999.
4. Keith Simmon, "Rich kids lose sight of mighty dollar, *USA Today,* "Snapshots," January 24, 2001.
5. Harry Balzer, NPD Group, research firm.
6. NFL research, *Orange County Register*, Sports section, January 29, 2001.
7. Wirthlin Worldwide survey, CWA—Family Voice, November/December 1999.
8. Walt Mueller, "What you see is what I am," CPYU newsletter, Spring 2001, p. 18.
9. *Cosmopolitan Girl,* "How to give a heavenly New Year's Eve kiss," January 2001.
10. Madeline Dalton, "Study: Cigarette smoking in movies," *Dartmouth Medical School,* January 2001.
11. Arthur Peterson Jr., lead researcher of the Fred Hutchinson Cancer Research Center, who conducted the experiment for the *Journal of the National Cancer Institute, USA Today,* December 20, 2000.
12. 1998 survey by the Center for Disease Control and Prevention, Social Science Research Center—www.ssrc.msstate.edu.
13. Arthur Cosby, "Smoking in America: 35 Years After the Surgeon General's Report," Social Science Research Center, September 2000.
14. Clive Bates, President of Action on Smoking and Health, co-author of "Teen cell phone sales rise, smoking falls," *British Medical Journal,* November 3, 2000.
15. Joseph Califano, CASA—Center on Addiction and Substance Abuse—Columbia University. November 3, 2000, Internet news report.
16. *Vanity Fair,* February 2001.
17. Richard Price, *Movieline,* October 1992.
18. Donna Leinwand, "Parents share their drugs with teens," *USA Today,* October 10, 2000.
19. Ibid.
20. The Republican Jewish Coalition, Fall 2000 report from Web site; "Facts about illiteracy in the USA," www.rjchq.org.

Chapter 12

1. Ted Turner, *LA Times* April 3, 1994.
2. Larry Poland, CEO of Mastermedia Inc. on *Death by Entertainment* video.
3. "Achievers," OC Family, February 2001, p. 16.

4. "Let's Connect," Philips Consumer Communications, CPYU, 2000, fall 1999.

5. Andy Warhol, *From A to B and Back Again* (New York: Harcourt Bryce, 1975).

6. Hilary Wasson, "Many kids watch TV unrestricted," *USA Today*, February 9, 2001.

7. The Kaiser Family Foundation report, *Kids and Media at the New Millennium*, November 1999, reported by CPYU, Paul Robertson in YouthCulture@Today, Spring 2001.

8. *Newsweek*, 10/18/99, reported by CPYU, Paul Robertson in YouthCulture@Today, Spring 2001.

9. Paul Robertson, *Making the young old before their time,* CPYU, Spring 2001, p. 10.

10. Ibid., p. 11.